SEEDS OF THE SIXTIES

· ·

Andrew Jamison
Ron Eyerman

UNIVERSITY OF CALIFORNIA PRESS
Berkeley · Los Angeles · London

University of California Press
Berkeley and Los Angeles, California
University of California Press, Ltd.
London, England
Copyright © 1994
by the Regents of the University of California

First Paperback Printing 1995

Library of Congress Cataloging-in-Publication Data
Jamison, Andrew.
    Seeds of the sixties / Andrew Jamison and Ron Eyerman.
        p.   cm.
    Includes bibliographical references and index.
    ISBN 0-520-20341-0
    1. United States—Intellectual life—20th century.   2. United
States—Civilization—1945–   .   I. Eyerman. Ron.   II. Title.
E169.12.J35   1994
973.92—dc20   93-9092
                                                               CIP

Printed in the United States of America
1   2   3   4   5   6   7   8   9
The paper used in this publication meets the minimum requirements of American National Standard for Information Sciences—Permanence of Paper for Printed Library Materials, ANSI Z39.48–1984. ⊗

In memory of our fathers, Alvin Eyerman and Saunders
Eliot Jamison, and to Jeff Alexander, our friend
and colleague, who continues the long march through
the institutions

History is a reservoir of human creativeness. Without the perpetual rediscovery and reinterpretation of history, without free access to that reservoir, the life of any single generation would be but a trickle of water in a desert.

Lewis Mumford, The Condition of Man (1944)

CONTENTS

Preface   xi

1 REINVENTING PARTISANSHIP   1

2 MASS SOCIETY AND ITS CRITICS: 30
   C. Wright Mills, Hannah Arendt, Erich Fromm

3 THE ECOLOGICAL INTELLECTUALS: 64
   Fairfield Osborn, Lewis Mumford, Rachel Carson

4 SHAPING NEW KINDS OF KNOWLEDGE: 103
   Leo Szilard, Herbert Marcuse, Margaret Mead

5 THE RECONCEPTUALIZATION OF CULTURE: 141
   Allen Ginsberg, James Baldwin, Mary McCarthy

6 MAKING POLITICS PERSONAL: 178
   Saul Alinsky, Dorothy Day, Martin Luther King, Jr.

7 CONCLUSION: Taking Sides in the Fifties   209

   References   225

   Index   231

PREFACE

One of the great myths perpetrated by activists in the American student movement of the 1960s was their historical uniqueness. It was central to the New Left's view of itself that it had burst on the scene as if from nowhere and that the "Old" Left, connecting back to the labor movement and political activism of the 1930s, had begun to evaporate after the Second World War and had largely disappeared by the 1950s. The wider social movements of the 1960s and beyond generally followed this ahistorical tack, stressing their break with the past and glorifying their spontaneity and "newness." As a result, the multifarious impacts of the new social movements on American society have tended to be downplayed by later analysts, and the sixties have all too often been depicted as a brief and somewhat strange historical parenthesis.

For the generation of Americans who grew up in the 1950s, a sense of being at the end of history seemed confirmed by personal experience. For the two of us, living in Brooklyn and suburban New Jersey, the 1950s were a quiet time, when baseball and basketball determined the seasons of our lives. The media focus on family values and patriotism far overshadowed the McCarthy hearings and the early stirrings of the civil rights movement. Even with the weekly civil defense drills at school, the world of politics seemed far away. For us, as for so many of our contemporaries, the links to the collective dreams of the 1930s had been effectively broken.

This book, then, is at once a voyage of self-discovery and an attempt to identify some of the intellectual roots of our generation. Our topic is the transformation of critical public discourse, what we call the critical process, in those quiescent cold war years. We do this through recounting the lives and works of fifteen persons who in the 1950s reinvented traditions of partisanship in American intellectual life. Our choice of individuals reflects the personal nature of this book. In most cases, the people we have chosen have been influential in our own personal development. There are many others we could have included—Paul Goodman, Pete Seeger, Dwight Macdonald, Irving Howe, Kenneth Boulding, Barry Commoner, Paul Sweezey, Lewis Coser, Leonard Bernstein, Ella Baker, Maya Angelou, and even Billie Holliday were all considered—and perhaps we will return to some of them on a later occasion. At this point, we merely want to stress that our book does not pretend to be comprehensive. Through the selective portrayal of individuals, we have sought to highlight a historical process. We do not claim that those individuals presented here were the only "few brave men and women" (Horkheimer) who stood up against the flowing tide, against the grain. They were not an intellectual elite who, in traditional aristocratic fashion, sought to distinguish themselves from their peers and the subservient masses. Rather, by describing the activities of these fifteen people, we want to remember the intellectual connections between radical generations and to begin to restore a sense of history—a usable past—for our own generation.

Seeds of the Sixties has been a very personal book to write. It began as part of a larger reflection on the significance of social movements in processes of social transformation, which, in two earlier books, *The Making of the New Environmental Consciousness* (1990) and *Social Movements: A Cognitive Approach* (1991), we approached in more detached sociological fashion. We directed our arguments primarily to our fellow social scientists, who until recently have tended to ignore the role of social movements in broader patterns of development. What became increasingly clear as our thinking progressed, however, was how difficult it was to separate our own engagement in the social movements we were discussing from the academic issues involved. From different routes we had both been active in the social movements of the 1960s and 1970s—the student movement and its various offshoots in the United States and Europe—and we wanted to find a way to bring that experience directly into our analysis. This, in turn, inspired a search for the roots of our own partisan stance and a reflection on our intellectual heritage. The book you are about to read is the result.

Many people have been helpful in this project. The Swedish Social Science and Humanities Research Council (HSFR) has been very generous in its support. Its financial assistance not only permitted us the necessary research time but also made it possible to visit the United States on numerous occasions as well as present versions of various chapters at seminars and conferences with friends and colleagues around the world. Several of the latter deserve special thanks. Jeff Alexander, Aant Elzinga, Johanna Esseveld, Pat Eyerman, Jonathan Friedman, Bengt Gesser, Margareta Gromark, Madelyn Holmes, Barbara Jamison, Martin Kylhammar, Christer Lindberg, Orvar Löfgren, Everett Mendelsohn, Conny Mithander, Torsten Nybom, Sheldon Rothblatt and Janet Ruyle (at the Center for Studies in Higher Education at Berkeley where the idea for the book first germinated), and Sverker Sörlin were especially helpful. We would also like to thank Barry Commoner and Irving Howe for sharing with us some of their recollections. The portraits we present are primarily based on readily available sources, and we would like to thank the excellent biographers who have supplied us with much of our "raw data." William Lanouette's new biography of Leo Szilard came out unfortunately after we had already completed our manuscript. The comments of the reviewers for the University of California Press were both encouraging and constructive in helping us think through the form and content of the manuscript. Stan Holwitz, our editor, was a great support, and the promptness of his transatlantic telephone calls helped bring the book into being far quicker than would otherwise have been the case. Thank you all. Contrary to the normal academic disclaimers, we have no qualms about letting you share the responsibility.

1

REINVENTING PARTISANSHIP

. . . .

This is a book about dissident intellectuals and the breathing spaces that they carved out of the postwar American landscape. They reinvented partisanship at a time when most intellectuals were falling in line. In an age of conformity, these people took sides against what C. Wright Mills called the main drift, defending the right to dissent and struggling to keep open the critical process of public debate. In dark times, they provided some rays of enlightenment that helped inspire the emergence of new political energy. They planted seeds of the sixties.

In the quiescent days of the 1950s, when American power was at its height, these people created new concepts—and contexts—of social criticism. They reaffirmed the intellectual commitment that had helped define the 1930s in both Europe and the United States but that had gone out of fashion. In the margins of the postwar society, they kept alive something of the spirit of the thirties and prepared the way for a new wave of radicalism in the sixties: they unwittingly connected radical generations. For some, the connection was obvious and direct; Mills and Herbert Marcuse, for instance, became cult figures in the 1960s, as their ideas articulated the unconscious assumptions of the alienated young. For others, the connection was far less obvious, as the seeds they planted were largely indirect; Hannah Arendt's provocative affirmation of the life of the mind and Lewis Mumford's outspoken rejection of the suburbanization of America inspired no cult following but served rather as living examples of intellectual engagement and dissent. It was more in their style than in the substance of their opposition that they helped stimulate the questioning of dominant values and institutional norms that was so much a part of 1960s social protest. We do not claim that these critical intellectuals created the movements of the 1960s, but we do contend that those movements would not have happened—and certainly would not have changed America as they did—if the intellectual groundwork had not been laid. The social movements of the 1960s, the formative experience of our generation, were not primarily an outburst of emotional irrational behavior, reducible to media happenings or political mobilizations. Nor did they represent the total break with previous critical traditions that the people in this book—the older generation—often accused them of being. We see the 1960s, rather, as a creative period that carried new ideas into American society.

In the 1950s, a small number of critical American intellectuals reconstructed radicalism, by addressing new issues, remembering classical traditions, reforming organizations, and reinterpreting American society: they reinvented partisanship. Some struggled to keep established institutions honest, working on the inside to maintain a space for critical thought and research. Others moved out of the mainstream to find other Americas in the nonhuman natural landscape and the dehumanized urban ghettos. In their writings and activism, they gave voice to the deviant and the downtrodden as well as to the silent rhythms of the natural environment. And although their ideas and practices were important in inspiring a more widespread revolt and criticism in the 1960s, many of our critical intellectuals later came to break with the movements they helped inspire. Their work, essential though it was, has tended to be overlooked in the voluminous literature that has been produced on the 1960s; this book tries to set the record straight.

American Intellectual Traditions

American intellectuals are usually treated as separate beings, strong heroic individuals standing aside from (or above) the rest of society pontificating on the basis of an inner authority, or even an inner calling. Whether they are seen as public intellectuals, serving as a

2

society's conscience, or as alienated outsiders, escaping from society to absolutize personal expression, the standard accounts portray intellectuals as a breed apart, a social group floating freely in an autonomous realm of "critical discourse." Derived from puritanism and filtered through the transcendentalists of the nineteenth century, an Emersonian ideal of self-reliance and independence has been a central component of American intellectual life. Ralph Waldo Emerson was a minister and a scholar who cast his spell on later generations of intellectuals, not so much through his specific ideas as through his moral example. It was the strength of the personality and the importance of independence that were central to the Emersonian ideal of the scholar, who was also seen as representing—and articulating—a distinctive form of national character. As the Emersonian tradition developed into the late nineteenth and early twentieth centuries, there emerged an intellectual ethos that blended craftsmanship, hard work, and moral strength into a stance of spiritual self-reliance. From William James to Lewis Mumford, this personalist sensibility has been an important presence in twentieth-century intellectual life.

Another tradition depicts intellectuals as an "intelligentsia" of progressive reformers identifying with universal ideals of brotherhood and social service. From Jane Addams to Dorothy Day and Martin Luther King, Jr., the progressive American intellectual has been a kind of missionary striving to infuse his or her "common" fellows with a sense of justice, equality, and reason. If America has ever produced an intelligentsia, a group or a class of individuals who define their common relation to the world in the collective mission of bettering the human lot through political and cultural activity, then Greenwich Village in the first quarter of the twentieth century was its cradle. As in Chicago, where Addams's settlement house served as a meeting place for socially concerned academics and came to inspire progressive reformers throughout the social sciences, New York drew idealistic college students and socially engaged writers and artists to what were essentially poor immigrant neighborhoods. Greenwich Village progressives like Randolph Bourne, John Reed and Thorstein Veblen—and their more established counterparts among the academic followers of John Dewey—redefined the relations between high culture and everyday life and between professional intellectuals and common people. In journals like *The Dial* and in institutions like the New School for Social Research, they helped diffuse a spirit of progressive reformism into American society. This tradition experienced something of a revival in the aftermath of the depression in the late 1930s, when the labor movement exercised a strong attraction for intellectuals.

With the rise of industrialism and the concomitant need for expert knowledge, a third tradition emerged, as a kind of hybrid outgrowth of the other two: scientific professionalism. Based on the ideals of science and strongly influenced by positivism, this tradition gained a strong foothold in American universities by the 1920s. The rise of the corporate foundations and industrial research laboratories provided scientific professionalism with an institutional base and a crucial social function in relation to American industry. In the 1930s, the New Deal and its various programs of social engineering further stimulated scientific professionalism, and by the end of the Second World War, the scientific-technical experts had come to dominate intellectual life in America. In the process, they had become strongly associated with the military as well as with the increasingly powerful private corporations.

In the 1950s, the tension between these traditions—the independent critic, the progressive reformer, and the expert—grew acute. With the expansion of the universities and the growth of "mass society" and "mass culture," intellect came to be pitted against intelligence. Meanwhile, the partisan intellectual role that had been imported from Europe added a new dimension to the indigenous critical and progressive traditions. The migration of anti-Fascist intellectuals gave new life to the few remaining adherents of American critical thought. In their time, the processes of recombination and reconceptualization were marginal to the main currents of American intellectual life. And yet, the ensuing revitalization of American criticism would prove to be crucially important for the social movements of the 1960s.

The Postwar Intellectual Context

After the Second World War, American intellectuals were confronted with a new set of social conditions in which to carry out their work. During the war, science and technology had become linked, irrevocably it seemed, to the military arms of the state. The combination of scientific expertise and state power in the production of weaponry, most especially the atomic bomb, as well as in the planning and organization of military operations had given the United States a place of leadership among the "free" nations of the "Western" world. America—and its various types of intellectuals—came to be governed after the war by a new regime and a new image, or conception, of intellectual life. Science, technology, and even the arts became strategic resources to be mobilized in the nation's quest for world dominance. Intellectual activity, which had so often in the past been castigated to the social margins with the intellectual taking on the role of the alienated outsider, was brought in from the cold and given a prominent place in this new scientific-technological state. For the first time in American history, the state took on the task of supporting, rather generously at that, the production of knowledge primarily—but not exclusively—for military purposes. A number of private corporations were transformed into "knowledge industries" largely dependent on state funding for their high growth rates. At the same time, the very notion of knowledge changed; after the war, knowledge came to be seen as something that could be manufactured along industrial lines, and its production could be subjected to standardized methods. The results of this "industrialized science" could then be bought and sold on the commercial marketplace. Thus both intellectuals and the fruits of their activity had become fundamentally altered in the wake of the Second World War.

The war had all but eliminated the critical intellectual, drawing even the most disenchanted free floater into supporting the struggle against fascism. Those contexts that had sustained social criticism—the small magazines, the leftist parties and sects, the avant-garde cultural circles that had been so widespread in the 1930s—either disappeared or were transformed into organs of the war effort. The literary life, with its public intellectuals and open-ended cultural discourse, grew more specialized and commercial. New worlds of mass culture and "public relations" created lucrative new opportunities and new avenues for applying those literary skills that earlier had been directed to critical reflection and social commentary.

These developments had a major effect on the universities, bringing them into what came to be termed the military-industrial complex and thus transforming much of academic research into an industrial-ized and bureaucratic kind of knowledge production—so-called Big Science. American universities had already before the war built up a system of department-based graduate education, and primarily through support from private foundations, discipline-oriented re-search had already begun to supplant broader cultural aims as the dominant preoccupation of academic life. It was the massive state-military involvement during and after the war, however, with its con-tract system and the infrastructure of research councils and advisory committees, that led to the triumph of the "research university." At least some intellectuals, that is, physical scientists and military engi-neers, were thereby given a vastly different status and social impor-tance than they had had before the war.

Most American intellectuals saw their increased social status—and incomes—as cause for celebration. The atomic bomb and the heroic physicists who had built it had brought the United States a unilateral source of power and new global responsibility. There was a veritable cult of science in the postwar years, as an ideology of scientific om-nipotence—scientism—spread among American intellectuals. There was relatively little critical analysis of the new situation and even less support for fundamental kinds of structural change. Almost from the outset, to be sure, there were critics who wanted the United States to give up its new weapon and/or subject its control and further devel-opment to some kind of world government. Many of the most out-spoken critics were those like Leo Szilard who had worked on the atomic bomb project during the war, and their criticism was thus of a special kind. They were expert critics, whose main activity was not in building up a mass constituency but in affecting political influence, most especially in the political control and administration of atomic energy.

A different kind of criticism of the scientific-technological state came from the dispersed remnants of what had, in the 1930s, been a significant social movement. Working primarily through ad hoc orga-nizations of the "popular front," the 1930s movement had sought, among other things, to develop a more popular approach to knowledge and art and critically assimilate modern technology into American ways of life. In the depression, when capitalism seemed to have outlived its usefulness, many American intellectuals had been inspired by the Soviet Union's efforts to plan the economy and socialize the intellect and had tried to fashion an indigenous socialism out of populist political traditions and pragmatic approaches to knowledge. Marxism had been stirred into the American melting pot to help create a substantial literature of social criticism and a wide range of socialist parties and sects.

The collective dreams of the 1930s tended to fade amid the exigencies of war, however, giving way to reassertions of individualist and competitive, that is, capitalist, values. And the military enlisted the services of many types of intellectuals—writers, linguists, historians, anthropologists, sociologists, political scientists, and economists as well as the famous physicists who built the atomic bomb—to help carry out the war effort. After the war, the American way of life was no longer seen primarily as an active, creative force in need of further development but as a source of patriotic rhetoric, embodying the virtues of free enterprise, scientific-technological power, and individual morality. Many of those who had been the critics of American society before the war became its apologists, transforming their Marxian-influenced social criticism of the 1930s into a specialized professional role as literary or cultural or academic critics. But a few tried to keep the critical spirit alive in the midst of the cold war. Let us briefly describe what it was they tried to keep alive.

The Rise and Fall of Populist Pragmatism

It was during the 1930s, when President Franklin D. Roosevelt sought to inspire a "new deal" in American society as a way to overcome the severe economic depression, that a new kind of intellectual emerged in the United States. Combining elements from American traditions of pragmatist philosophy and populist politics with imported European ideologies, these "movement intellectuals" of the 1930s articulated a new social criticism as part of the radical movements that were so dominant at the time. This intellectual activity filled some of the gaps that had historically existed between intellectuals and common people in the United States. At the time of the New Deal, there was a strong interest on the part of many intellectuals to identify with a particular American way of life. As Warren Susman (1984: 179) has said, "In the 1930s, it might be argued, the self-conscious American intelligentsia set out to become 'an unlearned class,' to assimilate the culture of the 'people' into the inherited European tradition."

The pragmatic philosophy had been developed around the turn of the century: Charles Peirce, the idiosyncratic mathematician, had made the basic conceptual formulations of "pragmaticism," as he called it, in largely unpublished papers already in the nineteenth century. In the first decades of the twentieth century, William James had expanded on Peirce's ideas and applied pragmatism to various facets of human behavior, Charles Beard and others had applied them, after a fashion, to history, and George Herbert Mead and others of the "Chicago school" had developed a pragmatic approach to sociology— all affected, in various ways, by John Dewey, who applied pragmatism to education and just about everything else and served as a "symbol of liberation and integrity to a long generation of intellectuals" (Perry 1984: 368).

Until the 1930s, however, pragmatism was a largely academic philosophy. It had provided a common frame of reference, or world view, for many of the reformers in the progressive period in the early years of the century, which might be considered a precursor to the social movement of the 1930s. Although there were populistic tendencies in that earlier period, it was during the depression that the urge among academics and other intellectuals to reunite with the "people" took on significant societal proportions. In the process, pragmatism, or certain tenets of pragmatic philosophy, was combined with elements of populist political behavior to form a distinct cognitive praxis and a direct counterpoint to the technocratic and scientistic ideas that had been so dominant in the period after the First World War.

The 1920s had marked the coming to maturity of the "American system" of manufacturing, with its principles of mass production and rationalization. Henry Ford's conveyor belts and Frederick Winslow Taylor's time and motion studies, or scientific management, were the cornerstones of a distinct model of technological, economic, and even social development. With the engineer as the cultural hero and infinite progress as the guiding vision, the technocrat burst on the scene to do the bidding of the Fords, Edisons, Carnegies, and Rockefellers and man their research laboratories and corporate foundations. In response, writers and artists fled in droves to the cafés of Europe, from where they looked in disdain at the intellectual "wasteland" that their country had become in their eyes. Some wandered even farther, seeking in India—or, like Margaret Mead, in the South Seas—a spiritual alternative to their decadent technocratic homeland. While the technocratic vision was dealt a severe blow by the stock market crash of 1929 and the ensuing economic depression, many of the intellectual exiles were forced back home by the rise of fascism and nazism—themselves an outgrowth of economic decline.

The economic crisis created the basis for reinterpreting older visions and traditions and recombining intellectual practices into new syntheses. The failure of the corporate model was there for all to see in the bread lines and soup kitchens. Even scientists and engineers were out of work in record numbers. As the government stepped in to fill the gap and provide jobs in its public works programs, many intellectuals returned to their roots, and even the alienated writers were set to work to seek out and document the culture that still remained alive in the midst of depression. But they brought new methods with them, the engineers translating scientific technology into electrification and electronic communication and the artists translating European ideology into popular literary experimentation. The American worker, who had all but been reduced to a cog in a machine in the 1920s, emerged as a new cultural hero, and the intellectual himself became a worker like any other in the service of radical, even revolutionary transformation.

There was also an interest on the part of various ethnic minorities to include their paths of cultural development in the mainstream of American public life. This latter interest was fostered, no doubt, by the new technologies of communication—radio, phonographs, movies, and so on—but it was also a result of social and demographic changes brought on by the depression: the movement of blacks to northern cities, the westward migration to California from the "dust bowl," and not least the rise of the industrial cities of the Midwest with their working-class populations. In any case, the fascination with the "people" and the subsequent commercialization and successful exportation of a particular American mass, or popular, culture during and after the Second World War owes much to the combination of populism and pragmatism that characterized the New Deal era and the narrowing of the gap between intellectuals and the masses. By the 1950s, however, most intellectuals had returned to their traditional separation from popular culture, and the masses were left to the commercial forces of the marketplace for their entertainment.

In the second half of the 1930s, along with the well-known labor and community activism, writers became journalists, many scientists became politically active, the government supported programs of cultural and economic reconstruction and public works, and the appeal of socialist and Communist parties and organizations was at an all-time high. However, it would be a mistake to characterize the movement that crystallized in the late 1930s as something specifically leftist. For there were pragmatic populists, seeking cultural solutions to social problems, on both the Left and Right. Conservative southerners, the so-called southern agrarians, for example, developed a distinctive style of sociology, as well as regional planning, literature, and art. For a time, ideological differences—and the class distinctions that went with them—were less important than the active "re-cognition" of American cultural identity. The contribution of the movement would be, more than anything else, a reinterpretation of American society through new cultural concepts and approaches that would be diffused throughout the society in the ensuing years. As in Germany, but in rather different ways, a national culture was contrasted to a capitalist civilization that was seen to be in need of fundamental overhaul. For Susman, "a key structural element in a historical reconstruction of the 1930s [is] the effort to find, characterize and adapt to an American way of life as distinguished from the material achievements (and the failures) of an American industrial civilization" (1984: 156).

As with many, if not all, social movements, what was central to the movement of the 1930s was what we have elsewhere called "cognitive praxis," the active relations to science, to technology, to nature, and to society that were articulated and practiced, often in innovative organizational forms (Eyerman and Jamison 1991). The movement of the 1930s took the ideas of populism and pragmatism that had been developed by intellectuals and applied them to the various facets of social life. The movement provided a new audience but also a new organizational context for the development and recombination of ideas that had been associated with progressive intellectuals. Influential books like Reinhold Niebuhr's *Moral Man and Immoral Society* (1932), Ruth Benedict's *Patterns of Culture* (1934), John Dewey's *Liberalism and Social Action* (1935), Lewis Mumford's *Technics and Civilization* (1934) and *Culture of Cities* (1938), and Robert S. Lynd's *Knowledge for What?* (1939) provided a terminology and a way of thinking that could serve to guide, among other things, the assimilation of machine technology into American life.

The idealization of the worker was particularly prominent in literature, among the so-called proletarian writers associated with the Socialist and Communist parties. The "masses" were discovered as a source of artistic inspiration as well as the main vehicles of progressive historical change. The novels of James T. Farrell, John Steinbeck, and perhaps especially John Dos Passos gave life to the working class while applying new techniques of literary creation. For them and countless others, the movements of the 1930s opened up a new range of opportunities for the intellectual as artist; the writer could refine his craft while contributing to the cause of radical social change. For a time, the cultural and the political reinforced one another, as the artist provided identity and self-confidence for the masses and the masses provided inspiration, even legitimation, for creative innovation. In the case of Dos Passos, the combination of journalism and literature and the pioneering use of the montage technique as well as the mixture of fact and fiction were lasting legacies of the 1930s movement to American culture.

Like all social movements, this was a temporary one; and yet its cognitive identity, its combination of populism and pragmatism, was, for a few years, a very important force in American culture. In considering its significance, Norman Birnbaum has recently reflected that "radical movements may be understood as schools—from which the students graduate not quite the same as when they entered. They also, of course, affect and influence far more persons than their members." For Birnbaum, the movements of the New Deal period "enlarged our conception of politics. . . . The New Deal at the very least encouraged another American public ethos" (1988: 140–143). Already with the debates over entering the war at the end of the 1930s, however, the common assumptions, what Birnbaum calls the "uneasy amalgam" of "progressivism, Catholic social reform and Keynesianism," began to split apart. Largely as a result of the exigencies of war, the project that had tried to take "from both the liberal and socialist traditions those ideas that seemed most appropriate for a post-capitalist civilization" began to fragment.

The Postwar Cult of Science

The war was not a time for nuances. The active and constructive re-cognition of American culture that had occupied so many people during the 1930s could not survive Pearl Harbor. The simpler and more traditional values of individualism and self-interest reasserted themselves, and the ideas of the 1930s diffused into American society in fragmented and often simplistic ways. The concern with American culture gradually became an American superiority complex, as writers during and after the war celebrated a mythology of America rather than seeking to understand and redefine those myths. Populist pragmatism tended to lose its luster during and after World War II, as American intellectuals in ever-increasing numbers came to subscribe to new imported philosophies from Europe: logical positivism, neo-Thomist theology, existentialism, and so on. Many consciously sought to distance themselves from the mass culture that came to take form in the television-watching suburbs of postwar America. By the late 1940s, the cognitive praxis of the 1930s had largely been transformed into an anti-ideology of anticommunism, on the one hand, and patriotic celebration of American greatness, on the other. As with other social movements before and since, the synthesis of disparate ideas that provided a cognitive identity was differentiated into its component parts, leading to new dualisms and dichotomies of thought. Pragmatism was replaced as a unifying social cosmology, or world view, by logical philosophies of science, on the one hand, and new idealistic theologies, on the other. A critical cultural assessment of technology gave way to a technological culture of scientific expertise and economic abundance. And an innovative populism, seeking to bridge the gaps between intellectuals and the common people, was replaced by a reaffirmation of academic professionalism and a commercialization of popular culture.

As Mills was to bring to the nation's attention in 1951, America had come to be dominated by an amorphous collection of "white-collar" workers—in the various layers of corporate management, in the media, in the public sector, and in the universities. The expansion of the state and the growth of the mass media provided employment opportunities for many previously unattached—and unemployed—intellectuals, but in the process, the very idea of the intellectual was transformed. A good many of those who had been the partisan intellectuals of the 1930s became the white-collar workers of the 1950s. At the same time the universities were restructured in the image of the modern corporate conglomerate. Upholding academic freedom gave way to a business mentality among a new generation of university presidents and administrators, who refashioned curricula and overhauled disciplines so as to compete more effectively for students and research funds. Higher education and academic research grew into substantial industries in an academic marketplace that was unimaginable before the war.

As such, public life in the United States was scarcely intellectual at all when it came time to confront the scientific-technological state; even many American intellectuals had come to be colored by that deep-seated anti-intellectualism and entrepreneurial spirit that has formed such a central part of American history. Just at the time when anti-intellectualism was at its height in the form of aggressive anti-communism, the status of professional expertise and of science had never been higher. Science was thus seen not primarily as an intellectual path to national and individual enlightenment but rather as a magical bag of tricks, a path to national and individual power. Science, we might say, was assimilated into American culture in an anti-intellectual way. By a kind of reductionist sleight of hand, the pragmatic "method" had been transformed into the blind faith of technocratic social engineering, or instrumental rationality, as Marcuse was to call it. Practice, in good American fashion, remained the criterion of scientific truth, but it was a limited, scientific-technological practice that determined value, not the practical experiences of ordinary men and women. As such, pragmatic populism got turned on its head into a cult of science. And science came to take on the character of a religion.

Postwar America has been called the "era of the expert." With the virtual elimination of social movements and their innovative barrier-breaking movement intellectuals, corporate America propelled the elitist expert to a position of power and influence. With so many people moving out to the suburbs and leaving behind both historical tradition and a sense of community, experts moved in to fill the gap with new kinds of professional advice. From Benjamin Spock to Norman Vincent Peale, the lonely crowd of postwar America was socialized into a new scientific age. Even sports entered a new professional era with the rise of mass communications and the further expansion of advertising. Indeed, sports provided a kind of surrogate community spirit to replace the traditions that had existed in the prewar small towns and ethnic urban villages. As Elaine Tyler May (1989: 155–156) has written, "The postwar years marked a heightening of the status of the professional. Armed with scientific techniques and presumably inhabiting a world above popular passions, the experts had brought us into the atomic age. Physicists developed the bomb, strategists created the cold war, and scientific managers built the military-industrial complex. Science and technology seemed to have invaded virtually every aspect of life, from the most public to the most private."

Science became, in the telling phrase of Vannevar Bush, the new "endless frontier" for postwar Americans to explore and glorify. Bush had been director of the wartime Office of Scientific Research and Development and, in 1944, had been asked by President Roosevelt to suggest how science could be supported after the war was over. His report, published in July 1945, set the tone for much of the immediate postwar discussion. "Advances in science," Bush wrote, "when put to practical use mean more jobs, higher wages, shorter hours, more abundant crops, more leisure for recreation, for study, for learning how to live without the deadening drudgery which has been the burden of the common man for ages past. . . . But to achieve these objectives—to secure a high level of employment, to maintain a position of world leadership—the flow of new scientific knowledge must be both continuous and substantial" (1945: 5).

The cult of science inspired a scientistic faith and a concomitant dismissal of the populist spirit that had characterized the culture of the 1930s. But it took time before its hegemony was established. What it involved was a transformation of one ideal of knowledge into another. Rather than deriving their methods and approaches from an indigenous progressivism, sociologists and historians and psychologists and government officials increasingly came to model themselves on the natural sciences. Atomic physics became the ideal of knowledge that set the standard for the humanities and the social sciences, not to mention popular culture and private life. The scientistic spirit that had dominated the social sciences in the 1920s came to the fore again, but this time its self-confidence and sense of superiority over other ways of thinking were even stronger than before. The scientific spokesmen sought to replace the populist enthusiasms of the 1930s with a positivist belief in the future. Scientific progress was seen as the key to American greatness and the main source of economic and industrial expansion.

The transformation was often largely unconscious and was for many intellectuals more like following a new fashion or trend than making an explicitly political decision. The general assumption was that the world had changed: the programmatic statements stressed the irrelevance of the prewar enthusiasms to the postwar world. The prewar, populist concern with an American way of life came to be criticized for its national and inward-looking provincialism; with the end of the war, American intellectuals had a responsibility to uphold the broader values of Western civilization. The responsibility was no longer to help "create a great American nation," as the president of the American Historical Association put it in December 1945, but to provide moral leadership for what came to be called an Atlantic community. "Of such an Atlantic community and the European civilization basic to it, we Americans are co-heirs and co-developers, and probably in the future the leaders. If we are successfully to discharge our heavy and difficult postwar responsibilities, we shall not further weaken but rather strengthen the consciousness and bonds of this cultural community" (Hayes 1946: 208).

With the diffusion of scientism, those who would uphold the populist pragmatism of the 1930s tended to be marginalized and had difficulty in formulating a critique of the scientific-technological state. In the writings of the elderly John Dewey and the young C. Wright Mills as well as in those of the increasingly embittered middle-aged Lewis Mumford, the militarization of American culture was criticized, and the incorporation of intellectuals into business and politics—what Mills called "Brains, Inc."—was castigated, but there was little space for such viewpoints in the general atmosphere of the cult of science. The three volumes by Mills that we will discuss in the next chapter— *New Men of Power* (1948), on the labor unions, *White Collar* (1951), on the middle classes, and *The Power Elite* (1956), on the new military-corporate rulers of American society—stand relatively alone as a comprehensive corpus of social criticism in the decade following the Second World War.

The critics themselves are at least partly to blame. Mumford's first published response to the atomic bomb was an article entitled, "Gentlemen: You are Mad!" And his tone grew ever more frustrated and extreme as the postwar era progressed. With the coming of McCarthyism and the cold war, the few progressive critics who had retained their critical values were all but silenced; and the younger generation of social scientists and writers were themselves a part of the American celebration. Later in the 1950s, pragmatic populism, emerging out of the southern black churches in combination with pacifists and moral reformers, helped fuel the civil rights movement, but even then it was considered "un-American" in a time when Americanism had come to stand for aggressive anticommunism rather than an open-ended egalitarianism. As we shall see, however, the radical ideas of the 1930s played an important role in Martin Luther King, Jr.'s moral crusade as well as in Saul Alinsky's community organizing.

The Return to Professionalism

During the war, the enthusiasms of the 1930s came to be seen by many intellectuals as dangerous departures from objectivity and transgressions of professional standards of behavior. The elitism and specialized professionalism of the natural scientist became the norm, and although criticism was tolerated, partisanship was not. The norms of science that the sociologist Robert Merton characterized in 1942 stressed the inner cohesion of the "scientific community" around the values of universalism, disinterestedness, organized skepticism, and commun[al]ism, and those values placed the partisan intellectual outside the doors of academe. As such, the kinds of social criticism that were acceptable in the postwar years were much more limited than those that had characterized the 1930s. The days of the omniscient generalist were over; even a critical thinker as public and active as Mills prided himself on his sociological expertise (although he thought of it as craftsmanship) and his adherence to a sociological tradition epitomized by Max Weber. What many of our dissident intellectuals practiced was an alternative professionalism, reinventing the partisan engagement that had characterized intellectual life in the 1930s—and in the European resistance. The alternative professionalism often led, however, as we shall see, to academic marginalization; the battle to defend social criticism was, in most cases, won at the cost of scholarly respectability.

In the social sciences, the cult of science included the propagation of a specialized ideal of knowledge, dividing social reality into separate academic disciplines. In this respect, scientism transformed the pragmatic interest in the scientific investigation of society into an institutionalized social "role." Science was seen, in the framework that came to dominate sociological thinking, as part of a functionally differentiated social system. In the words of Talcott Parsons, who was to become the dominant social theorist of his time, "Social science, as a system of human activity, is an integral part of a larger social system. Because it is inevitably involved in a complex balance of forces, the maintenance and promotion of its standards and functions are inherently precarious. Stability cannot be taken for granted, but must be accomplished by continually vigilant adjustment to a changing situation." Parsons sought to inculcate a professional ethic into social science, distinguishing it from the more amateurish social studies that had flourished before the war. "In maintaining a balanced and steadfast orientation to technical standards, the social scientist must hold a model of purely scientific work continually before him. He must have a clear realization of the importance of genuinely technical work in making possible his own applied functions" (1948: 105). Parsons's structural-functionalism served as a theoretical legitimation for the new regime of scientific expertise. In his social system, everyone had his or her proper function and "social role." Stepping out of line, or transgressing disciplinary boundaries, was dysfunctional and thus inefficient in terms of the smooth operation of the social system as a whole.

One important implication of this theory of society was the differentiation in social science between what Mills called "grand theorists" and "abstracted empiricists" and the development of a technical ideal of research. Theory itself became a technical operation, generating formal concepts and thus reducing social process to logical relations. Such a theory fit well with the ongoing transformation of social science into an applied research activity. Many social scientists—even some of those who would later become critics—conducted opinion surveys and other forms of applied research during the war, and afterward, a statistically based and individually oriented empirical orientation came to take on increasing importance in many academic social science departments. In this regard the role of the large private foundations, such as the Rockefeller Foundation, was particularly important. The Carnegie Foundation support for "area studies," for "social relations" at Harvard, and for educational research, the Rockefeller Foundation's support for "international relations" and development economics, and the Ford Foundation's support for "behavioral studies" helped redefine the social sciences in significant ways. Besides serving ideological functions, these programs favored empirical research of a survey variety and thus encouraged particular methodologies and research approaches. The result of these as well as of more "internal" forces within the academy—such as Parsons's and Merton's theories in sociology, Milton Friedman's and Paul Samuelson's theories in economics, Robert Dahl's theories in political science—tended to marginalize critical thought.

Even those who would criticize in the guise of academic expertise were subject to the norms of disciplinarity. Criticism came to be fragmented according to the specialized competence of the critic. The atomic scientists could criticize the uses of atomic energy, economists like John Kenneth Galbraith and Robert Heilbroner could criticize the productive economic uses—and abuses—of scientific research, sociologists like Robert Merton could criticize the institutional aspects of scientific work, and cultural critics like Dwight Macdonald and Irving Howe could criticize the vulgarities of mass culture. But the kind of all-encompassing social concern that had been articulated in the 1930s was no longer respectable, for it was not considered sufficiently scientific. The almost total academic rejection of Mumford's *The Con-*

dition of Man (1944) and *The Conduct of Life* (1952), the third and fourth volumes in the Renewal of Life series that he had initiated in the 1930s, is one of several indications that a new scientistic climate was fast achieving a hegemonic status as the cold war intensified.

Intriguingly, the scientistic hegemony of intellectual life fostered, almost in spite of itself, a subjectivist mirror image of romantic anti-scientism that would, in the 1960s, inspire a counterculture that posited heightened subjectivity and personal liberation as a great refusal of the Great Society. The sources of the counterculture included both the studies of alienation and subjectivity, such as Arendt's *The Human Condition* (1958), Marcuse's *Eros and Civilization* (1955), and Erich Fromm's *The Sane Society* (1955), and the more mystical explorations of Eastern religion, especially Zen Buddhism, undertaken already in the 1950s by people like Allen Ginsberg and Gary Snyder.

Perhaps even more important was the discovery by writers and artists of what might be termed the underlife of American society: the deviants, criminals, drug addicts, and sexually promiscuous. William Burroughs, James Baldwin, Jack Kerouac, and Allen Ginsberg glorified another realm of existence beyond the antiseptic scientific official culture. In the margins of America—the jazz clubs of Harlem, the slums of Chicago, and on the roads between the idylls of suburbia—the hard life of direct experience formed the stuff of the Beat writers and the rhythms of the new electrified blues music.

With the scientification of academic life, several of the "activist" or movement intellectuals of the 1930s either accepted the new "technical standards" or distanced themselves from the academy altogether, finding, like Macdonald and Mary McCarthy, niches for themselves as professional (cultural) "critics" for popular magazines or, like Mills and Mumford, becoming professional outlaws, with their social criticism—and their criticism of fellow intellectuals—growing ever more alienated. Both Mills's and Mumford's criticism would be influential in the 1960s in inspiring the student revolt with its rejection of what Mumford called the megamachine and its eventual rediscovery of romantic passion.

On another level, however, the professionalization of criticism represented a kind of breakthrough into the commercial media. Watered down and accommodating as they might have been, the articles by James Baldwin and Macdonald in *Esquire* and *Playboy* and the columns by Mumford and Howe in the *New Yorker* and *Time* gave birth to a new kind of journalism, directing critical, literary attention to popular themes. At the same time, the infusion of qualified critical voices into the popular media challenged the hegemony of the formal academic cultural experts, indeed, challenged the academic culture altogether. While many academic humanists distanced themselves from the reality around them by escaping into a world of abstract techniques and scholarly jargon, coteries of cultural critics writing in the popular media questioned the values and conventional wisdom of their time. The spaces that they managed to carve out within the established culture would provide some of the models for the alternative media that would develop in the 1960s.

The emphasis on science as the source of social and economic development was part of a more general transformation taking place in American society, which we can term the shaping of a technological culture. It corresponded to a period of rather unproblematic economic expansion and the coming to prominence of new technologies based on cheap oil: plastics, petrochemicals, synthetic textiles, and so on. The "long wave" of economic and technological development that was ushered in by the Second World War and that continued into the 1960s was based on a new technoeconomic paradigm. The paradigm was characterized by both "scientification," that is, the direct infusion of scientific research into the production process, and militarization, the domination of military priorities over technological development; and it came to be steered by new kinds of diversified multinational, or transnational, corporations, which in the postwar period developed their own systems of knowledge generation, production, and diffusion. As with the earlier long waves of capitalist development, this postwar wave also had a cultural component—the creation of an appropriate set of values and beliefs in the general public that were congenial to and acceptant of the new products and production processes.

The propagation of general education and popular science was a widespread strategy in the postwar years to infuse a scientific-technological value system into American culture. Unlike the writings of the 1930s that had often sought to show how science grew out of practical needs and practical problems, the postwar writings tended to present the scientist as a man apart, a great man of thought and ideas, more a magician than a technician. This view was reproduced in the literature—and, not least, the films—of science fiction, which reacted to the challenge of the scientific-technological state by resurrecting Frankenstein images of the mad scientist or developing new alien images to contribute to the anti-Communist crusade. While science fiction gave vent to otherwise repressed fears, popular science writers glorified the new scientific-technological elite and their discoveries, and on television, children were introduced to the scientific method by a jovial and pedagogical "Mr. Wizard." Not only was science useful but it could also be fun.

But even here the hegemonic culture opened spaces within which critics could operate. As the 1950s progressed, the popularization of science took on a critical edge, and, in 1962, Rachel Carson, one of the most successful of the postwar science writers with two best-selling books on the oceans to her credit, was able to use her talents to help shape a new environmental opposition. Popular writing about science grew more critical, especially after the Soviets launched their space satellite in 1957, and there developed a widespread fear that the American scientific-technological state was falling behind. That soul-searching produced President Dwight D. Eisenhower's famous warning about the insidious power of the "military-industrial complex" in his farewell address in 1961 as well as the awakening of environmental concern.

The Remaking of Partisanship

While most intellectuals in the postwar period came to renounce their youthful enthusiasms, a vocal minority tried to keep the ideas of the 1930s alive. Some of these partisan intellectuals had been students in the 1920s and 1930s; others contributed actively to the intense debates about the future of America in a world on the road to war. The social movements of the times provided them with more than a supplement to formal education; for many, the experiences of social and political activism offered a much richer and more relevant education than any university course could hope to give. The war continued this schooling in reality, by bringing almost all Americans together in a common struggle against fascism and widening the range of their horizons. The war both fostered an international outlook that was less ideological than had often been the case in the 1930s and mixed people from different backgrounds and regions together for a brief, intensive period. But unlike their contemporaries who willingly wandered after the war into the expanding wasteland of the American empire, these intellectuals struggled to maintain and redefine their partisanship within the new intellectual and personal contexts that emerged.

This book will move between biography and history in tracing the intellectual roots of the 1960s. The people we write about are not merely the symbols or abstractions or role models that they often seem to be for commentators on the 1940s and 1950s; we are concerned with them both as representatives of larger historical patterns and as distinct human beings existentially constructing their own lives. It is a particularly appropriate way to approach the American postwar era, an age that was so strongly colored by the conflict between individual freedom and totalitarianism and perhaps more than anything else witnessed the loss of Emersonian man into the lonely crowd of mass society.

Our method is that of collective biography, grouping apparently disparate individuals around a common thematic category—society, nature, knowledge, culture, politics—each of which formed the basis for the emergence of social movements in the 1960s and 1970s. Re-conceptualizing these categories at a particular historical juncture is what our subjects have in common. They share contextual and generational commonalities, even though their life histories often went separate ways, marked, as they have been, by an often aggressive struggle for autonomy and individuality.

As individuals, these partisan critics of postwar America were all concerned with intellectual craftsmanship and with breaking down academic boundaries and distinctions. In this they differed from their mainstream contemporaries, who found congenial the new conditions of big science and corporate culture. While many, if not most, academics were becoming organization men, partisan intellectuals were reasserting their independence, or at least attempting to keep a distance from the new range of opportunities for intellectual labor. Their self-appointed task was to ask uncomfortable questions, identify fundamental problems, and try to put the pieces together into new patterns of understanding and meaning. They gave radical witness.

In the process they strayed across disciplinary borders and partook of intellectual comradery as compensation for the movements that were suddenly no longer available. Few of the critical intellectuals worked in isolation; they found sustenance in small groups and journals as well as in small, temporary spaces in and around the universities. In helping to lead a new generation out of the "wasteland," they were themselves marginalized by the established centers of cultural influence and success. But in combining homegrown radicalism with European ideas, they opened the door to new paths for achieving both fame and fortune.

Much of the criticism that will concern us in this book was embodied in refugees, like Hannah Arendt, Leo Szilard, Herbert Marcuse, and Erich Fromm, all of whom had come to America to escape fascism. Outsiders by necessity, they often found support and friendship in outsiders by choice, people like Allen Ginsberg and James Baldwin. Still others, like Lewis Mumford, Mary McCarthy, and C. Wright Mills, managed to stay inside the academy or the popular media while rejecting the values that came to dominate those institutions. And a few, like Fairfield Osborn, Dorothy Day, and Saul Alinsky, created new organizational spaces for their critical work.

From our perspective, the 1960s cannot be adequately explained or understood without examining the formative role played by these and other partisan intellectuals. The 1960s, we contend, were not merely significant as politics; indeed, the political battles have been overtaken by history. Today they seem anachronistic. But the ideas of the 1960s live on, as sources of inspiration in a variety of scientific fields, in popular culture, and as a paradigm for life at once autonomous, free, and committed: the "personal is political." The importance of the 1960s is largely symbolic, or, in our terms, intellectual. Like other social movements, it is the cognitive praxis—the new ideas and the new intellectual contexts—that gives the movements of the 1960s and after their main significance. The power of the ideas that emerged—and, indeed, the continuing power of the 1960s as an inspirational idea itself—cannot be comprehended unless those ideas are looked at in formation, as emergent processes of rediscovery and recognition.

In this book, we want to explore how the cognitive praxis of the 1960s first emerged out of the activities of critical intellectuals. It was, we claim, a small number of relatively isolated individuals who set the stage—and much of the conceptual framework—for 1960s social activism. In the 1950s, as so often before in American history, intellectuals were under attack by forces of anti-intellectualism or conformity, which gives many of their writings a special power and a renewed relevance for contemporary American society. With the purported closing of the American mind and the recent resurgence of American military might, it is important to remember the cold war critics of the 1950s.

The Structure of the Book

Five main intellectual areas or themes concern us in the pages that follow: Society, nature, knowledge, culture, and politics. These areas do not cover the entire range of ideas that were spawned by the movements of the 1960s, but they capture at least most of what has continued to be important and influential. We will approach them through the method of collective biography, presenting the activities of our critical intellectuals in a thematic way, mixing a portrayal of the person's life with analysis of the person's works.

We have chosen those intellectuals whose ideas and/or activities had a significant impact on the movements of the 1960s, although "impact," we admit, is a somewhat subjective term. In most cases, the impact is obvious; in others, the impact is both less obvious and less direct. In all cases, however, the impact that concerns us is personal as well as collective, for our subjects served both as bearers of traditions of intellectual partisanship and as formulators of ideas and issues. In addition to serving as examples of intellectual behavior, they provided many of the concepts and theories—and organizational forums—that lay behind the more public manifestations of social movement.

Impact and influence are double-edged, however. While some of the people who fill the following pages became heroes, even gurus for the movements that they spawned, others grew disappointed in what had been unleashed. Marcuse and Arendt offer contrasting patterns of interaction with the movements of the 1960s. Where the one found a new historical agent and personal recognition in a foreign intellectual environment, the other primarily found a failed opportunity and a repetition of the extremism and anti-intellectualism that had afflicted previous periods of radicalism in America. Between these poles of attraction and repulsion fall the more mixed relations of Mead and McCarthy and Mumford and Baldwin, keeping their intellectual distance while being nudged toward more critical positions, and Fromm, Alinksy, Ginsberg, and especially King, identifying with the new movements while seeking to play an independent intellectual role. Mills and Carson, who served as models for many of the activists of the 1960s and whose writings perhaps more than any others inspired the movements of student and environmental activism, died (in 1962 and 1964, respectively) before they had to take a stand.

The first theme that concerns us deals with the reconceptualization of society. America had traditionally been seen as a kind of open-ended frontier, dominated by small towns, family businesses and farms, democratic institutions, and Protestant values. In the twentieth century, however, America was transformed from a loosely connected confederation of communities into an increasingly urban, industrialized nation. The Second World War brought about the rise of a military-industrial complex and the domination of society by a middle class of white-collar workers. These changes were assimilated, if not accepted, by most social scientists, who saw their role primarily as analysts of the social problems or strains that the transformations had brought about. But a few outlaw academics and disenfranchised Marxists were able to provide the terms and concepts that were needed to comprehend this new mass society; in particular, we will indicate how the social theorists C. Wright Mills, Hannah Arendt, and Erich Fromm, from different intellectual vantage points and at different levels of abstraction, challenged the new mass society in their writings and their very way of living as critical intellectuals. Postwar industrial society, our critical intellectuals claimed, had become both authoritarian and repressive and steered by what Mills called a new "power elite"; their writings and actions inspired the New Left in its collective call for liberation and participatory democratic action. Arendt's fierce intellectual independence kept her from taking active part in the movements of the 1960s—indeed, she became an outspoken critic of most of them—but her uniquely philosophical journalism remained an important intellectual presence throughout the turbulent decade.

Our second theme deals with the reconceptualization of nature. The closing of the frontier and the spreading of industrialism transformed the American landscape from a largely untamed wilderness to an exploitable expanse of resources. With postwar suburbanization and the rise of the sunbelt industries, nature came ever closer to society; and the traditional interest in conservation gave way to a new world of nature re-creation. Postwar industrial development was based on science rather than on nature; plastics, synthetic textiles, and petrochemicals replaced natural processes with man-made techniques, but, as a result, their disposal created substantial new problems. The American consumer had become a "waste maker," and pollution was like a plague upon the land. It was in the 1940s and 1950s that a small number of nature lovers, writers, and scientists began to identify the new problems. We will focus on three individuals, as representatives for the range of ecological criticism that emerged. Fairfield Osborn, now largely forgotten, was one of the very first to warn of the new dangers in his book, *Our Plundered Planet* (1948), but he was also one of those who tried to put his critique into practice, through his work in conservation and zoological societies. Lewis Mumford transformed his human ecological philosophy into a more far-reaching and all-encompassing social criticism in the 1950s and 1960s, challenging the highway builders and the city planners and keeping the 1930s bioregional vision alive. Finally, we examine how the new conception of nature as a human environment came to be presented most dramatically and influentially by Rachel Carson in her book, *Silent Spring* (1962). These ecological intellectuals were among the handful of critics who planted the seeds for the new ecology movement. In the process, nature conservation was transformed into environmentalism, which continues to affect research agendas as well as American political life.

Our third theme deals with the reconceptualization of knowledge. It was the Second World War that would turn little science, a kind of artisanal activity, into the Big Science of corporate and military research. At the same time, a new breed of professional expert moved into government service and sought to give America a new position of leadership in the world of knowledge, encouraged by the emigration of many scientists and other intellectuals from Europe. This organized knowledge production became the basis for a range of new industrial products, but even more important was how the creative process itself became incorporated into the marketplace as universities and other academic institutions competed for talent and for government research contracts. The critics here would emerge from within the new institutions themselves; first, among the atomic scientists just after the war who were the first to outline the significance of the new "atomic age," and later, among the peace researchers and other intellectuals who would inspire the mass protests against the bomb in the 1950s and the movement against the Vietnam War in the 1960s. In the writings of Leo Szilard and in the pages of the *Bulletin of the Atomic Scientists,* the conception of knowledge was transformed from an autonomous small-scale activity into a form of societal practice; and the works of Margaret Mead and Herbert Marcuse introduced new approaches to understanding the consequences of this socialization of knowledge. Marcuse brought Marxism up to date, by reformulating its basic tenets in the light of the failed Soviet experiment and the victory of technocratic rationality in the West. His critique of "one-dimensional thought" was an important pillar of the New Left's theory of knowledge. Even more influential perhaps were the writings and personal example of Mead, drawing on the cultural anthropology of her friend, Ruth Benedict, and the experience of her own fieldwork to relativize the very idea of what knowledge consists of.

Our fourth theme concerns the reconceptualization of culture. During and after the Second World War, America was transformed into a mass consumption society of television-watching suburbanites, with serious effects on the common culture. On the one hand, television and mass media more generally produced an age of conformity and a degeneration of artistic standards. On the other hand, the hegemony of the new middle-class values tended to narrow the range of the common culture as a shared way of life and to exclude the various outsiders that not only did not disappear but actually increased in numbers after the war. Three types of responses were especially significant for what was to come in the 1960s and onward. On the one hand, there is the reaction of the successful novelist, typified for us by

Mary McCarthy, the established woman writer, who uses satire—a typical weapon of the oppressed—to poke fun at her masculine colleagues and provides a role model for other women to emulate. Her best-selling novels on the mores of middle-class women helped set the agenda for the feminists to come. On the other hand, James Baldwin, in his self-biographical novels and essays, presented what might be called the black counterpoint to middle-class culture and provided inspiration for the emerging civil rights movement; Baldwin, like McCarthy, relied on traditional literary forms to expand social consciousness. A third, more culturally radical response came from the Beats; William Burroughs, Jack Kerouac, and especially Allan Ginsberg, on whom we focus our attention, gave voice to the sexual, spiritual, and psychological repression intrinsic to the conformist culture. As fathers of the 1960s counterculture, the Beat writers reconceptualized in their very persons the meaning of culture in American society.

Finally, the idea of politics was reconceptualized; indeed, the new politics of direct action was what the 1960s came to stand for. With the debacle of the Wallace campaign in the presidential election of 1948, politics in America came to be frozen into mass parties, collections of interest groups rather than collectivities of active citizens. Community organizing, as practiced by Saul Alinsky in the streets of Chicago, became an important alternative in the art of doing politics. Alinsky's approach was to take on power directly over issues that affected the local community, and his "rules for radicals" would be a handbook for many activists in the new social movements. Dorothy Day, journalist and former cultural radical, brought to the antiwar movement a unique moral presence based on pacifist beliefs and missionary zeal. While her role has tended to be neglected in the many recountings of the 1960s, Day exemplified partisan intellectual practice through her catholic anarchism, living among the poor in New York and helping to shape the peace movement. A pacifist during the Second World War, Day kept alive a tradition of civil disobedience that was drawn on and revitalized in the 1960s and beyond. In her quiet devotion to serving the interests of peace and justice, she was one of the most important women who, often behind the scenes and out of the headlines, first served to make the political a matter of personal commitment. Martin Luther King, Jr.'s contribution was much more direct and obvious, constructing in his speeches and his organizing a bridge between the Old Left "popular fronts" of the 1930s and the antiwar movement of the 1960s. The civil rights movement that he helped carve out of the wilderness provided a space where the two radical generations could meet. Drawing on the social gospel of the 1930s and the moral example of Gandhi, King helped bring spirituality back into American politics.

. . .

In the 1950s, these different themes tended to be reconceptualized as separate discourses, and the reconceptualizers tended to live in separate intellectual universes: some wrote for popular consumption, while others worked within professional, more academic communities. Our partisan intellectuals, even those who had legitimate standing in the established political culture, were often isolated from their peers and their society. Small, marginal magazines and autonomous spaces could not replace what they most needed and craved—an audience to interact with and to act on their ideas, that is, a social movement.

The movements of the 1960s—civil rights, student activism, opposition to the war in Vietnam, and then environmentalism and feminism—provided that audience but, by so doing, took many of the reconceptualizers by surprise. In one sense, their very existence challenged some of the ideas that had been formulated; the movements disproved the contentions of conformity and one-dimensionality while bringing new social actors to the fore. Students, women, blacks, nature lovers became activists, but by becoming active, they also broke with some of the conceptual and organizational frameworks that had been constructed by our partisan intellectuals. Many felt neglected, even rejected. But some would eventually outlast the 1960s and help inspire a new generation of critics.

2 MASS SOCIETY AND ITS CRITICS

C. Wright Mills, Hannah Arendt, Erich Fromm

• •

In 1944, a twenty-eight-year-old refugee from Waco, Texas, armed with a Ph.D. in sociology from the University of Wisconsin and fresh from wartime Washington, settled in New York hoping to change the world. Eighteen years later he was dead, and if he had not exactly changed the world, he had certainly done more than most to change the way we think about it. On arriving in New York, C. Wright Mills had moved into a brownstone apartment in Greenwich Village that he had gotten with the help of Daniel Bell, the editor of the *New Leader*, a small socialist journal. Mills, who in his doctoral dissertation had tried to apply pragmatism to sociology, had come to New York in search of the kind of intellectual excitement and political commitment that had characterized the city in the 1930s but by 1944 was fading into memory. Bell would soon move on to *Fortune* magazine, and Mills would take up an academic post at Columbia University, but he would never renounce the reason for first coming to New York; almost singlehandedly in the 1950s, Mills would try to keep alive what he later called the sociological imagination in countering the drift toward conformity, homogenization, and instrumental rationality: in short, mass society.

Three years earlier, another refugee, fleeing the Holocaust and wartorn Europe, had come to New York to help her fellow Jews and to continue her lifelong search for answers to some of the more fundamental questions of human existence, the classical intellectual quest. Trained in philosophy by Martin Heidegger and Edmund Husserl, two of the most important figures of twentieth-century German thought, Hannah Arendt brought with her the best of the continental tradition as well as a commitment to justice and humanity that she would spend much of the rest of her life communicating to her new countrymen. She worked for a time for a publishing house, started by a fellow Jewish refugee, that spread the great works of German culture in English translation; and she eventually created for herself, in Jewish circles as well as among sympathetic New York intellectuals, a unique place in American postwar life. Like Mills, Arendt was never really accepted by the academic establishment, since she refused to confine herself to any one specific discipline. She remained an outsider and joined a number of other refugees of similarly generalist persuasion at the New School for Social Research. Yet she managed to keep the big questions alive in her weighty but highly popular books about totalitarianism, revolution, and the "human condition." And in questioning the moral legitimacy of a political order that no longer rested on active partic-ipation, she helped inspire, without really intending to, the quest for direct democracy that was to be so central to the revolts of the 1960s.

Erich Fromm brought the problems of mass society down to the personal level. Already in the 1920s, he had conducted a survey of "class consciousness" in the German working class with Max Hork-heimer, the founder of the Frankfurt school of critical theory, while simultaneously training as a psychoanalyst. Fromm's lifelong search for a sane society, combining psychological insight with social responsi-bility, began in the midst of the Weimar Republic and was colored by the confrontation with the Nazi apocalypse that affected the lives of so many middle-class Jews of his generation, bringing them out of a (false) sense of security. Not directly involved in the actual political struggle, Fromm managed to synthesize the teachings of Marx and Freud and make the results palatable to an American audience. His critical contribution was to articulate a moral stance and a humanism appropriate to modern society, a personal path out of the wasteland.

Mills, Arendt, and Fromm each bore with them different intel-lectual legacies and traditions. And they had each been personally affected by the anti-totalitarian movements of the 1930s. Of course, they were not unique in this regard; but because of personal strength and social circumstance, they were somewhat better able to sustain a sense of partisanship through the dark days of the cold war. Their particular contributions in sociology, political philosophy, and social psychology were colored by their involvement, however peripheral, in the social movements of the 1930s, and in America, they managed to find a space to continue to innovate and eventually inspire a new wave of movement activity. Their approaches differed, but they shared a common ambition to find a way of conceptualizing and criticizing the new mass society.

The Sources of Their Discontent

The 1930s ushered in a great economic, political, and social depression. An acute sense of crisis filled the air, as old ideas and visions no longer seemed to work. This sense of crisis was heightened by the coming to state power of reactionary social movements in Germany and Italy and by the consolidation of the Soviet revolution in Russia. From both the Left and the Right, it appeared that the masses had entered European politics to stay. To counter these challenges and to meet the demands of its own working class, some 25 percent of whom were out of work when Roosevelt took office in 1933, the American corporate establishment was forced to adopt a more liberal stance and offer a new deal to the American people. The 1930s were marked by experimental governmental programs, attempting to broaden the base of political legitimacy, but also by an enormous rise in labor activism and in political movements on both the Right and the Left. It was in such a context that Mills went to college at the University of Texas. And it was from a very different "mass movement," namely, German national socialism, that Fromm and Arendt had fled to America.

The outbreak of a second world war provided an escape from the sense of crisis as well as from the economic depression, as the nation was pulled back together in common cause. In addition to turning American attention to world politics, the war helped to accelerate some dramatic economic and demographic shifts under way since the outset of the depression. These shifts involved the movement of skilled workers, mostly white, from the industries of the northern and northeastern states to the west and southwest and the movement of farm labor, mostly black, from the rural south to the cities of the industrial north, especially Chicago, Detroit, and New York. The war created oppor-

tunities for skilled industrial workers in defense industries newly located on the West Coast as well as in the suburbs around New York,
where Grumman and Republic built their aircraft plants. The blacks
moved into the northern cities the whites abandoned for the suburbs,
helping set the stage for some of the great racial confrontations to come.

The rise in salaries in the overheated economy stimulated by the
war created a new buying public among skilled and semiskilled white
workers. The automobile made suburban living possible and was a
precondition for the building boom that would also stimulate the
postwar economy. Some two million new homes were built each year
during the 1950s, and in their little boxes in the suburbs, young families
entered the culture of abundance, with its endless supply of consumer
goods and that great new invention for home entertainment, television.

In terms of ideology, the centerpiece of this new suburban style
of living was the housewife, a specialist in consumption and in nurturing
a spirit of togetherness in the family as well as in the artificial community
of the suburban neighborhood. Higher wages and increased leisure
time made the home and the private sphere, rather than the work place
and the union hall, the center of attention. No longer, it appeared, were
class and work the stuff out of which personal identity was to be
constituted. Increased profits created money for advertising, as television became the new means of reaching the consumer, especially
housewives and children. At the same time, military spending rose from
$14 billion in 1949 to $44 billion in 1953, or to some 60 percent of the
federal budget. The culture of abundance needed to be defended.

With American involvement in the war—and then later in Korea—
production and productivity soared in both industry and agriculture.
A great wave of patriotism flowed over the United States, and volunteers
flocked to the armed forces and to the defense industries. Even the
former radicals in the labor unions and the socialist parties lined up
behind the war effort. Partly because of the shifts in the structure of
the economy and partly because of the new sense of national unity, the
"labor question" that had previously been at the center of American
domestic politics was replaced by concern with the American standard
of living. As Steve Fraser (1989: 57) has put it, "The struggle over power
and property, which had supplied the friction and frisson of politics
since at least the Gilded Age, was superseded by the universal quest

for more—goulash capitalism. Mass politics replaced class politics. Labor ceased to be a great question or even a mass movement containing within it the seeds of a wholly new future." The end of the labor question in domestic politics was accompanied by the transformation of Russia from ally to enemy and the rise of the Communist threat. The end of utopia was also the end of ideology as the labor movement shifted from social movement to interest group. The defining political issue became totalitarianism versus freedom, rather than capitalism versus socialism. Among the main articulators of the new dichotomy were C. Wright Mills, Hannah Arendt, and Erich Fromm.

From the Worker to the Lonely Crowd

The society that emerged out of the Second World War was given many names, as it evoked powerful images of conformity, loneliness, homogenization, standardization, and mediocrity. Individuals had become faceless figures in gray flannel suits, working in anonymous organizations and living in the little boxes made of ticky-tacky that Malvina Reynolds made fun of in her song. For intellectuals it almost seemed as if T. S. Eliot's nightmare vision had been realized: the open spaces, the wide frontier had become the wasteland of the mass society.

While many tried to diagnose the new conditions, only a handful tried to find a way out. New techniques in social research permitted the scientist to poll opinion, to study attitudes and tastes, and to help devise strategies of acceptance and accommodation. For the "lonely crowd" that David Reisman christened in his influential study of 1950, the sociologist could offer a range of new personality types and characterizations; and the psychologist and therapeutic expert could provide temporary relief (like the pain-killing tablets promoted in the jingles of radio and television advertisements). Eventually, the gyrations of a young singer from Tupelo, Mississippi, would awaken other paths to satisfaction, and there would be something of a nationwide obsession with deviance, violence, crime, and perhaps especially juvenile delinquency. The mass society bred alienation and rebellion, but it also led to new visions of American society and a new, postindustrial concept of community.

The social ideas that inspired the political activism of the 1960s emerged out of a new kind of dialogue between Europe and America that went beyond the older ideological categories and divisions between Right and Left. It may well have been the case that there had come an "end to ideology," as Bell contended; but that did not mean that Americans could avoid the insights, or the lessons, that could be drawn from the wholesale destruction of central Europe during the Second World War. From Europe, Arendt and Fromm brought the nightmare of totalitarian oppression in their own personal experience; and they reformulated the radical philosophies of Marx and Freud and applied them to postwar American conditions. They opposed the dominant modes of social interpretation that were so popular in American universities, joining with the academic outlaw Mills to connect the public and the private spheres in a new critical discourse about society.

The discourse provided a critical analysis of mass society and identified the new sources of power and authority in America—and in the world. The military-corporate alliance that emerged during the Second World War transformed American society and exerted a form of domination that was new in its inclusiveness and range. To oppose these new men of power, it was necessary to see society not as a set of balancing interests and functions but as an arena of conflict. It was especially Mills, as an academic critic, who attributed to conflict and social tension a central place in the constitution of social life, and it was Fromm who wrote of its repercussions in personal relations and individual sanity. Our critical intellectuals—perhaps because they had internalized the conflicts of the age more directly—managed to probe deeper into the roots of social action and the dangers of conformity and mass persuasion. But because of a broader intellectual register and a grounding in classical thought—and a willingness to transgress disciplinary boundaries—they could also suggest sources of renewal and regeneration for individuals as well as for the society at large. Arendt's resurrection of the Greek idea of polis, which she rediscovered in the American revolution, entered into the efforts at participatory democracy that characterized the 1960s movements, while Fromm's socialist humanism inspired, from an altogether different direction, the great refusal of students and activists to take part in the mass society and seek liberation wherever they could find it.

It was in the 1950s that long-term and nearly invisible changes in the structures of American society began to become visible and demand a name. While many names were cast about, one that stuck was "mass society." The concept first appeared in Europe around the turn of the century as part of the conservative reaction to Marxist theory and the breakdown of traditional society. In the interwar period, it had been taken up by social critics to refer to the changes in society brought about by technology and mass production. In America, it came to be used by left-wing critics in a way that was similar in terms of the ills it identified but different in terms of the remedies proposed. In the postwar American context, mass society was that form of society in which the autonomy of the individual, the basis of critical thinking, was said to be undermined by changes in work and family life. And where the new mass culture, instead of being the expression of well-grounded tradition or creative genius, now contributed to the formation of false consciousness rather than insight or enlightenment.

C. Wright Mills, the Academic Outlaw

Mills was one of the key advocates of the mass society thesis. In a series of books and essays that would become important to the formation of the New Left a decade after they were written, he outlined the new America with broad, passionate strokes. Born in Texas in 1916, Mills remained something of a westerner even after he made a permanent move to New York in 1944. During the war he had taught at the University of Maryland, near Washington, D.C., but he had been more interested in the political goings-on in wartime Washington than in his teaching. It was radical politics and social criticism, the praxis of the classic intellectual rather than the academic, that attracted Mills. When the possibility of moving to New York, the center of American intellectual life, presented itself, he did not hesitate to leave his academic appointment. Through the help of Daniel Bell and the forum provided by the *New Leader,* which Bell was then editing, Mills came in contact with other New York intellectuals like Philip Rahv, Dwight Macdonald, and Irving Howe who were connected to the *Partisan Review.* That loose network provided Mills with access to a small but influential circle of writers and journals. As Macdonald recalls, it was Mills who provided him with the name for the journal *Politics,* which he started in 1944 (Horowitz 1983: 77). And it was Bell who provided Mills with the connections necessary to attain a position at Columbia University's Bureau of Applied Social Research in 1944, when the wartime expansion created new opportunities for part-time researchers.

While the broader New York intellectual milieu provided Mills with his contacts and helped him develop his polemical writing style, it was the bureau that provided Mills with the necessary material for his reinterpretation of American society. Under the direction of Austrian émigré Paul Lazersfeld, the Bureau of Applied Social Research had grown rapidly as a war-related interest in practical social research was channeled in government money. With data and experience gathered while working on large-scale surveys at the bureau, Mills was in the unique position of being an outsider social critic armed with insider skills and information.

Mills came to Columbia at a time when the social and technical basis for producing knowledge was changing, when the scientist or man of knowledge was replacing the classical intellectual or man of letters. This new man was part of a bureaucratic organization with access to great masses of mechanically compiled data. This was a position not available to everyone, only those who met the requirements and who had mastered the sophisticated techniques of data gathering and interpretation. This was the "insider" part. On the other side, Mills tried to play the part of a critical intellectual, a type fast being phased out in favor of the specialized professional. It was the role of insider as outsider, or as he preferred to call it, academic outlaw, that Mills carved out in the new context. It was a role that would put him in direct conflict with many of his colleagues.

One aspect of the new context that faced American intellectuals in the postwar period was the expanding opportunities for intellectual labor. The increased interest shown by government and business in the production of knowledge was supplemented by the flood of students attracted to institutions of higher learning, many of them veterans supported under the so-called G.I. Bill. At the same time, formal higher education was becoming a necessary qualification as more and more occupations were in the process of being professionalized, including university teaching itself. Columbia University was at the center of this process of transition and growth. Despite making room for exiled Europeans like Lazersfeld, Theodor Adorno, and Lewis Coser, Columbia remained rooted in American academic traditions. The new technically enhanced means of acquiring knowledge may have deeply affected the ways its sociologists went about their business, but that business was still defined in terms of established scientific traditions or "norms" of objectivity, disinterestedness, universalism, and organized skepticism, as Merton, the leading intellectual figure of the department of sociology, formulated them.

In his role of academic outlaw, Mills was closer to Lynd, the odd man out in the department. Lynd was famous for his large-scale community studies in the 1920s and 1930s and through them was connected to that collective orientation and tradition of political partisanship that had all but disappeared from professional sociology. His collection of provocative essays, *Knowledge for What?* were even as they were being written a sort of swan song for the type of sociology Mills himself would produce. While Lynd was still an important figure at Columbia when Mills arrived, his star was fading.

While Mills would later entitle his critical book on the state of sociology *The Sociological Imagination,* after the work of another of his Columbia colleagues (Lionel Trilling's *The Liberal Imagination*), many of his arguments were derived from Lynd. Unlike Lynd and Trilling, however, Mills spent a great deal of his energy trying to distance himself from the academic world. Academics were not his prime audience. Lynd had aimed his polemics against the detached professionalism in the discipline, and Trilling, while continuing to write in smaller journals, adapted to the new academicism, as did many of the so-called New York intellectuals of the postwar era. Mills kept alive both the message and the spirit of the 1930s, as he continued to act as a public intellectual with a progressive, pragmatic approach to social science.

Knowledge for What? made many of the points Mills would later develop in his conception of mass society and the lack of sociological imagination. The theme running through that book was that sociologists were good at producing knowledge but weak at putting it into practice. This was a point of view that Mills elaborated in all his writings. Mills rejected, however, one of the underlying points of Lynd's book, namely, that social change would have to be engineered from above. Both Mills and Lynd seemed to agree that the formerly rugged individualist American citizens had become the "masses"; they had become conformist creatures of habit rather than free-thinking activists, but they parted company at the suggestion that this implied a need for social engineering with well-meaning experts to act in the public interest. In spite of the increasing complexity of society and his own growing pessimism, Mills continued to speak to and believe in the common man. He remained true to his populist origins even as he moved into the higher circles of American academic life.

In a series of three books, *The New Men of Power, White Collar,* and *The Power Elite,* Mills laid out his vision of America as a mass society, a society ruled over by the heads of giant organizations. He did this from within his own position as insider/outsider at Columbia University. As head of the Bureau of Applied Social Research's subdivision on work and workers, Mills had unique access to information on the working class in postwar America, but he was able to give a radical interpretation of this material. In Mills's particular combination of Weber and American populist pragmatism, the labor question was recast in terms of the twin processes of institutionalization and rationalization, an analysis that culminated in the announcement of a new type of labor leader: the head of a large bureaucratic organization, a part of a new power elite. The labor movement that had been the hope of radical intellectuals for half a century was now, from the perspective of the academic outlaw, part of the mainstream of American society.

By the time *White Collar* was published in 1951, Mills had moved to the department of sociology proper. The department of sociology at Columbia was by this time an expanding and important part of the new "scientific" sociology. Under the control of Merton, Lazersfeld, and Mills's former friend, the recently hired Daniel Bell, the department had attracted a talented and aggressive group of graduate students. Mills need not have worried; he never fit in. Even though *White Collar* was built around solid empirical evidence and again revealed Mills's ability to work with masses of quantitative material, his moral-political message and his polemical tone were out of step with the new trends at Columbia. In their overview of the developments in American sociology in the 1950s, two of the rising stars of the field, Seymour Martin Lipset (a product of the new trend at Columbia) and Neil Smelser (a product of a similar trend at Harvard), had this to say: "It must be reported . . . that [Mills] has little importance for contemporary American sociology, although his books are best-sellers outside the field and widely hailed in certain political circles. . . . If Mr. Mills cuts himself off from the sociology fraternity, he retains important outlets of expression in the more popular and commercial media, and thus manages to influence the outside world's image of sociology" (Lipset and Smelser 1961: 50–51).

Being on the margins, not only of the department but of the discipline itself, is reflected in Mills's work. The theme of *White Collar* is the transformation of the American middle class—of which Mills as a Columbia sociologist is clearly a member, at least objectively. But subjectively, he sought to free himself from a middle-class identity. The new middle class in America had become rootless and amorphous. It was a group whose status and power did not rest on anything tangible. This was truly a class in the middle, uncertain of itself, caught in between an elite above and a greater mass below. Unlike the old middle class, whose power and status gave rise to political conservatism, the new middle class was a class without bearings. It was a class in the position of a mass, faceless and rudderless, in search of direction. From the viewpoint of the academic outlaw, these were dangerous tendencies that should be curbed. This was why he continued to write for the wider audience and why he turned his back on his more professionally bound colleagues.

The contrast between this new reality and the rough-and-ready working class that carried intellectuals through the depression cannot be more clear. As Mills put it, "The white-collar people slipped quietly into modern society. Whatever history they have had is a history without events; whatever common interests they have do not lead to unity; whatever future they have will not be of their own making" (1951: ix). Unlike the collectively organized carriers of the hopes of the 1930s, the new middle class was split internally, "fragmented and dependent upon larger forces. . . . Even if they gained the will to act, their actions, being unorganized, would be less a movement than a tangle of unconnected events." Not much here to pin one's hope on.

Yet it is important to understand this new actor on the scene, because, though fragmented and powerless, the new white-collar worker represents both the present and the future. This is the reality that American intellectuals of the 1950s had to face. The idea born in the nineteenth century and nurtured through the 1930s, that the working class would be the bearers of a new, more progressive social order, must be erased from the mind and a new image put in place.

> By examining white-collar life, it is possible to learn something about what is becoming more typically "American" than the frontier character probably ever was. What must be grasped is the picture of society as a great salesroom, an enormous file, an incorporated brain, a new universe of management and manipulation. By understanding these diverse white-collar worlds, one can also understand better the shape and meaning of modern society as a whole, as well as the simple hopes and complex anxieties that grip all the people who are sweating it out in the middle of the twentieth century. (xv)

For Mills, white-collar workers were the everyman of modern society, and getting to know them and their condition was to get to know oneself, a kind of self-reflection. "The troubles that confront white-collar people are the troubles of all men and women living in the twentieth century" (xv). As opposed to manual laborers, who for an earlier generation typified all that was wrong with capitalist society, the new white-collar worker suffers not material hardship but rather a form of psychological hardship. Taking his cue from the title of Hans Fallada's novel of the subordinated clerk in Weimar Germany who symbolized the supporters of the Nazi movement, Mills wrote, "The new Little Man seems to have no firm roots, no sure loyalties to sustain his life and give it a center. . . . Perhaps because he does not know where he is going, he is in a frantic hurry; perhaps because he does not know what frightens him, he is paralyzed with fear" (xvi).

Drawing on the sociological tradition of Max Weber and Emile Durkheim, Mills located the source of the white-collar malaise in a loss of moral purpose and vision, a condition that Durkheim, in speaking of another great social transformation, had described as *anomie*. "The uneasiness of our time, is due to this root fact: in our politics and economy, in family life and religion—in practically every sphere of our

41

existence—the certainties of the eighteenth and nineteenth centuries have disintegrated or been destroyed and, at the same time, no new sanctions or justifications for the new routines we live, and must live, have taken hold. So there is no acceptance and there is no rejection, no sweeping hope and no rebellion" (xvi). There is only indifference, and this is the danger of the times. Indifference leads to apathy and apathy to passivity in relation to the new men of power.

In place of a cultural tradition that might offer some sort of immunity against this apathy, the new white-collar masses were given mass culture. "Newly created in a harsh time of creation, white-collar man has no culture to lean upon except the contents of mass society that has shaped him and seeks to manipulate him to its alien ends." But this only puts him at the mercy of the new men of power in another way: he is open to their manipulation in leisure as well as at work. "For security's sake, he must strain to attach himself somewhere, but no communities or organizations seem to be thoroughly his. This isolated position makes him excellent material for synthetic molding at the hands of popular culture—print, film, radio, and television" (xvi).

Mills's reconceptualization of America as mass society culminated with the publication of *The Power Elite* in 1956, a book that many would later see as a bible for the student movement of the 1960s. Mills returned to themes that had preoccupied him since the 1940s: the increasing powerlessness of people being confined "to projects not their own" (1956: 3). The appeal is again made to the "common man," the everyman caught in the web of modern mass society. Positions in this web, however, are not equally confining. Not everyone, Mills writes, is at the bottom looking up; some are less ordinary than others. "As the means of information and of power are centralized, some men come to occupy positions in American society from which they can look down upon . . . and by their decisions mightily affect, the everyday worlds of ordinary men and women."

The idea that modern society was like a complex web that spun its nets of duties and responsibilities around its inhabitants had been brought to the United States in the 1940s, when Parsons and Mills himself translated Weber's writings into English. Liberal theorists like Parsons made use of this notion to argue that new forms of human interactions, like voluntary groups from parent-teacher associations to locally based political organizations, would ensure that democracy would not only survive the interwoven complexity of modern society but would indeed flourish. Mills took Weber's vision in another direction. He saw the cohesiveness of modern society as a new form of domination, a social system in which power was more diffuse and less visible than in early forms of social order. Rather than the direct power exerted by the factory owner over his employees and the autocratic ruler over his subjects, modern power had become bureaucratized and thus less easy to locate and recognize. *The Power Elite* was Mills's attempt to put a face on the faceless, to visualize the invisible.

The new face of power in mass society was a corporate one, an interlocking hierarchical system. In traditional America, Mills wrote, the family, the school, and the church were the main institutions around which social order congealed. In modern America, these had been replaced by the corporation, the state, and the army, each embedded in a technology, a system of interlocking processes. As systems, rather than institutions, these processes were known as the economy, politics, and defense: in short, as the "military-industrial complex," as Eisenhower named it. When Eisenhower made this astounding claim in his 1961 farewell address to the nation, he was speaking, perhaps unwittingly, in the voice of Mills and Weber.

Already in 1948, Mills had envisioned an America divided between the men of power and the masses. His vision was not as pessimistic then as it would be in 1956, as the main drift toward the concentration of power had continued unabated. Rather than the conspiracy theory that could be drawn out of *The Power Elite, The New Men of Power* had called attention to largely invisible processes at work behind the backs of actors, creating the conditions under which an active and organized power elite could rule over a passive mass. Here Mills's concern lay with making the process visible to its victims, as a first step toward organized political action, as had been attempted in the 1930s. A necessary condition for such action was the recognition that as it approached midcentury, America was not as it had been before the war. What had changed was not only that new men had come to power but more important that the labor movement that had helped focus political activity in the 1930s had become bureaucratized and that there was precious little to distinguish its leaders from leaders of other bureaucracies, like the army, the government, and worst of all, private business.

This is the same theme that had been developed in *The Power Elite,* only now with more pessimistic overtones. The hope for alternative movements had disappeared. In the late 1940s, Mills still hoped for the emergence of an American labor party along the lines of the British, where intellectuals and workers could fight the drift toward mass society together. By 1956, Mills recognized that he had been wrong in predicting that labor leaders would become more important in American society and also in his vision of a labor party that could encompass progressive left-wing intellectuals like himself and the power of organized labor in a progressive social force. What remained central to his hope for the future was the role that mediating groups of the politically aware—intellectuals and small publics organized around magazines and journals—could play even in a mass society. It is this vision of an active public sphere that united him with other critical intellectuals and helped bridge the gap between the 1930s and the 1960s.

The Sociological Imagination was Mills's parting shot at professional sociology. Again assuming the voice of the common man, Mills outlined his complaints against a discipline that left its promise unfulfilled. The book opened with this:

> Nowadays men often feel that their private lives are a series of traps. They sense that within their everyday world, they cannot overcome their troubles, and in this feeling, they are often correct: What ordinary men are aware of and what they do are bounded by the private orbits in which they live; their visions and powers are limited to the close-up scenes of job, family, neighborhood; in other milieux, they move vicariously and remain spectators. And the more aware they become, however vaguely, of ambitions and of threats which transcend their immediate locales, the more trapped they seem to feel. (1959: 3)

The promise of the sociological imagination—and the task of the sociologist—was to provide the common man with insight into the causes of his feeling of being trapped. Sociology's promise lay in its all-encompassing framework, a vision of society in its totality, within which the common man could better understand the structural and historical basis of his feelings and frustrations. The sociological imagination was a form of self-consciousness that would allow the individual to "understand his own experience and gauge his own fate . . . by locating himself within his period, [so] that he can know his own chances in life . . . by becoming aware of those of all individuals in his circumstances" (5).

The task of sociology as Mills formulated it built around his own synthesis of ideas taken from two founding fathers of the discipline, Karl Marx and Max Weber, incorporated into a native American pragmatism. From Marx, Mills took the idea that social theory ought to provide insight into the social conditions of existence; from Weber, the thought that these conditions offered a series of limited "life-chances." From pragmatism came the notion that knowledge ought to have a practical outcome for the individual, that it should provide the basis for making decisions concerning the range of possible actions and eventually for changing the very conditions that limited those choices. In an age lacking in collective solutions, an age in which social movements did not exist, it was the task of sociology to provide the frustrated individual with the necessary tools for understanding how society worked and to translate, as Mills put it, "personal troubles into public issues, and public issues into the terms of their human meaning for a variety of individuals" (187). And this was precisely what the professionalized social sciences were not doing.

In his final years, Mills completely ceased to address his professional colleagues after outlining their promise and their failure. As he gave up on the social sciences, he searched for sources of critical insight outside the United States, in the social movements emerging in the Third World, especially in Cuba. This further alienated him from his colleagues and, more important perhaps, from his remaining contacts among intellectuals. Macdonald wrote, "Mills soon began to make up his mind, 'to get his head together,' and his stuff became rather too clear and one-sided: he judged capitalist America with a severity he didn't apply to socialist competitors like Castro's Cuba. The double standard is as unattractive in politics as in sex" (quoted in Horowitz 1983: 282). As with the criticism of academic colleagues, such comments were to little effect. Mills had a personal mission and a much wider audience. The popular success of his books brought him national and international attention: he appeared on television in both the United States and Europe and was invited to the Third World countries he championed. Two books directly addressed to a popular audience, *The Causes of World War Three* (1958) and *Listen, Yankee! The Revolution in Cuba* (1960), sold very well and increased both his popularity and his alienation. In a sense, the two were necessarily connected. Had Mills chosen to debate his colleagues and to address a more professional audience, he would almost certainly have been drawn into the main drift of American society and thus lost as a critical voice. In choosing the other path, he became a spokesman for the next generation, seeking a way out of the wasteland and keeping alive the task set out in *The Sociological Imagination.*

Hannah Arendt and the Public Sphere

"The European visitor simply cannot perceive the political realities of the United States because they are so well hidden by the surface of a society whose publicity and public relations multiply all social factors as a mirror multiplies light so that the glaring facade appears to be the overwhelming reality." So wrote Hannah Arendt in 1948. She had arrived in the United States in 1941, not as a casual visitor but as a refugee fleeing Hitler's holocaust. Among her luggage was a tradition of European social theory that she would find useful in filtering the "glaring facade" of the American reality she encountered. Schooled in classical philosophy and in modern German thought by the great teachers of the interwar years, Husserl, Heidegger, and Karl Jaspers, Arendt applied a distinctly European perspective to her new experience. Her first major work in English, *The Origins of Totalitarianism* (1951), would have an enormous—and in many ways unexpected—impact on its American audience.

Written in New York between 1945 and 1949, *The Origins of Totalitarianism* addressed what appeared to be essentially European concerns. In attempting to come to grips with the dramatic events leading up to the Second World War, the book's conceptualization was idiosyncratic and extremely personal. "It must be possible," Arendt wrote in her preface, "to face and understand the outrageous fact that so small (and, in world politics, so unimportant) a phenomenon as the Jewish question and anti-semitism could become the catalytic agent for first, the Nazi movement, then a world war, and finally the establishment of death factories." Comprehending this "outrageous fact" meant facing up to the dark side of human reality, the existence of absolute evil. It also meant a recognition that the grand ideals of human history that had grown out of the Enlightenment tradition and fostered liberalism, socialism, and communism were, if not dead, at least in serious trouble. As two other German Jewish refugees, Horkheimer and Adorno, had written in a book published around the same time, but with much less impact, the recent events had revealed that the "dialectic of enlightenment" could as easily end in tragic catastrophe as in human emancipation.

The Origins of Totalitarianism grappled with the question of how such quintessential human attributes as reason and action could end in the concentration camp, which for Arendt, herself a victim, was the essence of totalitarianism. At the same time, she pondered how politics, which was the human capacity to act in public, could result in mass political movements of the Right, in fascism. She condemned all totalitarian societies and included both Stalin's Soviet Union and Hitler's Germany. The political movements, Fascist and Communist, that were supposed to lead mankind into a new glorious future by eradicating class differences had instead ended in atomization and homelessness. Rather than realizing the potential of human action, modern politics ended in totalitarian society; instead of creating a higher form of human community, mass society created isolation, terror, and loneliness. "Loneliness, the common ground for terror, the essence of totalitarian government, and for ideology or logicality, the preparation of its executioners and victims, is closely connected with uprootedness and superfluousness. . . . To be uprooted means to have no place in the world, recognized and guaranteed by others; to be superfluous means not to belong to the world at all" (Arendt 1951: 475).

These powerful and foreboding words threw cold water in the face of postwar American euphoria. Rather than concerning events in Europe, *The Origins of Totalitarianism* was seen by many of Arendt's American readers as an interpretation of their own experience. She seemed to be evaluating tendencies in their own society as well as in the modernization process in general. Coming at a time when the cold war was just beginning to make itself felt, Arendt's equation of Stalinism and Nazism seemed to confirm the belief of some American critics that there was really no alternative, for better or worse, to the emerging American way of life and that choosing the West, as the terms were then being put, was really no choice at all. At the same time, Arendt's analysis implied that massification, aspects of which were becoming visible in American society, was a step toward totalitarianism and that the new mass society in the West was in danger of converging with the totalitarian East. Thus, Arendt warned her American colleagues, even if one must choose the West, as Macdonald had done in 1952 when recanting his earlier political radicalism, one must also recognize—and criticize—tendencies toward massification in American society.

Further, Arendt's analysis of totalitarianism offered another way of interpreting existentialism, the philosophy that was then so in vogue and in which Arendt was herself trained. The form of existential loneliness that Arendt described as part of the human condition in mass, totalitarian society was a long way from the heroism described by Sartre or Camus, or, closer to home, by Saul Bellow in *Dangling Man,* published in 1944. Both the drift toward mass society and the new forms of thought that could be coupled with it were in need of thorough reconsideration, in America as well as in the Europe that gave birth to them. *The Origins of Totalitarianism* offered no easy solutions and little solace to American intellectuals. Tracing the origins of totalitarianism was not a way of making propositions about the present. Arendt offered no answers to the questions she raised; she had no better vision to offer and no new solutions to old problems. Her aim had rather been to look backward as a way of preparing the groundwork for analyzing contemporary problems. The answers would come in her later works, partly through the stimulation provided by unexpected events like the Hungarian revolution in 1956 and partly in reaction to events in America itself.

The first set of answers came in *The Human Condition,* published in 1958. Here, mass society itself was at the center of focus. In *The Human Condition,* Arendt traced the concept of society to its classical origins, defining it as "an alliance between people for a specific purpose, as when men organize in order to rule others or to commit a crime" (1958: 24). As originally conceived, she argued, the concept meant a corporation, a humanly designed organization to achieve consciously conceived ends, whether within a small group or among an entire people. In contrast to modern society as the basic form of social organization, Arendt outlined the classical Greek notion of the polis, where collective identity and purpose emerged not so much from organization as from active participation, from human action. A central theme of *The Human Condition* is that structure and action, the two basic forms of human life, once distinct, had in modern times been conflated. That distinctly human form of political action permitted in the loosely structured environment of the polis had all but disappeared in the highly administered politics of modern society. It was a case of structure crushing action, of organization killing humanity.

From the point of view of a later generation of social critics, *The Human Condition* was one of the most important books published in America in the 1950s. In it was laid out the concepts for understanding the basic conditions of human life against the background of an emerging modernity. Arendt's theme was the old humanist idea that the origins of Western culture could be traced back to ancient Greece, to a way of life that sharply distinguished between activities concerned with biological reproduction, which man shared with other animals, and those that uniquely expressed human creativeness.

What made Arendt's reconceptualization of the old ideals important was both its timing and the analytical tools she provided: her categories of labor, work, and action provided the philosophical basis for radical social criticism in what many of her contemporaries considered the age of conformity. Her powerful portrayal of the degradation of creative work into labor and of politics into administration and manipulation gave sustenance to intellectuals at a time when they most needed it. But more than that, Arendt helped to recall a concept of human society that was in danger of being extinguished: society, she pointed out, was created through the actions of people, through their active participation in all spheres of life. It was this theme that would prove to be the most long lasting in Arendt's work, making *The Human Condition* a book that would be taken up by the younger generation as a source of inspiration in challenging the established order.

The Human Condition presented tools not only for the reconceptualization of society but, on another level, for the personalization of political questions. Like Mills, Arendt made personal problems and choices the basis of political theorizing. Her theoretical reflections grew out of thought experiments designed "to capture experiences and find the experiential base of positions, decisions and policies" (Young-Bruehl 1982: 309). Political reflection begins in human experience and with the questions, "What would I do in that situation" and "What should I do in this one." Following Immanuel Kant, Arendt argued that all men, not just philosophers and kings, are legislators of their own actions. Men are not only responsible for their actions, as the then exceedingly popular existentialism argued, but are also capable of judging their actions. She thus refused to distinguish between the knowledgeable few and the ignorant masses, the rulers and the ruled. However, she also warned that mass society was creating the conditions that made such distinctions all too real. This standpoint concerning the human condition and the grounding of politics in responsible human action was to prove central to the new social movements of the 1960s. In the 1950s, however, it was more the source of controversy among intellectuals than a stimulus for wider social activism.

Arendt's writings about society, totalitarian or otherwise, contrasted two notions of collective identity and political life that had competed with one another since the Enlightenment. The idea that social life should be the conscious construction of human beings was one of the pillars on which the Enlightenment *philosophes* had based their criticism of traditional French society. For Voltaire and Rousseau, human reason was a better guide to social interaction than the authority of church and state. What later came to cause differences of opinion among them, however, was how widely distributed among the populace this Reason should be. Here viewpoints differed according to whether active participation in the rational reconstruction of society was to be the work of everyone or an elite. By the time they reached the 1950s, these differing viewpoints tended to be seen in terms of competing conceptions of the role of the intellectual in society as well as in terms of differences in the meaning and degree of participation by the masses in culture and politics. While the 1930s had encouraged an activist answer to these questions on the part of intellectuals, the

1950s suggested a more passive approach. In the 1930s, intellectuals had sought to move the masses to participate in the reconstruction of society, in the wake of the collapse of the old order in the depression. The 1950s were more a time for reconceptualization than for activism, for trying to make sense of the changes that seemed to be occurring behind the backs of actors. Like Mills, Arendt was more concerned with the effect of the main drift of society and the common man than with her own role or that of the intellectual as such, a concern that engaged many of her colleagues. She had been too much the victim of historical circumstance to give way to such indulgence.

Born in 1906, the daughter of wealthy, assimilated Jews in Königsberg in what was then East Prussia, the easternmost city of Europe and a stopping-off point for travelers in both directions, Arendt studied philosophy in Marburg with Heidegger and in Freiburg with Husserl. She thus experienced the heady days of the Weimar Republic through the categories of existential phenomenology. It was Jaspers, however, who was to make the most lasting impression on her intellectual development. Perhaps more because of the complications that arose from a love affair with Heidegger than any intellectual disagreement, Arendt wrote her doctoral dissertation under Jaspers rather than Heidegger. The two men were friends, and it was Heidegger who directed Arendt to Heidelberg and to Jaspers. The move proved significant for Arendt's developing philosophical and political views. Jaspers was just beginning to work out his own philosophical position when Arendt arrived in Heidelberg, and she was thus able to participate in its creation. Jaspers was influenced by Weber, his mentor at Heidelberg, especially by Weber's method of identifying "ideal types" of world views and tracing their effects on human behavior. It was this linking of fundamental outlook and everyday life experience that formed the basis of Jaspers's "existence philosophy" and of Arendt's own approach.

Arendt arrived in New York in 1941, after having fled Germany in 1933 for Paris, where she worked for a Jewish youth organization and became attracted to Zionism. In New York, she continued her involvement with Jewish refugees and her interest in Zionism, finding work as editor at Schocken Books, headed by another refugee from Germany. As for Mills, New York provided Arendt with an intellectual environment and a space for activism. In addition to being a source of the themes she discussed in her work, the local Zionist organizations provided Arendt with a stimulus for her intellectual reflections. The small magazines like *Commentary* and the *Partisan Review* and their publics, which provided Mills with a forum and an outlet, served Arendt as well. Early versions of *The Origins of Totalitarianism* appeared as shorter pieces in journals like *Jewish Social Studies* and *Review of Politics.*

Like Mills, Arendt moved on the margins between the intellectual social critic and the professional academic. Keeping her pen sharp by writing in public interest journals and more popular magazines like the *New Yorker*, she became for a time professor at Princeton University, the University of California, and the University of Chicago, before finally settling in New York once again, at the New School for Social Research, where she taught until she died in 1975. Even as an (always reluctant) academic, however, she never abandoned her engagement in issues of broad public appeal or lost her desire to influence the general public. While Columbia University only added to Mills's alienation from the drift of American life, the New School, with its roots in Dewey's pragmatism and Veblen's cultural radicalism and its focus on adult education, provided a perfect setting for Arendt to develop her particular synthesis of classical European and American thought.

As the home away from home for émigré European intellectuals fleeing fascism in the 1930s, the New School for Social Research had from its beginnings been designed to provide a setting for mixing European and American intellectual traditions. Founded in 1919 by a group of intellectuals and academics connected to the *New Republic*, the New School aimed at preserving radical and liberal intellectual traditions. It engaged Dewey, then a professor of philosophy at Columbia but dissatisfied with the trends in American higher education, and Veblen, the economist and social critic and author of *The Theory of the Leisure Class.* The New School opened its doors to German and Italian intellectuals in the 1930s. With the help of private foundations, the University in Exile was established in 1933 as part of a program to support refugee scholars and to open a forum for intellectual integration and exchange. The University in Exile would soon change its name to the Graduate Faculty of the New School for Social Research. Throughout the 1950s, the New School provided Arendt with a forum for presenting and debating her ideas about totalitarianism and the human condition. She was hired on a permanent basis at the New School in 1967.

Hannah Arendt cannot be claimed as a direct, personal supporter of the new social movements as they emerged in the United States in the late 1950s and early 1960s. The contrary is more the case. When in 1957 the civil rights movement caught national attention with the televised attempt to integrate the public school system in Little Rock, Arkansas, Arendt was moved to outspoken criticism. In "Reflections on Little Rock," finally published in *Dissent* in 1959 after having been commissioned by *Commentary* two years earlier but refused publication because of its controversial content, Arendt criticized Negro parents for using their children for what she characterized as their own ends. Children are not revolutionaries, she wrote, and should not become fodder in their parents' dreams of economic and social advancement. As Arendt later acknowledged when Ralph Ellison wrote a moving rebuttal to her charges, she misinterpreted the motives of Negro parents by perceiving them through the prism of her experience of German Jews and their false hopes of assimilation into German society. This was a position that, when developed in a series of articles in the *New Yorker* on the trial of Adolf Eichmann in Jerusalem in 1963, would place her in the midst of public controversy.

Her inspiration for the new social movements was not her personal stance on particular issues. In fact, she was more or less dismissed as a hopeless conservative by movement activists. Her importance was rather in the ideals she so passionately defended. The most important of these ideals was that action was the central human attribute and the ground of human existence, a position she outlined in *The Human Condition* and further developed in *On Revolution* (1963). The latter offered an eloquent defense of the revolutionary tradition in European and American politics and was a great source of inspiration for student activists in the Free Speech Movement in Berkeley when it was published. Arendt argued that revolutions re-created the public spaces in which critical reflection could take place. They suffered, however, from a failure to institutionalize their great political innovations, the council system, based on direct participation in political decision making. "It would be a great loss to humanity," she wrote, "if this great tradition faded from memory because the spirit of revolution—a new spirit, and the spirit of beginning something new—failed to find its appropriate institution. There is nothing that could compensate for this failure or prevent it from becoming final, except memory and recollection" (1963: 280). To this end, the book's last chapter, "The Revolutionary Tradition and Its Lost Treasure," was a long and passionate call for social renewal through revolution and "participatory democracy," an ideal and a phrase that would reverberate throughout the 1960s.

Another source of inspiration was her passionate personalization of politics. In *The Human Condition,* she had defined politics as a form of collective self-disclosure, in which people revealed themselves through public action. As she herself revealed in the controversy surrounding her "Reflections on Little Rock," she based political judgment on an ability to place oneself in the position of an actor. Although she developed these ideas through historical and philosophical analysis, not in direct political activity, her thoughts contributed, against her own will perhaps, to one of the central themes of the new politics of the 1960s: the personal is political. In direct confrontation with activists, she argued vehemently against feminists, who in her view conflated the private and public domains of intimacy and action, just as she had argued against Negro parents, who in her view confused social and political aims. However, Arendt's reflections on personal political judgment and the importance of symbolic public acts became extremely influential in the new social movements.

Arendt's notion of society as collective disclosure added an important communicative dimension to what had traditionally been conceived of as a domain of self-interest. Her work linked two domains that had been kept separate in modern social theory: culture and politics. More important, in its own context her work provided a way of thinking about politics, as a sphere of meaning and symbolic action, that would inspire new political actors as well as new political acts.

Erich Fromm and the Individual in Mass Society

The last thing, it seemed, that Americans wanted to think about in the 1950s was conflict. After the hot wars in Europe and Korea and the cold war with the Soviet Union, the national mood was to turn inward. International conflict was to be avoided, and domestically the theme was peace on the labor market to get on with making up for the lost time and opportunity of the war years. In the academic world, the ideals of harmony and integration reigned supreme, just as long as one pledged loyalty to the flag and took part in the anti-Communist crusade. Parsons had published an enormous work on the structure of social action in 1937 in which he developed the outlines for a new perspective on society, a structural functionalism in which the various social institutions all served to ensure consensus and equilibrium. In this world where harmony of interest prevailed, conflict was seen as something abnormal and deviant, a social dysfunction, rather than the normal state of affairs, as Marx and other theorists of capitalist society had earlier claimed. In the real world of politics and in the theorized world of academic social science, the key word was "equilibrium," and the search was for consensus rather than contradiction.

Impulses against this mainstream came from Europe as well as from academic outlaws like Mills. In a way not lacking in paradox, Europe, the site of the last great conflict, sent émigré intellectuals to America in search of peace, yet bringing a social theory in which conflict was the core idea. Erich Fromm was one such émigré, perhaps the most influential of all in popularizing the insights of Marx and Freud for a mass audience, making accessible the teachings of the two major prophets of social and interpersonal tension. As a practicing psychoanalyst, Fromm focused on the inner conflicts of the individual psyche; as a Marxist, he located a prime source of conflict in the class struggles of modern capitalist society; as a social critic who sought to combine Freudian and Marxian insights, he focused on the disturbing effects of conflict-laden mass society on the development of the individual. With this perspective, Fromm added a psychological dimension to the reconceptualization of society, thus implanting a dimension that would prove to be extremely important to the social movements of the 1960s.

Fromm was born in Frankfurt in 1900 to a wealthy, deeply religious Jewish family. Unlike the assimilated environment in which Arendt grew up, Fromm was saturated in Jewish tradition. As a teenager he was greatly attracted to messianism, and in his twenties he was one of a group of Jewish intellectuals (including Leo Lowenthal, Siegfried Kracauer, and Martin Buber) who organized an academy for the study of Jewish thought. This background would be crucial to Fromm's later social theory. While he would leave orthodoxy behind, he would never give up a religious orientation in trying to make sense of the relations between the individual and society. The basic idea that Fromm developed out of his religious orientation was that human nature was the product of an interaction between man and his environment as well as between human beings themselves. In the political mode in which he was to reconceptualize this idea, Fromm interpreted such interaction in terms of conflicts and as occurring in this world and not above or beyond it. As opposed to others attracted to psychoanalysis at the time, Fromm came to the field through sociology and philosophy, not medicine, having received his Ph.D. from the University of Heidelberg in 1927, with a dissertation entitled "The Sociology of Jewish Law," written under the direction of Alfred Weber, a cultural sociologist and the brother of Max Weber.

In the late 1920s, Fromm joined up with other like-minded social critics at the Frankfurt Institute of Social Research, and there his interest in the conflicts between the individual and society took on a more concrete, as well as political, direction. Under the direction of Horkheimer, Fromm conducted a series of empirical investigations on the "formation of class consciousness." His research was quite different from anything that had ever been done before. What previous Marxian-inspired political activists had given little attention to became the focus of the Frankfurt concern: the subjective side of politics. Fromm and his colleagues wanted to know why the German working class had largely failed in its attempts to take over German society. The failure of working-class revolutions in Germany and Hungary ten years earlier, when popular support for revolts led by small cadres of activists did not materialize, raised important questions for Marxist theory. Class consciousness, the awareness of common exploitation and common interest among the exploited, was now seen as problematic. It could no longer be taken for granted as a function of social position. For Fromm, an important medium in the formation of consciousness was the family, which was an important source of an individual's character structure. This insight into the importance of the family in the formation of consciousness was the direct result of the use of Freudian theory in political analysis. And in this Erich Fromm was a pioneer.

In 1929, Fromm carried out a study of the political beliefs and psychic structure of blue- and white-collar workers in Germany, as a way of providing scientific grounding for political practice. Fromm and his co-workers sent out a questionnaire with 271 questions to 3,300 persons; of these, they received more than 1,000 replies. When interpreted though the analytic framework provided by a synthesis of Freud and Marx, the results called into question the "truth" they sought to test: even some of the most "objectively" revolutionary workers, members of both the working class and left-wing political parties, revealed a strikingly nonrevolutionary, "authoritarian" set of attitudes in areas traditionally regarded as nonpolitical, such as child rearing and women's fashion. The Freudian-Marxist framework allowed Fromm not only to explore these working-class attitudes but also to argue for their political significance. Fromm argued that "character structure" was the underlying foundation of psychological identity and thus the prime factor in consciousness and that it affected and was affected by family life and interpersonal relations, as much as by the relations of production, in the classical Marxian formulation.

For Fromm the ground of individual experience, the filter through which an individual interprets and constructs her reality, is character structure. It unified all the contradictory needs, desires, and impressions of everyday human experience. In a class society, one that is both hierarchical and contradictory, a particular character structure was formed in which these hierarchical and contradictory conditions were embodied. Character structures, according to Fromm, were class-specific and not universal, as Freud thought. The medium for the formation of an individual's character structure in Fromm's account as well as Freud's was the family. Here again, however, Fromm incorporated Marxian insights about the historical and class-specific nature of social institutions when he described the family as a set of social practices that vary within the social class hierarchy, thus producing particular class-related character structures. The nearly universal condition that did connect the historically specific family practices was male domination and authoritarian family relations.

In explaining the behavior of the German working class, Fromm pointed to the necessity to distinguish between those who merely supported and those who really believed in the Nazi movement. The problem, as Fromm saw it, was in interpreting the indifference expressed by the majority of the workers to the obvious threat that Nazism represented to their organizations and their way of life. His explanation of why the workers did not actively resist the Nazis was given in *Escape from Freedom* (1941). Here he argued that the answer lay not in the traditional appeal to false consciousness, that is, in an inability to perceive real interests, but in a loss of will. "By the beginning of the 1930s the fruits of its [the German working class] initial victories were almost completely destroyed and the result was a deep feeling of resignation, of disbelief in their leaders, of doubt about any kind of political organization and political activity. They still remained members of their respective parties and, consciously, continued to believe in their political doctrines; but deep within themselves many had given up any hope in the effectiveness of political action" (181). The explanation for this essentially psychological failure was thus historical and political: the German working class had suffered too many defeats. As a class, German workers knew where their interests were, but as individuals, they were no longer willing to fight for them.

In this and later analyses of Fascist movements, Fromm described the authoritarian character structure as containing the contradictory need both to dominate and to be dominated, a combination of sadistic and masochistic tendencies. Out of the political turmoil of the Weimar period, the Nazi social hierarchy was constructed so as to allow each person a social position from which he could dominate another and himself be dominated; the contradictory desires of the authoritarian character structure found their expression. Fromm was careful to point out, however, that he did not see the psychological conditions he described as the causes of Nazism; rather, they "constituted its human basis without which it could not have developed" (188). The type of false consciousness produced by this character structure made it impossible for members of the lower middle class or workers who typified it to distinguish more emotionally rooted short-term interests from longer-term economic or political interests.

As a consequence, these individuals and groups became the prey of political forces that would eventually destroy them.

The results of Fromm's path-breaking early work were not published in English until the 1980s. But they were not lost to either his early Frankfurt school colleagues or his own later work. *The Working Class in Weimar Germany* (1984) formed the model for later institute studies on the "authoritarian family" and the famous American study, *The Authoritarian Personality* (1950). Fromm continued his interest in character structure and the psychological dimension of consciousness formation, as well as the wider problem of the interaction between individual formation and social setting, even after he moved to the United States in 1934, to help establish the Institute of Social Research in exile. In part because of internal conflicts within the exile community, the Frankfurt institute set up its headquarters in New York at Columbia University and not the New School for Social Research. While key members of the institute, Horkheimer and Adorno, lectured at Columbia, Fromm lectured at the New School, where psychoanalysis and cultural criticism were more in vogue and where his subject-oriented political theory was more acceptable.

From our perspective, one of Fromm's most influential books was *The Sane Society* (1955). Here Fromm asked the provocative question of whether an entire society can be unhealthy. The very question, as he stated in an early chapter, would be impossible to ask within the mainstream sociology of the time. "To speak of a whole society as lacking in mental health implies a controversial assumption contrary to the position of sociological relativism held by most social scientists today. They postulate that each society is normal inasmuch as it functions, and that pathology can be defined only in terms of the individual's lack of adjustment to the ways of life in his society" (1955: 12). Contrary to this sociological relativism, Fromm described his own position as "normative humanism," which argued that there were indeed universal criteria for mental health. Here again, Fromm drew on his Freudian-Marxian theory of human nature as the outcome of a conflict between individual psychological characteristics and social conditions, to develop criteria for mental health that could be used as a basis for criticism of contemporary American society. From his theory of human nature developed in his early work on the German working class, Fromm argued that modern social conditions hindered and distorted basic human needs. As he wrote in *Escape from Freedom,* "While it is true that man is molded by the necessities of the economic and social structure of society, he is not infinitely adaptable. Not only are there certain psychological needs that imperatively call for satisfaction, but there are also certain psychological qualities inherent in man that need to be satisfied and that result in certain reactions if they are frustrated" (1941: 315). Mass society, Fromm argued in 1955, denied the inherent human need for creative and productive work by turning man into a cog in a great machine of his own creation. Mass society turned man into a commodity like any other, where "his value as person lies in his salability, not his human qualities of love, reason, or his artistic capacities" (1955: 356). In mass society, man becomes alienated from himself, from his own human nature. From this viewpoint, it is not a sane society.

With the great transformations it brought about in the way of producing the necessities of life and in the forms of private and public life it encouraged, the new mass society, Fromm suggested, fostered new personality types. David Reisman, a patient in Fromm's psychoanalytic practice and close follower of his thinking, wrote *The Lonely Crowd* (1950), the first popular academic book to attempt to map out these changes. Beginning with Fromm's assumption that societies tend to produce the individual personality types they require so as to be able to reproduce themselves, Reisman offered a character typology of mass society. In what would soon become catchwords for almost every educated person, Reisman mapped the shift from traditional to early industrial to modern mass society as the shift from tradition-directed to "inner-directed" to "other-directed" character structure.

Fromm elaborated on similar themes in *The Sane Society* and in later works like *The Art of Loving* (1956), which is curiously deceptive in its accessible and friendly tone; even today, however, it retains its power as a critique of American values. Written in the format of a self-help manual, the cover of the 1970 paperback edition proclaims "The world-famous psychoanalyst's daring prescription for love." Here Fromm reveals not only his writing skill but also his penchant for turning social criticism into language everyone can understand. It was this very capacity and the paperback packaging of his criticism that caused some, like Marcuse, to dismiss Fromm as a mere social reformer. The medium, after all, was the message. But anyone picking up Fromm's book off the supermarket or drugstore shelves and seriously reading it could not help but be moved by the power of his critique of contemporary society. Love was described as an art, one that required discipline and practice but that was nearly impossible to achieve in a modern, commercially dominated capitalist society, which turned everything, including the deepest of human emotions, into commodities to be bought and sold. The art of loving, presumably, would require the revolutionary transformation of American society. Not exactly the normal supermarket fare.

Supporting himself through his private practice as an analyst and by lecturing at the New School, Bennington College, and the University of Mexico, Fromm wrote books in a popular style for a mass audience. Like Mills and Arendt, he remained on the fringes of academic life and tried to continue to keep his political beliefs alive. No longer was it easy for outsiders to find their way into the academy or for ideas other than those approved by the professional community to be voiced in the classroom. It was not Joseph McCarthy alone who would police the universities in the 1950s; the academic profession was fast developing its own mechanisms for ensuring conformity. That conflict could have a positive function in society was not one of the approved ideas of the time. To rediscover this lost perspective, Fromm, like many other émigré scholars, reached back into European social theory. Through them the new social movements of the 1960s were provided with a rich field of radical ideas to harvest.

By addressing himself to serious topics in an easily accessible manner, Fromm introduced central themes of European social and psychological theory into American culture. His socialist humanism drew attention to the alienation and psychological distress that a competitive capitalist society brought about. Like Mills and Arendt, Fromm aimed at providing the educated American public—and perhaps especially those in the process of being educated—with insights into the conditions of its own existence, the human condition in mass society. Their books were widely read in the 1950s, often to the annoyance of professional colleagues, but the real effects of their work did not become visible until the next decade, when new social actors were able to turn their isolated voices into new forms of collective political action.

· · ·

C. Wright Mills, Hannah Arendt, and Erich Fromm can all be considered midwives of the new social movements that would erupt in the 1960s. Each in their own way transformed the legacies of the 1930s— and even before—and made radical social thought relevant to the conditions of the postwar era. In so doing, they provided categories that helped make the new mass society comprehensible. Opponents of the professionalism that swept through the intellectual world, they were freer than most of their colleagues to transform inherited modes of thought into a new critical framework. As outsiders, they could more easily resist the general celebration of America's new position in the world as well as the academic shift from collective to individual-oriented social theory. Trained in America's heartland, in the Midwest, Mills formulated his critique of mass society in the wider moral terms provided by the populism he learned in Texas. He infused populist pragmatism with an original view of the sociological mission. Arendt remained faithful to the classical German philosophy she carried to America even as she assimilated an American concern with individual rights and freedom. In the postwar context, she confronted the ideal picture America had of itself with the new reality. Starting from a very different standpoint, she arrived at conclusions similar to those of C. Wright Mills. But she refused to abdicate her personal philosophical autonomy. When radicalism arrived on the scene in the 1960s, Arendt remained aloof but, at the same time, passionately engaged, upholding independent political judgment and reaffirming an autonomous life of the mind. Her importance was in the power and eloquence with which she displayed that judgment and the individual strength she showed in confronting her opponents.

Trained as a psychotherapist, Fromm resisted the drift in his profession toward an exclusive focus on the individual. He insisted on a moral as well as a historical standpoint in interpreting the character structure and personality patterns in the new mass society. Individual adjustment to external stress was not his concern, as it was for most of his professional colleagues. His opposition to the main societal drift and his professional marginality allowed him to keep alive a critical intellectual attitude in new surroundings. Like Mills and Arendt, Fromm's conception of the individual was that of a person actively involved in the critical process of constructing the conditions of his or her existence. His synthesis of Freudian and Marxian thought within a moral-humanist framework added a crucial psychological dimension to the social criticism of Mills and Arendt.

While their social criticism grew out of different intellectual traditions, Mills, Arendt, and Fromm shared the formative experience of the upheavals and the social movements of the 1930s. Out of this experience emerged a common perception of the role of the intellectual as partisan, as one who takes sides on the issues of the day and raises fundamental questions of human existence in dialogue with a knowing public. While the actual content of this public may have differed at the beginning of their lives, they never lost contact with a larger public, and all three came to direct their social criticism toward the mass American public. This was not simply a choice they made but rather a result of historical contingency. As Arendt wrote of her own intellectual development, history was not always a welcome intruder on her own theoretical meditations. Try as one might, one could not remain "above the world," especially in dark times. Participation in social movements—Zionist in Arendt's case, socialist in the case of Mills and Fromm—widened their perspective on the aims and goals of intellectual activity. An intellectual must be involved in society to be able to address the crucial issues of an age in an accessible language. Much as they might dislike the transformations they described, including the explosive growth and importance of the mass media, they actively sought to use these media to spread their message. It was a rare occasion when Mills, Arendt, or Fromm addressed purely professional concerns. All suffered the wrath of their more professionally oriented academic colleagues for this alleged popularization or "vulgarization" of science. In the choice between professionalization and popularization, which confronted all intellectuals in the 1950s and which in many ways characterized the age, they clearly chose the people.

3 THE ECOLOGICAL INTELLECTUALS
Fairfield Osborn, Lewis Mumford, Rachel Carson

• •

In March 1948, the sixty-one-year-old president of the New York
Zoological Society did something that intellectuals do: he published a
book. Dedicated "to all who care about tomorrow," *Our Plundered
Planet* by Fairfield Osborn was one of the first—perhaps the very
first—of what would later grow into a minor industry, namely, popular
environmental books; by the end of the year, it had been reprinted
eight times, and in the next few years, it would be translated into
thirteen languages. Osborn's message was that the global role that
America had assumed in the aftermath of the Second World War had
an important but neglected environmental dimension. In a polemical
but reasonably calm tone and using a large number of well-chosen
examples from the various regions of the world, Osborn showed how
man's "silent war" with nature was causing a wasteful destruction of
natural resources and leading to serious economic difficulties, especially in what were soon to be called the developing countries.

The son of a famous geologist/paleontologist, Osborn in 1935, the
same year his father died, had left a career in investment banking to
devote the rest of his life to conservation. Perhaps because of his
background, conservation for Osborn meant something broader than
the traditional concern with nature preservation that had for so long
dominated conservation circles. He did not consider nature as a separate realm outside of society; he focused on the interactions between
nature and society. As he wrote in his book, "Nature represents the
sum total of conditions and principles which influence, indeed govern,
the existence of all living things, man included" (1948: viii). And

although there would be others in the postwar years who came to adopt a similarly "ecological" conception, Osborn was one of the very first to present it to a wider public. Even more significantly, he put the new ecological philosophy into practice and, by so doing, helped to draw some of the organizational contours of what would emerge as an "environmental movement" in the 1960s and 1970s. The seeds he planted were more in the solid ground of practical activity than in the theoretical compost of ideas and theories. Nonetheless, in establishing the Conservation Foundation, which supported some of the significant pioneering environmental research of the 1950s, as well as in the more mundane work with the ecological renovation of the Bronx Zoo, Osborn was one of those who helped implant an environmental consciousness in his fellow Americans.

Lewis Mumford's contribution to environmentalism was both more indirect and all-encompassing. When the Second World War ended, Mumford was fifty, entering what would be perhaps the most difficult period of his life, both privately and publicly. He was the epitome of the self-made man, an extremely productive and highly vocal public intellectual who had by then written eleven books and countless magazine articles on architecture, technology, cities, and literature. His latest book, *The Condition of Man*, had been published in 1944 to less than universal acclaim and in September his only son Geddes had been killed in action in Italy at the age of nineteen. His mood did not improve when he heard of the dropping of the atomic bomb; the new weapon indicated for Mumford that those in power in America had literally lost their minds. Mumford was to be a vigorous opponent of the emerging military-industrial complex, bringing to the task—and into the postwar era—his own special mixture of Emersonian idealism, organismic philosophy, and social, or human, ecology. Having been active in interwar movements for regional development and garden cities, he would become one of the most outspoken critics of postwar America, as he saw his countrymen drifting ever farther away from traditional values into a mass acceptance of what he would later call the "myth of the machine." On the personal level, Mumford was turning into something of a country gentleman, having moved already in the mid-1930s his base of operations to the small town of Amenia about one hundred miles north of his native New York City.

By 1945, he had come to respect both the pace and the style of country living and had even taken up gardening. In the 1940s and 1950s, he was one of the fiercest opponents of the highway builders and the generals and the organization men, trying to keep the spirit of Emerson and Thoreau alive in dark times. He wrote and spoke against atomic weapons, and, in his architectural column for the *New Yorker,* he regularly bemoaned the transformation of the urban landscape into an increasingly sterile, artificial environment. Through his writing, as well as through his personal example, he would come to provide a sense of history and an intellectual role model for the new environmentalism.

Rachel Carson, whose book *Silent Spring* (1962) is generally considered to be the single most important contribution to raising the American public's environmental awareness, spent her war years writing nature pamphlets for the government and taking bird-watching excursions. She was a traditional kind of nature lover who succeeded, at the end of her life and almost in spite of herself, in turning nature-loving into politics. Her first book, *Under the Sea Wind,* had come out a week before Pearl Harbor, and its eloquence about life in the oceans was all but ignored as attention came to be focused instead on death in the oceans, the wholesale destruction taking place in the Pacific. After the war, Carson would have better luck; *The Sea Around Us,* an unusual best-seller, which also became an award-winning documentary film, brought her fame and fortune in 1951, and she could then leave her editing chores at the Bureau of Fisheries to write on a full-time basis. She could also buy a house on the shores of Maine so as to be better able to commune with her beloved ocean. Perhaps most crucially, the celebrity status that she achieved with *The Sea Around Us* assured her of an audience when she was ready to awaken her countrymen to the new chemical challenges to nature that had come in the wake of the war. As a nature writer, Carson transgressed the boundary between the two cultures of the postwar era, combining the poetic imagination with the scientific. In her writings, she tried to express that sense of wonder that she had felt for the natural environment since childhood, when she walked with her mother in the woods of rural Pennsylvania. Nature, for Carson, was not an abstraction or, for that matter, an escape from daily concerns. The beauties and details of nature were, for her, what gave life meaning; the sense of wonder involved in the reverence of the mysteries of nature was a central part of human experience. "There is symbolic as well as actual beauty in the migration of birds, the ebb and flow of tides, the folded bud ready for spring," she wrote. "There is something infinitely healing in the repeated refrains of nature—the assurance that dawn comes after the night and spring after the winter" (quoted in Hynes 1989: 59). Carson drew not merely on the scientific understanding of nature to awaken her countrymen to the environmental crisis; through the manner of her writing, she could also strike deeper, more spiritual chords.

From their different points of departure, Osborn, Mumford, and Carson planted some of the most important seeds of the many-branched tree that we now call environmentalism. They were not alone, of course. A number of other nature writers and scientists also helped in the course of the 1950s to transform what had been a somewhat marginal and even elitist conservation movement into the much bigger and more broadly based "new social movement" of environmental activism. Osborn, Mumford, and Carson illustrate something of the range and depth of the new ecological wave as well as the flavor of its intellectual practice.

Osborn as an institution builder, Mumford as an independent social critic, and Carson as a "counter expert" carved out different intellectual roles in postwar America, transforming the narrower conservation concerns of the 1930s into the broader environmentalism of the 1960s and 1970s. They were generalists and popularizers, writing not for academic colleagues so much as for wider publics; and they were outsiders who not only managed to keep critical traditions alive in the postwar natural sciences but helped remodel those traditions to suit the times. They reconceptualized the relations between "nature" and "society" by focusing on their interactions and on the flows of energy and materials that pass through the "ecosystems" that link nature and society together. As such, the ecological intellectuals altered the way in which we think about our surroundings—and, in a fundamental sense, the way we think about life itself.

Osborn, Mumford, and Carson gave voice to a new kind of criticism in postwar America. They looked in dismay at the American landscape, seeing the waste and ugliness as symbols of a much larger problem, a change for the worse in the human spirit. For them, the environmental crisis was not merely a matter of pollution or the result of a growing population, although both were important; it was, above all, a crisis in humankind's mode of interchange with nature. Science itself was to blame in the way it reduced the reality of life to chemical formulas and in the way its practitioners allowed themselves to be steered by commercial interests. Nothing less than a new science, a science with a different, more ecological approach to reality, would suffice.

The postwar environmental consciousness took shape as a reaction to the new mode of production that emerged out of World War II, when science had been called on to provide ever more powerful instruments of destruction. It was in large measure because so many of the new products—the chemical fertilizers and insecticides as well as atomic energy—were science based and the results of laboratory research that they threatened the very survival of life: being man-made, they challenged, even replaced, fundamental natural processes or life-support systems, thus disturbing what came to be called the ecological balance. And even if ecological patterns and systems had been subjected to challenges and threats before, what was new in the postwar era was the scale, the dimension, and the intensity of the new technological urge. In Mumford's terms, the "megamachine" had taken over the landscape. Humankind, or at least those men who wielded political and economic power, seemed set on transforming the world around them into something of their own making, something artificial. The technological imperative appeared to have become all-encompassing and insatiable, and the endless technical creation of new needs and products had become a goal in itself, rather than the means to achieve human ends. In a book that appeared in the same year as Rachel Carson's—but that was never given the attention it deserved—the ecological anarchist Murray Bookchin described America as a "synthetic environment," a place where an entire new range of diseases and dangers to both human and nonhuman health appeared as the counterfactual results of technological development, the unintended price to be paid for progress (Herber/Bookchin 1962).

The postwar patterns of living and producing encouraged a new attitude to nature, for now natural surroundings were seen as something to be consciously manipulated by man. Nature could no longer be a mysterious realm outside of human control and intervention when certain men had learned how to rearrange natural processes into new useful packages. This idea of controlling or manipulating nature for man's benefit had been around for a long time; it has now become customary to associate its emergence in its modern form with Francis Bacon's philosophy in the early seventeenth century and with the Puritans who tried to put his teachings into practice (many of whom fled to colonial America after their defeat in the mid-seventeenth-century revolution in England). But it was the atomic bomb and the new forms of energy and production that emerged after the war that brought the idea or the vision of a man-made nature down to earth. Older concepts could not really encompass the new realities; what seemed to be needed, at least for a handful of critical scientists and science writers, was a new ecological conception of reality in which nature and society were linked together in common patterns and processes.

Making us see and begin to understand why the new threats to the natural environment mattered was the work of a few disenchanted intellectuals, like Osborn, Mumford, and Carson, who managed to use some of the new channels of popular communication and entertainment as critical forums in which to articulate the new issues. Their writings and practices would inspire the activist scientists and intellectuals of the 1960s, like Bookchin, Barry Commoner, and Paul Ehrlich, who would be directly involved in shaping the new environmental movement.

While drawing on ideas from the nineteenth century and even earlier, the new environmentalism was something different from classical nature-loving and wilderness appreciation. It contained a much more explicit social philosophy, propagating alternative technologies and patterns of consumption as well as offering new "paradigms" for science and politics. Today it is all around us in the form of national and transnational environmental organizations and among the environmental lawyers and engineers and scientists. Its message has perhaps lost something of its radicalism, as many environmentalists have left the movement behind in pursuit of more immediate political and economic gain. But in the 1960s, environmentalism represented something new and transcendent, helping to carve out a public space in which new kinds of issues became political and an ecological perspective or world view became, for many, a way out of the wasteland.

The Historical Legacy

Nature in America had traditionally been seen as the open frontier, the wide open spaces of western movies and popular legend. The country had grown by taming its vast natural expanses, conquering a rough nature through ingenuity, technology, and hard work. But the experience of conquest and domination had given rise to two rather different conceptions of nature, one that might be called romantic and one that might be called utilitarian. Where the one image tended to respect nature, at times even glorify the beauty and tranquillity of certain natural areas, the other saw nature as a kind of enemy of human development, a foe to be outwitted and exploited for economic benefit. Both images helped give nature conservation a place in the nineteenth-century political discourse. But they provided the early conservationists with a different set of arguments to justify their activities. The romantic, or pastoral, image led to ideas of tending and cultivating the natural environment and eventually to living in "harmony with nature" and preserving parts of nature from further encroachment and human use; the pragmatic or frontier image, in contrast, came to justify exploitation, even domination, of nature, setting the rugged individualist—first the woodsman and then the inventor and entrepreneur—the task of taming a wild, belligerent nature. In time, utilitarian exploitation turned into efficient management, but the underlying image remained largely the same. The images have coexisted uneasily throughout American history, at times contending with each other for the allegiances of intellectuals, at other times combining into new constructive syntheses. In the battle between the images, we can see the roots of the conflict between culture and civilization and even more perhaps a tension between a Puritan "work ethic" and community spirit and sense of limits, on the one hand, and a militaristic ethos of growth and expansion, on the other. At the turn of the century, in the progressive era when Theodore Roosevelt was president, conservation became institutionalized in federal agencies for national parks, fisheries, wilderness, and so on, and conservation itself came to be justified on pragmatic grounds. Preserving natural resources became a part of the Progressive Era's "gospel of efficiency," but by the 1920s, short-term gain and exploitation had once again come to characterize the dominant American attitude to nature (Hays 1959).

It was in this as in other respects that the 1930s were a period of active reform and marked something of a return to the earlier progressive principles. Among the activities of the New Deal era, some of the most lasting were the efforts made to preserve nature. This was the period when the old conservation movement can be said to have come of age. The area set aside for national parks was substantially increased, and access to the parks was considerably improved due to various programs at Harald Ickes's Department of the Interior. Campgrounds were built, bridges and access roads were constructed, and paths were cut through the wilderness areas, so that the dramatic American landscape could be enjoyed by many more people than had previously been the case. Access to nature brought with it an increased understanding as well as an increased market for nature writing, photography, and so on. There was also a growth of membership in hunting and fishing organizations, and for many members of the National Wildlife Federation, which is still today the largest environmental organization in America, there emerged a concern with rational "game management."

The heightened utilization and increased access to nature fostered among some nature lovers a new, more radical mood. In the 1930s, the romantic or pastoral American conservation tradition, associated in the nineteenth century with people like Henry David Thoreau and John Muir, came alive again. With the end of the frontier, it seemed to many Americans even more essential to preserve virgin wilderness areas, to protect particular animal and plant species, and to revitalize earlier, preindustrial methods of forestry and agriculture. There was a move back to the countryside on the part of many an urban dweller; and there was a move, as well, to a conception of the countryside as a community, a bioregion, or a distinct landscape. Two writers who were important in this regard were Lewis Mumford and Aldo Leopold. They were two of the most important transmitters of an ecological consciousness into American culture. Both were children of the Progressive Era; and in the 1930s, they were among the proponents of a social or human ecology, Mumford through his writings on regional planning and technological development and Leopold through his activities in game preservation and in founding the Wilderness Society.

The word "ecology" had been coined in 1867 by the German biologist Ernst Haeckel. And as it traveled through Europe in the late nineteenth century, it took on distinct national colorations. In Scandinavia and England, the homeland of Carolus Linnaeus and Gilbert White, respectively, ecology became associated with native natural history traditions, and by the early twentieth century, there were schools of plant sociology in Denmark and Sweden and influential animal ecologists in England focusing not on single species but on ecosystems, or communities. Meanwhile, in Germany and other countries, ecology was part of a broader interest in nature and natural spirits as a counterforce to industrial materialism. Rudolf Steiner experimented with biodynamic agriculture and also resurrected Goethe's alternative natural science of form and color.

In America, ecology found fertile soil for its cognitive growth, and, as with other sciences, European ideas were imported into America both through emigrants and through returning American students who had gone off to Germany and Britain to escape the Roaring Twenties. By whatever channel, however, ecological approaches came to be quite popular among both biologists and sociologists in American universities in the 1930s. The regionalism that was an important part of rural reconstruction schemes, the urbanism that was a central aspect of social planning doctrines, the managerial conservationism that was fostered by governmental programs—all were based on ecological ideas.

It was an ecology different from the one that emerged in the 1960s, however. In the 1930s, nature was still something out there, separate from society, and, as such, it remained something primarily to be managed and controlled. For most Americans suffering under the Great Depression, nature was nothing to be preserved for its own sake, and while the conservationists developed a more radical wing, for the vast majority, nature was still primarily a resource base for material development. The huge hydroelectric dams on the Columbia River that Woody Guthrie was asked to write songs about served as the symbol for progressive use of nature's bounty, and the Tennessee Valley Authority, with its community control of resources, became a model of ecological engineering. Natural beauty could inspire the poet or the artist, but it had, in the 1930s, little political importance. In keeping with the pragmatic orientation of American history, nature was something to be used by man, for pleasure, benefit, and wealth. It was only when that ambition proved to have such disastrous consequences and implications—first with the atomic bomb and then with the making of the physical wasteland of postwar America—that a new way of thinking gradually emerged.

The postwar conception of the environment grew out of the movements of the 1930s in several ways. For Leopold and Mumford, the 1930s were a period of experimentation and exploration, as they sought ways to apply an ecological perspective to social development. After the war, both men came to see those planning efforts as morally limited and philosophically questionable. Leopold in his final years tried to articulate some of the ethical or moral aspects of conservation, and he spent a good deal of his time bringing to life a piece of land he had bought in northern Wisconsin, commemorated forever in his musings, published shortly after his death in 1949 as *A Sand County Almanac*. Leopold stressed the limits that the natural surroundings imposed on human life and moved beyond the managerial perspective that he had propagated earlier. Mumford after the war spent more time at his country house in upstate New York, enjoying in middle age the slower life-style of a rural existence; and he raged first against the atomic bomb and then against the ugly sterility of postwar American cities. He came to see, more clearly than he had earlier when he had criticized conservationists for their wilderness romanticism, that nature did not exist merely for man and that there were limits to what man could legitimately do in the name of progress. For both of them, as well as for other activists in the 1930s, the new environmental ideas developed as a kind of critical reflection on the earlier period.

Osborn was one of a new generation of more professional and public-minded leaders who came into the conservation movement in the 1940s. He wanted to bring nature into the urban realm and into the schools, and he also saw, perhaps more clearly than anyone else, the need for an international orientation among conservationists. For

Carson, environmentalism, or an ecological perspective, grew out of a sense that there was no longer a wild, untouched nature to escape to. Their different backgrounds, as well as their different relations to the earlier movements, strongly colored the way that our ecological intellectuals came to interact with the new environmentalism of the 1960s and 1970s. While a kind of despair mixed with old age overtook Mumford, keeping him from interacting directly with the new movements he had helped inspire, Osborn, in his various organizational activities, played a somewhat more formative role, even though he too was well on in years (he died in 1969 at the age of 82). Carson, perhaps because she was in many ways a child of the older conservation movement who had been too young to play a formative part in the interwar activities, could more easily translate the older conservation ideals into a new language with the tools of mass communication. In any case, she was more successful than any other single individual in transforming the older, more romantic image of nature into the ecological image of the environmental movement. After Carson's death in 1964, she would rightly be considered the primary intellectual source of inspiration for the new environmentalism.

Fairfield Osborn, Conservation's Organization Man

Fairfield Osborn wrote books, but his importance as a critical intellectual in helping to shape the environmental movement perhaps derives more from his institution building and reforming than from his writings. He was one of the key individuals who broadened the focus of the various conservation organizations that had, in one way or another, defended nature from the encroachment of American industrial society. David Brower of the Sierra Club, John Baker of the Audubon Society, and Howard Zahniser of the Wilderness Society all shared with Osborn a more professional orientation and, like Osborn, modernized their organizations after the war to reach out to larger audiences and more effectively influence government policies. When Osborn became president of the New York Zoological Society in 1940, he launched a series of programs to renovate the Bronx Zoo and to create a modern aquarium in New York City. By the mid-1950s, both institutions had become popular tourist attractions, and the society had also taken on a number of new research and educational tasks. As with many of the other conservation organizations, the society's magazine and publishing activity more generally was overhauled and made more popular in the 1940s and 1950s; Osborn had changed the title of the organization's publication (from *Bulletin of the New York Zoological Society* to *Animal Kingdom*) on assuming the presidency in 1940, and through the years, he brought the range of new environmental concerns into the pages of the magazine. Osborn also took the initiative for creating the Conservation Foundation in 1948, which supported research primarily on some of the "newer" conservation issues: pesticides, natural resource use in developing countries, population control, international environmental research, and so on. He also helped to found an environmental consulting firm, Resources for the Future, and never tired of speaking—"I hate to call it lecturing," he once wrote, for it sounded so pretentious—on environmental issues at gatherings of businessmen, educators, politicians, and even scientists. He represented a new breed of conservationist, at once international and local, acting locally but thinking globally.

As a writer, Osborn was among the very first to identify the environmental costs of the postwar culture of abundance. In his two books, *Our Plundered Planet* (1948) and *The Limits of the Earth* (1953), Osborn provided readable introductions to the misuse of the soil, forests, and other natural resources. In his first book, he took what he called the long view, following the lead of his paleontologist father into the fossil records, sketching, in popular language, a history of man's relations with his natural surroundings. He criticized the "flattery of science," the idea that new techniques and new chemicals could substitute for careful husbandry of nature, and he pointed to case after case of environmental destruction—from the American dust bowl of the 1930s to the starving masses unable to feed themselves in India and China. Osborn tried to place the "war with nature" in a social, even political, context, questioning, for example, the substantial loan given by the American government to Greece, since it was not based on an analysis of the real environmental situation in that country. "The question comes down to this," he wrote. "Is the loan being made with an adequate consideration of the land situation in Greece, and have arrangements been concluded for a thorough long-term program to build up the land base from which the living resources of that country are derived?" And then he made the more general point, "that the time has come when international questions cannot be dealt with intelligently unless governments are prepared to recognize that the usage and condition of the land are essential elements in the world problem" (Osborn 1948: 103).

Osborn thus linked, possibly for the first time, the issue of nature conservation to international politics. *Our Plundered Planet* can be read as an attempt to internationalize nature, to show that natural resources mattered, not just for national economies but for international relations as well. It can also be read as a plea for national resource planning, or at least for a continuation and extension of the policies that had governed the conservation activities of the Roosevelt administration during the 1930s. Osborn directed much of his most aggressive language to the private ownership of public lands; when he reached his own country in his global survey, he singled out for attack the "maneuvers of the powerful minority groups of livestock men, skillfully supported by their representatives in Congress" who "having taken over virtual control of the Federal Grazing Service . . . now are attempting similarly to control the Forest Service." As he put it, "The powerful attacks now being made by small minority groups upon the public lands of the West have one primary motivation and one consuming objective—to exploit the grazing lands and these last forest reserves for every dollar of profit that can be wrung from them" (182–184).

As a former banker, Osborn had no illusions that businessmen had any other interest than making money. He thus understood that private ownership of the land could not be publicly beneficial. He pointed to the need for government action, for a strengthening of conservation programs at all levels of government. For Osborn, as for many of the postwar environmentalists, the Tennessee Valley Authority was an impressive illustration of what could be done by public coordination and planning of resource use. "Ably administered," he wrote, "it has, within the span of little more than a decade, justified itself not only as a social experiment but as an effort to harmonize human needs with the processes of nature. Above all, it provides an example from which lessons can be drawn for the solution of the problem that faces the entire country" (1948: 192–193). Osborn described, critically but sympathetically, some of the projects in land use planning being carried out in Russia, and he returned, again and again in his book, to the need for coordination and public control of natural resources. His message was presented calmly but with a great deal of radicalness, although he made every effort to sound responsible and reasonable.

In this he differed somewhat from William Vogt, whose book, *Road to Survival*, was also published in 1948 but was written in a more alarmist tone (and perhaps for that reason sold more copies than Osborn's). Vogt revived the way of thinking about human population pressures that Thomas Malthus had propagated in the early nineteenth century. For Vogt, as for Malthus, the central problem that the world faced was overpopulation and the imbalance between world food supplies and population growth rates. In making his claims, Vogt offended many of those he most wanted to influence, as he argued for the imposition of birth control in Catholic countries in Latin America as an absolute necessity. Like Malthusianism in general, Vogt's influence on the later environmental movement would be questionable. Population growth was certainly important; but politically, it was probably more effective to see it as one factor in the ecological problematique rather than the main cause of environmental crisis. In much the same way that certain technological critics (such as the French theologian Jacques Ellul) came to blame machines for the destruction of the environment, neo-Malthusians like Vogt saw the population "explosion" as a kind of abstract force beyond human control that had to be stopped, if necessary with coercive measures. After his book, Vogt went on to work for Planned Parenthood and to continue to speak and write about population problems; and Paul Ehrlich, author of *The Population Bomb* in the late 1960s, traced his own Malthusian beliefs to a lecture he heard Vogt give when he was attending college in the early 1950s. Interestingly enough, however, it was Osborn's book, rather than Vogt's, that found its way onto Ehrlich's reference list.

Osborn's arguments were presented more calmly, and one can argue that he was thus able to influence more people. He apparently never came to be viewed as an extremist, and throughout the 1950s, he succeeded in raising money among businessmen and private foundations for various environmental projects. In his book, he stressed a public control of the land, rather than population control, as the main plank in any ecological policy or philosophy. Much like Leopold, whose ecological ethic played a formative role in Osborn's own thinking, Osborn did not deny population pressure, but neither did he single it out as the dominant cause of environmental deterioration. His was, in many ways, the voice of the New Deal, with its state interventionism and active public policymaking, carried into a new era. "There is nothing revolutionary in the concept that renewable resources are the property of all the people and, therefore, that land use must be co-ordinated into an over-all plan," he wrote in his book. But the program of reform and national planning that was necessary was still "awaiting formulation," he claimed. In the postwar era, calls for national planning and public ownership of the land were perhaps "revolutionary" after all. In a country that was soon to be afflicted by a kind of social obsession with anticommunism, Osborn's call for national planning and coordinated land use disappeared from the political agenda, to return, with a vengeance, in the late 1960s. As the economy went into a new upswing in the 1950s and a more conservative political tone spread across the land, Osborn's message faded away: it was Leopold's personal and philosophical view of nature, rather than Osborn's version of social democratic environmental politics, that grew in popularity as the decade wore on.

As Osborn put it in his book, one of the main barriers to an environmental consciousness was lack of understanding. With over half of the population living in cities and thus separated from the land, Americans were "apathetic" and unconcerned about the sources of their own abundance. They "either do not realize what is going on or are lulled into a false sense of security by misleading reports regarding the status of our life-supporting resources that are inspired by groups having special interests in such properties as timberlands, cattle and water rights" (1948: 199). Education at all levels, in the formal school system as well as in other public spaces, was required. "It is extraordinary that with a few exceptions there is no such thing as the general teaching of conservation in our schools and colleges" (200).

Osborn tried to do something about the problems he described in his books. In his work with the zoological society, he tried to put his message into practice. His reform program as president of the society had several ingredients, but all centered around the task of bringing the environmental crisis home. Osborn tried to make the abstract and all but invisible problems of resource depletion understandable for modern urban Americans. He took part in some of the controversial conservation struggles of the 1940s and 1950s, serving on the board of the Save the Redwoods League and joining in the campaigns to protect wilderness areas in both America and Africa from further exploitation. Research that he helped support was important in providing evidence for the later assertions of Bookchin and Carson as well as Commoner and Ehrlich. But his main contribution, one that we by now take more or less for granted, was in making the urban environment more ecologically meaningful. He was a pioneer in the ecological renovation of city zoos and aquariums. It may not seem very much in the 1990s, when ecology is a household word and the global environmental crisis appears on television on an all-too-regular basis. But in the 1940s and 1950s, most urban Americans were not aware of either ecology or international resources exploitation. In his own nonpolitical but substantial way, Osborn helped to bring the message home.

He had always loved animals. His father's collections at the American Museum of Natural History fostered an early interest in nature, and he had a number of pets from far-off places already as a child. He had even accompanied his father on excursions while still in school, a source perhaps of his later internationalism. He chose not to pursue a scientific career, however, and after college, worked for a time as a railway worker before pursuing a business career on Wall Street. Even so, he did not forget his beloved animals, serving as a trustee from 1922 at the New York Zoological Society that his father had helped to establish at the turn of the century. And in the 1930s, the New Deal struck some chords in the socially conscious Osborn, who worked as a director in the National Youth Association and then, in 1935, left banking for a new life at the zoo.

His first major initiative for the New York Zoological Society was working with an exhibit for the World's Fair in 1939. "The entrance of the Society into the World's Fair," he wrote in the society's bulletin, "provides a peculiarly fitting occasion for working towards certain objectives that we have had in mind for some time. Principal among these is the exploration and development of new methods of presenting the truths and limitless wonders of Zoology to the public" (*Bulletin of the New York Zoological Society* XLII, no. 1 [1939]: 3). Osborn had a vision of a modern zoo as much more than a place of recreation; for him, a zoo was a place from which visitors should depart as changed people, with a better understanding and appreciation of the natural world. As he sketched his plans for the exhibit at the World's Fair, he gave his vision a somewhat more general form and started to articulate his program.

> There is a great opportunity for a scientific institution such as ours to develop better methods of presenting and interpreting the study of Zoology in a way that the man in the street can understand. For too long, scientific institutions of a public nature have failed to concentrate sufficiently on the invention of that particular alchemy which blends their knowledge—resources into the thought processes and comprehensions of the public. Too often the man whose primary job is the dissemination of scientific knowledge, keeps himself nevertheless in a sort of "Holy of Holies," bulwarked by techniques, safe within the wire entanglements of Latin derivatives. . . . When it comes to the processes by which we can reach the public at large, we must further develop a language in which the listener as well as the talker may find pleasure and understanding. (3–4)

As his reform activity unfolded during the war and in the immediate postwar period, Osborn and his staff focused especially on placing animals in natural habitats, taking them out of their cages and letting them roam freely among trees and plants. When the "African Plains" were opened at the zoo in 1941, the mayor of New York and many other notables came to hear Osborn tell of his vision. "The basic conception upon which our plans for the future are formulated is that the animal collections, to the greatest degree possible, should be shown grouped as they are in nature" (*Bulletin of the New York Zoological Society* XLIV, no. 3 [1941]: 69). This meant that African animals should be grouped together on the African plains and that Latin American and Asian animals should similarly be shown in an appropriate continental setting. Osborn saw such a principle as more suitable for the animals themselves, but even more important, such a natural zoo would have a much greater educational value. He seemed to be most interested in using the zoo as a vehicle for public consciousness raising. "I am not glorifying animals," he argued. "I am merely saying we should do well to know more of their scheme of things; we in turn will get a better understanding of our own scheme of things" (65).

Other innovations followed quickly on the heels of the African plains. In 1942 came the farm-in-the-zoo, which Osborn claimed was the "first completely stocked farm in any zoological park." Osborn wanted to give city people a taste of the country, and by developing educational programs and youth camps in relation to the zoo's farm, he tried to provide some hands-on experience of country life for city children. When he later took on the construction of a new aquarium on Coney Island, raising over a million dollars for the purpose, he also stressed the educative role of his efforts. But with the aquarium, as eventually with the zoo, Osborn also developed new contexts for scientific research itself, setting up scientific laboratories for research into the "conditioning factors" of fish and wildlife.

For the future environmental movement, the most significant institutional activity that Osborn was involved in was probably the creation, together with Samuel Ordway and George Brewer, of the Conservation Foundation in 1948. Osborn obtained funding from Laurence Rockefeller, an active member of the zoological society, to support research and education, particularly in international environmental issues, as well as to sponsor travel and international exchange among environmental scientists. The foundation, which Osborn headed until 1962, has been given credit for providing much of the scientific groundwork for the later campaigns against chemical fertilizers and insecticides. The foundation provided a source of funding and, eventually, information for many of the environmental groups and actions that started to emerge in the 1960s. Through his role as president of the foundation, Osborn took part in many international meetings and also served as an adviser to the Department of the Interior, where he lobbied for stronger environmental laws and more effective environmental administration. Russell Train, the first chairman of the national Council on Environmental Quality, had learned much about environmental protection while serving as director of the Conservation Foundation.

Fairfield Osborn tends to be forgotten when the history of environmentalism is written. But in his writings—and even more perhaps in his organizational activity—he planted many of the intellectual seeds that would later grow into environmentalism. Perhaps because he was so early in his international orientation and in his pioneering efforts to "urbanize" nature and ecology, he tends to be overlooked. But reading *Our Plundered Planet* some forty years after its initial publication, one is struck by how contemporary it sounds. Osborn was one of a handful of organization men who did not fall victim to the 1950s spirit of conformity. He used his organizational skills to provide a counterpoint to the age of abundance and criticize his countrymen's wasteful war with nature. By so doing, he provided important connections between the older conservation movement and the newer environmentalism of our day.

The Disenchantment of Lewis Mumford

The contribution of Lewis Mumford to the new environmentalism is also seldom recognized, even though his was, in many ways, the strongest and most influential American voice that came to be raised against the environmental consequences of the postwar technological culture. The neglect of his environmentalism, if it can be called that, is probably due to the range of his interests and the variety of his concerns; for while he wrote often in his typically colorful way about the new environmental problems and offered a number of suggestions on how to deal with them, he wrote about so many other things as well. In an age of specialists, he was the quintessential generalist, and even though he seemed to many of his postwar critics to be an anachronistic trespasser in the new frontier of scientific expertise, what he had to say about technology—particularly in the 1940s and 1950s—was especially significant in framing the way in which the new environmental consciousness came into being. Because he was an outsider, he could challenge the experts and not care what they thought about him.

It was Mumford who could more passionately than almost anyone else question the technological optimism of the times because he had been one of the first to delve seriously into its historical and cultural roots. We might say that his critique of postwar technology was important because much of his previous work and life had prepared the way for it. He had grown up in New York at the turn of the century, and, as an intellectually minded youngster living alone with a mother whose own self-absorption left him largely to develop for himself, fostering an unusually strong sense of self-discipline, the city had been his school. He studied technical subjects and loved to read classical literature, but mostly he spent his youth exploring his city and its environment, walking, sketching, thinking, visiting its museums, and finding a home in its Central Library. He never received a university degree, having dropped out of City College before he was drafted into the navy in 1917. In his twenties, he became a writer, inspired by the Scottish biologist-ecologist Patrick Geddes, whom he came to refer to as his "master," to turn his interests and talents to the reform and improvement of cities, not as an expert but as a philosopher. In 1919, he joined the staff of *The Dial*, one of the new journals of the Progressive Era. There he met Thorstein Veblen, a new source of inspiration, and soon he was beginning to publish what would become a long line of books on literature, architecture, technology, cities, and the "conduct of life." Geddes, Veblen, and Ralph Waldo Emerson were probably the most important sources of Mumford's unique vision, each of them independent and somewhat idiosyncratic writers who transgressed disciplinary boundaries as they wrote and acted morally and passionately on social issues.

Like his mentors, Mumford never really had an established place of work throughout his long life (he died in 1990 at the age of 95). In 1923, he was appointed secretary of the Regional Planning Association of America, and for the rest of the decade, he served as spokesman and organizer for garden cities and urban reform activities of various kinds. He also took part in producing the *American Caravan* yearbooks that fostered a rediscovery of American culture. And he wrote about classical American literature and culture—*The Golden Day* (1926) was one of the key works of the American "renaissance"—as well as about one of his favorite authors, Herman Melville.

His technical side led him into a more serious study of architecture, and he taught a course in 1923 at the New School for Social Research which he then turned into his second book, *Sticks and Stones*

(1924; his first book, *The Story of Utopias*, was published in 1922). In 1931, he was asked to write an architectural column for the *New Yorker*. As he became better known, he was asked to teach at more prestigious universities, and he continued to use his lectures as the first drafts of what would later emerge as books. *Technics and Civilization* (1934) started life as a course at Columbia University, and later books similarly grew out of lectures at MIT, Stanford University, and the University of Pennsylvania. But even though he visited universities and, in later life, was offered more permanent positions (which he always eventually rejected), Mumford was first and foremost a writer for the general public, not a professional academic. He represented a type of intellectual that has by now all but disappeared from American society, an independent man of letters, who had much to say and even more to write on almost all areas of knowledge. Never a modest man, his oeuvre is difficult to grasp and discuss briefly; and its relevance to environmentalism is spread throughout. For our purposes, two themes—themes that go through both the life and the writings—are of particular importance.

The first has to do with the overall cosmology or world picture, the organismic philosophy that Mumford has been associated with. The second theme has to do with his attitude toward technology. His writings on both themes follow a trajectory of disillusion, almost embitterment, as his youthful optimism and enthusiasm came to be challenged and eventually replaced by a more somber, even pessimistic view of man's future. The rise of what he termed "post-historic" man, rejecting history and refusing to recognize limits and constraints, represents for Mumford the victory of the forces of death. But his response to that victory was never to give in; rather, in his unique, intellectual way, the task became to delve even more deeply into man's soul, to master even more realms of specialized knowledge, to trace the roots of contemporary predicaments even farther back into history.

From *Technics and Civilization*, Mumford's first major work on technology, to the two-volume *The Myth of the Machine*, written in the 1960s, a most interesting process of intellectual transformation takes place. A utopian optimism becomes an almost dystopian pessimism. Mumford in the 1930s contrasted the culture of medieval Christianity to the darkness of the nineteenth and early twentieth centuries. He portrayed medieval technology in sympathetic terms, stressing its more limited impact on the environment, its reliance on natural materials like wood and plants, and its use of natural energy sources like wind and water. The eotechnic era, as he called it, represented a more harmonious time between man and his techniques; and, as he looked ahead into the future, he pointed to ways in which the more systematic use of science in material production, then just beginning, could signify a kind of return to a more organic technological regime. "We have now reached a point in the development of technology itself where the organic has begun to dominate the machine," he wrote. "One can now say definitely, as one could not fifty years ago, that there is a fresh gathering of forces on the side of life. The claims of life, once expressed solely by the Romantics and by the more archaic social groups and institutions of society, are now beginning to be represented at the very heart of technics itself" (1934: 367, 368).

Following Geddes and the English philosopher Alfred North Whitehead, Mumford in the 1930s came to be a proponent of a new organicism to oppose the mechanical philosophy that had governed science since the seventeenth-century scientific revolution. There was an interest, from both quantum physicists and biologists, to uncover more general, systemic processes in nature, and there was a feeling that the old machine metaphors and models had run their course. This holistic revival, which included also an interest in Eastern religions and art, had a strong influence on intellectual and political life in the interwar years. In architecture and literature, as well as in the visual arts, the free flow of organisms and natural rhythms provided new models and ideals for artists and writers, increasingly skeptical of the machine and mass production capitalism. In the social sciences, there was also a related interest in regionalism and urban ecology, and, in the course of the 1930s, Mumford came to be one of the most vocal and articulate proponents of organismic thinking in city and regional planning. His book, *The Culture of Cities* (1938), provided an ambitious history and conceptual framework for the experiments in regional development and urban reform that were such an important part of the programs of the New Deal era. His human ecological vision was propagated by regional planning groups and initiatives, like the famous Tennessee Valley Authority. But he disliked the experts even then, not so much for their programs as for their utilitarianism and their materialist values. And in the postwar era, his critique of materialism and the materialist world view that had come to dominate American culture grew ever more extreme and aggressive.

His books of the 1950s, *The Conduct of Life, In the Name of Sanity, The Transformations of Man,* contain much harsher judgments of his fellow Americans and their life-styles than the prewar works. At the same time, his faith in an idealistic metaphysic, a belief in organic personality and wholeness, grew, according to some critics, more dogmatic. Certainly, his books got more repetitive as he grew older; and his use of organicism as a guiding philosophy tended to grow more abstract and all-encompassing. It was his metaphysics, rather than his politics, that, according to Leo Marx, "accounts for the increasingly apocalyptic tenor of his writing about technology after World War II" (quoted in Hughes and Hughes 1990: 180). Rather than real social or political agents, Mumford came to believe in the individual personality as some kind of superhuman force, without which the world could not hope to avert disaster. His "politics" became metaphysical and deeply personalist, presaging some of the "deep ecological" ideas of recent years. As the human personality seemed threatened by extinction, Mumford became more extreme in his formulations and more outspoken in his desire to rescue humanity from the claws of the megamachine, with its regimentation, uniformity, and instruments of death. "About any and every machine, above all about the technical process itself," he wrote in 1954, "the critical question is: How much does this instrument further life?" And he went on, "The restoration of the organic, the human, the personal to a central place in our economy is essential if we are to overcome the forces that, without such over-all direction and control, are now driving our society ever closer to internal disintegration and external destruction" (Mumford 1979: 290).

There were also personal reasons for his increasingly pessimistic view of life. In 1944, Mumford's son Geddes was killed in Italy, fighting to defeat the Fascist "barbarism" that Mumford had reacted so strongly against in the closing years of the 1930s. He had been close to Geddes, whose strong feelings for nature and rural living he immortalized in his book, *Green Memories* (1947). Geddes, for Mumford, had "renewed the spirit of Thoreau" as he himself had renewed the spirit of Emerson, and his death affected him deeply. It only added to the sense of isolation and frustration that he increasingly felt in the years immediately after World War II. In calling on America to join the war effort in the late 1930s, Mumford had broken with many of his fellow Left-leaning intellectuals and a good many close friends, who had adopted an isolationist position before Pearl Harbor. Then, as always, he had not minced words; he had attacked the corruption of liberalism almost as strongly as fascism. Putting his words into action, he and his longtime friend Waldo Frank resigned in protest from the editorial board of the *New Republic,* where they had both served since the late 1920s.

The dispute over American intervention in the war brought to a head a critical attitude that Mumford had long felt toward what he termed "pragmatic liberalism." Pragmatism was a philosophy of means, Mumford contended already in 1926. It reflected the American infatuation with technology but neglected questions of meaning and value. Mumford's own voluminous writings were concerned with the ultimate goals of human activity. His first book told the "story of utopias," and in the interwar years, he carved out a niche for himself in the literary world, as he uncovered the hidden values of American art and literature, Western technology, urban development, and building design and construction. Perhaps more ambitiously than any other single author, Mumford had tried to formulate a comprehensive social theory for the twentieth century, weaving organismic philosophy, human ecology, and intellectual history into a unique and highly personal vision. During the war, he worked on the third volume in his Renewal of Life series. In this volume, with the typically immodest title, *The Condition of Man,* he explored, with some well-chosen examples, the links between personality and society.

With the wartime mobilization, however, such ideas became increasingly unpopular among social planners and scientists. The technological and regional transformation that Mumford had envisioned in the 1930s was stopped in its tracks, and a new kind of transformation took place instead—toward the megamachine, the pentagon of power. In the 1940s and 1950s, Mumford became one of the most outspoken critics of the new technological civilization. In his books and articles, as well as in his relentless and forceful campaigning for social control of atomic energy, Mumford questioned the dominant technological optimism, the belief in the machine. He criticized the false promises, the screwed up expectations, the unintended social consequences. And it was as part of that critique that Mumford pointed to the effects of this new technological regime on the natural environment. In a characteristic statement from 1956, Mumford made clear his disenchantment with the contemporary landscape.

> In contrast to the organic diversities, produced originally in nature and multiplied by a large part of man's historic efforts, the environment as a whole becomes as uniform and as undeviating as a concrete superhighway, in order to subserve the uniform functioning of a uniform mass of human units. Even today, the faster one moves, the more uniform is the environment that mechanically accompanies movement and the less difference does one meet when one reaches one's destination: so that change for the sake of change, and swiftness for the sake of swiftness, create the highest degree of monotony. (Mumford 1979: 381)

Mumford was not specifically concerned with environmental destruction; he was concerned with the destruction of life. But he did single out a number of elements of the postwar landscape for his own special kind of critical attention. In his architectural column for the *New Yorker*, he went after the skyscrapers and, more generally, the homogenization and deterioration of the urban architecture that he knew so well. In his commercially most successful book, *The City in History* (1961), he also subjected the new suburbs to severe attack. But perhaps more than anything else, he opposed the dominance of the automobile over postwar American life. He saw the private motorcar as the new American religion; and he waged his own kind of intellectual war against New York City's Robert Moses and other postwar city planners who had given the automobile a "sacred right to go anywhere, halt anywhere, and remain anywhere as long as its owner chooses" (quoted in Miller 1989: 480). Mumford challenged the plans of those who would turn cities over to highways and cars and in 1958 organized a political action group to stop a proposed highway that would have run through Washington Square in New York City. This rather unusual case of political activism on Mumford's part can be seen, in retrospect, as one of the seeds of the urban environmental activism that would play such an important part in the making of the later environmental movement.

More than any single issue, however, Mumford provided environmentalists with a sense of history. The seeds he planted were of a different sort than those provided by Osborn or other conservationists. Mumford offered—and still offers, for that matter—a personal view of human history and an emphasis on personality in the shaping of history while centering around the transformations between human societies and their natural environments. His works on cities and on technology are still unsurpassed as source material for understanding how natural conditions influence the making of human settlements and human behavior more generally. From this vantage point, much of his later writing can be seen as illustrations or further developments of themes originally outlined in the 1920s and 1930s. His more detailed treatment of some of his "heroes"—George Perkins Marsh, William Morris, Albert Schweitzer—that appear either as essays or as chapters in his later writings build on and specify the frameworks of analysis, the overall schemes of ecological history, that he presented in his early works. Ramachandra Guha has recently suggested that Mumford was also, in his later years, trying to evaluate his own contribution to history when he described the works of precursors he admired. Marsh, the nineteenth-century American geographer and author of the classic *Man and Nature* (1846), had, for Mumford, managed to combine "the naturalist's approach with that of the moralist and humanist," something that Mumford himself had always tried to do; while Morris was portrayed, as Guha puts it, as an early appropriate technologist "who sought to keep alive or if necessary to restore those forms of art and craft whose continued existence would enrich human life and even keep the way open for fresh technical achievements" (quoted in Guha 1991: 86–87). In the late nineteenth century, William Morris had inspired with his wallpapers and utopian lectures both the arts and crafts movement and the British socialist movement, and he is mentioned repeatedly in Mumford's later writings. Morris came to represent a lost polytechnic tradition that respected the artisan craftsman and sought to put the machine in its place, a tradition that Mumford felt was sorely needed in the late twentieth century. "Because we failed to foresee as clearly as Morris the consequences of automation, we now lack competent artisans or even fumbling handymen," he wrote with his typical sense of exaggeration in an essay in 1968. But, perhaps even more important, Morris, for Mumford, had been a man who had lived his life to the fullest and who had dared to dream utopian dreams; he had "cheerfully mastered every detail of each technical process, but sought to outline the kind of life that would still be possible, if other men shared his vision and his hope" (Mumford 1979: 213, 212).

In *The Conduct of Life*, Mumford had written about Albert Schweitzer in similarly glowing terms. "Schweitzer's moral greatness derives from the fact that he has shown that it is feasible, without renouncing the methods and insights of modern science, to achieve that which no science, no philosophy, no religion as yet adequately teaches: the possibility of becoming a whole man and of living, even under hostile circumstances, a whole life" (1951: 214). In pointing to individuals who had managed to live the organicism that Mumford preached, he was not merely providing role models for the later environmental movement but was also indicating that individual resistance and achievement could be important forces in social change.

In more general terms, Mumford opened up an ecological approach to history by showing how changes in resource use and energy supply strongly shaped cultural patterns and long-term social processes. Particularly valuable were his treatments of the medieval city and of medieval technics; *The City in History* is his magnum opus in this regard, providing a work of reference but also an interpretation of the history of Western civilization that centered on the ways in which human beings organized their interaction with nature. As a result, Mumford's writings took some important steps toward what Bookchin would later term social ecology, and his works have come to be the starting point for the writings of many an environmental sociologist or ecological social critic. By examining how technology had been adapted to local conditions and how a kind of regional imperative manifested itself in the rise and fall of urban communities, Mumford showed something of the ecological rationale of historical change, saving much of the detailed explication for later scholars. Never a systematic thinker, his writings offer a stream of hypotheses and speculations that can keep generations of human ecologists working for a good long time.

Mumford welcomed the rise of environmental activism without directly taking part in it or in any of the other movements of the 1960s. He spoke out against the Vietnam War as he had against the atomic bomb, and he was encouraged by the rebelliousness of the students in the 1960s. But he was getting old, and he recoiled from the extremism and the drift to violence in the more militant events of the late 1960s. Perhaps most pleasing to him, as he watched the movements that his writings had done so much to spawn, was the emergence of the "flower children" who came in the late 1960s to "return to the garden." Speaking in 1968, he said that "mere survival is not good enough: we must devise a strategy to ensure the further development of plants and men. . . . Not by accident, the young, who are in revolt against our power-stricken and machine-regimented society, have seized upon the symbolism of the flower and call themselves 'flower children.' In a very innocent, simple-minded, sometimes downright silly way, they have used the flower symbol to express their rejection of this automated and computerized and life-hostile technology. We too," the 73-year-old Mumford told his audience, "must learn to be flower children again, and rejoin the old procession and pageant of life" (1979: 493).

Mumford's writings helped to inspire many of those who have since tried to humanize the machine, either by writing its history or by exploring alternatives and potentialities. In an article in the 1950s, Mumford drew a distinction between the then-dominant authoritarian technics, motivated by power and dominance, and a democratic technics, responding to practical problems and existing at a modest, human scale. There were two traditions of technological development, Mumford argued, and as he traced the historical roots of democratic technics, he was also urging its continued relevance for a time that had grown all too dominated by the megamachine, the pentagon of power. In the late 1960s, many of those, in and out of the environmental movement, who moved to the countryside to develop more appropriate technologies found support in his vision and his "dialectical" view of technology. In many ways, Mumford can be said to have rearticulated or reformulated the legacy of technology criticism for the environmental movements of the late twentieth century. He brought into the postwar world the minority position on technology that had been expressed by the romantic poets and the socialist populists of the nineteenth century as well as by the conservationists and philosophers of the early twentieth century. When he died in 1990, Casey Blake noted in an obituary that Mumford's arguments "stand accused today of a 'pastoral nostalgia' or, worse, of a naive humanistic 'essentialism.' Maybe so," Blake wrote, "but it's hard to see how any equally inspiring vision of radical change has replaced the promise of self-fulfillment and democratic community that Mumford passed on to us from Blake, Morris, George and others" (Blake 1991: 190).

The Strange Success of Rachel Carson

While Mumford criticized the postwar technological landscape primarily on historical and philosophical grounds, Rachel Carson's opposition was that of a scientist and nature lover. Growing up in rural Pennsylvania, she brought a different sensibility, an emotional, yet scientifically based love of nature, to the postwar environmental challenges. Like Mumford, Carson also honored Schweitzer and his "reverence for life," but she seems to have been most directly influenced by women. She thus brought, perhaps unconsciously, a feminist perspective into the environmental movement. First her mother, who passed on to her daughter the unique dual interest in literature and nature, and then Mary Skinker, her biology teacher in college, who convinced her to switch her major from literature to biology, gave Carson strong female role models as well as respect for life processes. Carson studied biology in the 1920s when not too many women were active in natural science, and when she went to graduate school at Johns Hopkins University, her mother moved to Baltimore to help her pursue her scientific career. In the 1930s, Carson got a job for the Bureau of Fisheries as a research scientist, and at the same time, she also managed to develop her passion for writing, by producing articles on fish and underwater life, thus beginning a double career as scientist and writer. During the war, she wrote booklets for the bureau and by 1949 had become its director of publications, then renamed the Fish and Wildlife Service.

Silent Spring, Carson's book about pesticides published in 1962, is generally considered the start of the international environmental movement, but it is sometimes forgotten that Carson herself had become an international celebrity already in 1951, when her book, *The Sea Around Us,* became a best-seller and was translated into more than thirty languages. Carson was not alone in the postwar era in popularizing science for a general public or in waxing poetic about the wonders of life and nature; but she was, in many respects, the best of the lot. While other scientists took on popularization as a sideline, Rachel Carson turned science writing into a full-time profession. She helped fill in the gap between science and society, translating the ever more esoteric and voluminous findings of the scientists into a language that could not only be understood but appreciated.

Carson's success as a science writer rested on her own personal talents, but it also points to the fact that a new kind of literary market had developed in the United States, a new context for intellectual communication. Science occupied a particular place of pride in postwar America, and those who could write colorfully and informatively about its secrets—either as science fact or as science fiction—were given new kinds of career opportunities. Popular science entered into cultural magazines—both *The Sea Around Us* and *The Edge of the Sea* (from 1955) as well as *Silent Spring* appeared in condensed form in the *New Yorker* before being published as books—and even the visual media grew interested in science. *The Sea Around Us* was turned into a film in 1952 and won an Academy Award for best feature documentary. And after *The Edge of the Sea* brought new fame and prizes, Carson took time off from book writing to write a television script on clouds, "Something on the Sky." Her writing and film work in the 1950s paralleled that of other writers, like Arthur Clarke and Isaac Asimov, who wrote both factual popular books about the wonders of science and ambitious literary works of scientific imagination. Science had grown too important to be left to the scientists, and people like Rachel Carson were a new type of go-between.

Another development was the use of nature photography and films in the activities of the conservation societies. Nature books filled with color photographs became an important source of revenue for the

Sierra Club, in particular, as Ansel Adams and David Brower teamed up to produce impressive books on the deserts and forests of the American west. Nature writing and science journalism took on a new significance and could reach wider audiences through new production techniques and media as well as through the new methods of dissemination and communication. In a way, they were beneficiaries of the massification of culture in postwar America. What made Rachel Carson's story particularly important, however, was what she managed to do with her success and with the new contextual opportunities: she used them as a platform for social criticism.

Most of the other science writers were propagandists for the technological projects they wrote about. The best and most productive among them, like Asimov and Clarke, were visionaries, describing scientific breakthroughs in one book and speculating about future prospects and imaginary worlds in the next. In the postwar American culture, science and technology were seen as symbols of modernity, and the task of popular science writing and science fiction, as well, for that matter, was to "inform" the public about the new products and research results that science and technology provided. Popular science writers were enthusiasts of the new technological culture, and they generally neglected to inform the public that science itself was a social process and that the choices involved in making scientific priorities were social choices, not technical ones. In their enthusiasm for science—and many of them had come to writing from a scientific or technical background—they took on the role of public relations agents, "selling" science to the public rather than evaluating its social significance and consequences.

Perhaps because Carson was both a woman and a biologist, her science writing was of a fundamentally different order. She shared the fascination of her male colleagues, but she added a note of respect, even awe, for the natural processes and phenomena she described. Even more important, her perception of nature was historical and holistic; from her first book to her last, she stressed the cycles, the changes, the long-term processes at work in the world around us, and she portrayed the patterns of interdependence and interrelation that were at work under the sea as well as at its edge. Both *The Edge of the Sea* and *Silent Spring* focus attention on environments, rather than single species, and they present natural processes in interaction with human processes, not in the kind of sublime isolation that characterized the portrayal of nature in most preenvironmentalist nature writing. An ecological sensibility was central to all her work, but she grew more concerned about the negative influences of man on nature as the 1950s wore on.

Rachel Carson was able to bring to the traditional genre of nature writing insights and understanding emerging from the latest scientific findings. In this respect, she can be said to have brought the older pastoral image of nature up to date. But she also changed it, or at least transformed that image into one in which people had an important place—the people who studied and analyzed nature as well as the people who wreaked havoc on it. She also added a social or political awareness, fostered not so much by an ideological taking of sides as by a partisanship for life against death. She added to the ecological ethic emergent in the work of Lewis Mumford and Aldo Leopold the investigative skill of the journalist and the methodical research capability of the scientist.

The ecological way of thinking that she was so successful in spreading to her fellow countrymen was nurtured and sustained by changes that had taken place in American society in the postwar years. For one thing, many Americans found themselves living in a suburban middle ground, or no-man's-land, between nature and society. The new suburbs were neither cities nor countryside but a consciously planned hybrid, a man-made nature that was, at the same time, visibly, even painfully, artificial. On their television sets, Americans had come to experience the remotest reaches of wilderness in the comfort of their own homes, as nature was domesticated through an active and eventually colorful process of electronic communication. Driving in their cars over the expanded interstate highway system, many more Americans were able to visit national parks and forests and other bits of nature and take part in the increasingly popular and accessible activities of fishing, camping, hiking, and the like. In the words of Samuel Hays, "An increasing number of personal or media encounters with the natural world gave rise to widely shared ideas about the functioning of biological and geological systems and the relationship of human beings to them" (1987: 27).

Throughout the postwar period, Carson's letters give evidence of a growing awareness of the changes taking place in the landscape and a growing political consciousness. When she left the Fish and Wildlife Service in 1953 to write on a full-time basis, her director, Albert Day, was dismissed by Benton McKay, a former automobile salesman whom President Eisenhower had appointed secretary of the interior. Day's dismissal, she wrote in a letter published in *Reader's Digest*, "is the most recent of a series of events that should be deeply disturbing to every thoughtful citizen." The policies of the Republican administration represented a real threat to nature. "For many years," she wrote in 1953, "public-spirited citizens throughout the country have been working for the conservation of the natural resources, realizing their vital importance to the Nation. Apparently their hard-won progress is to be wiped out, as a politically minded Administration returns us to the dark ages of unrestrained exploitation and destruction" (quoted in Brooks 1972: 155).

She admitted that the coming of the new challenges to her beloved nature was difficult to accept. "The old ideas die hard, especially when they are emotionally as well as intellectually dear to one," she wrote. "It was pleasant to believe, for example, that much of Nature was forever beyond the tampering reach of man: he might level the forests and dam the streams, but the clouds and the rain and the wind were God's" (9–10). The fact that nature was now no longer free from human intervention was a fundamental point of departure for Carson, not just in *Silent Spring* but also in *The Edge of the Sea*, the book she wrote in the mid-1950s. There she wrote of plant and animal life on the shores and coastlines, but she also wrote about pollution and other human threats to the natural coastal environment.

Equally important as contextual background for the perspective that Carson presented in *Silent Spring* were the changes that were taking place within production. There was a shift in the postwar era, throughout the American economy, from an older set of products that were directly derived from nature—both in agriculture and industry—to a new science-based and synthetic production system. Plastics, synthetic textiles, chemical fertilizers and pesticides, and household chemicals proliferated enormously in the postwar period, and the general expansion of the economy was based in no small measure on these and other products that had been created in industrial research laboratories. These products were certainly wonderful in many ways, as consumers were often reminded in the television commercials that were used to sell them (and that themselves became a form of pollution). But they were not natural, which meant that they could not easily be disposed of by natural processes of degradation and decomposition; they thus became garbage, dumps, waste, pollution. The accumulation of waste and the physical deterioration of the landscape were, of course, nothing new for the postwar era; but the expansion of consumer commodities and the exponential growth rates of certain chemical and plastic products brought these problems increased visibility.

They also fundamentally changed the scale and dimension of the pollution problem. What Rachel Carson came to write in *Silent Spring* about pesticides was also the case for many of the other new pollutants. "For the first time in the history of the world, every human being is now subjected to contact with dangerous chemicals, from the moment of conception until death. In the less than two decades of their use, the synthetic pesticides have been so thoroughly distributed throughout the animate and inanimate world that they occur virtually everywhere" (1962: 24).

Even more serious perhaps was the fact that many of the new products were unhealthy, and the "risks" involved in their use were hard to locate and hard to prove. In the words of Rachel Carson,

> The new environmental health problems are multiple—created by radiation in all its forms, born of the never-ending stream of chemicals of which pesticides are a part, chemicals now pervading the world in which we live, acting upon us directly and indirectly, separately and collectively. Their presence casts a shadow that is no less ominous because it is formless and obscure, no less frightening because it is simply impossible to predict the effects of lifetime exposure to chemical and physical agents that are not part of the biological experience of man. (168)

Many of the new products of the postwar era were dangerous to have around the home, as well as dangerous for workers to make. The new pollutants thus altered the very meaning of health, transforming what had come to be seen as something largely individual into a growing public concern. Environmental pollution as well as traffic accidents and urban degradation became the undesired and unexpected "side effects" of postwar prosperity.

In the course of the 1940s and 1950s, the production of waste had become systematized; production was now based on the idea of disposability, as new products were not meant to last forever. The "affluent society" that Galbraith described in 1958 was one that was set on growing forever, with constantly rising demands and expectations for prosperity and personal wealth. In his best-selling exposé in 1960, the journalist Vance Packard showed how the postwar culture of abundance presupposed a society of "waste makers," making and buying an endless proliferation of soon to be discarded products. Packard disclosed how corporations actually planned for their products to become obsolete and through advertising fostered a life-style of conspicuous consumption with increasing disregard for quality and durability. He also noted that the postwar economy had grown ever more dependent on raw materials from other parts of the world, as Fairfield Osborn had pointed out a decade earlier. Packard began his own chapter on "vanishing resources" with a quote from Osborn's second book, *Limits of the Earth.* "We Americans," Osborn had written in 1953, "have used more of the world's resources in the past 40 years than all the people of the world had used in the 4000 years of recorded history up to 1914. . . . Man is becoming aware of the limits of the earth" (Packard 1960: 170). By 1960, that awareness had largely disappeared from popular consciousness after years of renewed exploitation and Republican deregulation of land use and forestry.

In the 1950s, many scientists pointed out that the American style of production with its insatiable appetite and inefficient production processes put serious pressure on natural resources and fostered increasingly unequal material relations between the United States and the rest of the world. Harrison Brown's widely read book, *The Challenge of Man's Future* (1956), offered a sober appraisal of the resources situation and, like many studies of the 1950s and 1960s, stressed the need for greater limiting of the use of nonrenewable resources, especially the fossil fuels. Brown, however, shared much of the technological optimism of his scientific colleagues, foreseeing in nuclear power and other new technologies various kinds of solutions or technical "fixes" to resource limitations.

Originally Rachel Carson thought to counter the technological optimism of the times with a critique of the entire chemical and technological war against nature. The working title of the book she had originally envisaged in the mid-1950s was *Man Against the Earth*. But she realized, as she started her research in 1958, that it would be more effective to focus attention on one particular chemical pollutant. She also thought that it would be faster to write it if the focus was on chemical pesticides in agriculture rather than on chemical products more generally. As it turned out, *Silent Spring* was some four years in the making, as she gathered documentation on the effects of pesticides on nature and human life. She realized that it would be highly controversial, and she conducted an even more thorough research investigation than she had for her previous books. The result of her efforts has been likened to a lawyer's brief, piling up evidence of harm and abuse collected from research journals, correspondence, and travels. The "big book on ecology" that she had wanted to write after her successful volumes on the seas became a very different and much more political book than anything she had ever written before; as she followed a reader's request to write about the dangers of chemical pesticides, her research took on a life of its own. Better than a general or philosophical work, *Silent Spring* specified the dimensions and the intensity of the environmental crisis by examining one critical area in detail.

What also made it valuable and useful for the movement that eventually took form around its message was its discussion of the alternative ecological solution, "the other road" of the book's final chapter. As she put it, "A truly extraordinary variety of alternatives to the chemical control of insects is available. . . . All have this in common: they are *biological* solutions, based on understanding of the living organisms they seek to control, and of the whole fabric of life to which these organisms belong" (1962: 244). As she outlined those alternatives, she once again, as in all her writings, let the scientists themselves speak, bringing not only people but dispute, contradiction, difference of opinion into the world of the expert. Perhaps even more important than the particular conflict she wrote about—

between chemical and biological insect control—was the presentation of conflict itself. The experts were themselves divided, and the environmental movement built its identity on that premise. "The road we have long been traveling is deceptively easy," Carson wrote, "a smooth superhighway on which we progress with great speed, but at its end lies disaster. The other fork of the road—the one 'less traveled by'—offers our last, our only chance to reach a destination that assures the preservation of our earth" (244).

Carson was not, of course, the only one to draw that distinction, but she was the one who made it stick. The impact of *Silent Spring* was rapid and enormous and worldwide. Within months after its publication, it was the subject of a barrage of criticism from the industries she attacked as well as the recipient of prestigious awards. Even more significant, the book led to practical, immediate reforms and to an environmental control administration in the United States and in most other industrialized countries. There was apparently nothing terribly organized about it; Rachel Carson was not explicitly political, it seems, nor did she have much time for social and political causes. She was concerned about the dangers to her beloved nature emanating from the new kinds of technologies that were used in agriculture and industry. The concern can be traced back to the war, when she saw some of the effects of the newly invented DDT while working for the Fish and Wildlife Service. That concern matured and grew, not by becoming shrill and aggressive but by gathering force and information. What made Carson successful was her ability to distinguish between good and bad science but even more, her capacity to bring the older identification with nature up to date. When the wilderness was no longer wild, its defenders needed a new language to express their concern. Rachel Carson's strange success was to fashion such a language and take on the powers of American industry with a single, impassioned voice.

· · ·

Our three ecological intellectuals, Fairfield Osborn, Lewis Mumford, and Rachel Carson, were certainly not the only sources of inspiration for the contemporary environmental movement, but each provided crucial role models for the new activism that took form in the late 1960s. Carson indicated that diligence, clarity, and commitment devoted to what has later been called public interest science could lead to institutional reform, legislation, and regulation measures as well as to social activism. She opened up a space for environmentalists to work within and eventually help construct a public arena of regulatory hearings, courtrooms, expert debates, and scientific information. Her book became the first of a long line of environmental critiques, in which problems were identified and changes were proposed and around which action groups and eventually new organizations were formed. Ralph Nader's *Unsafe at Any Speed* became one of the more influential examples of the genre as it developed in the later 1960s, leading to changes in automotive design as well as a host of regulatory and legislative measures. By the end of the 1960s, the public information "wing" of the environmental movement had taken on almost all the major polluting industries of American society and was beginning to marshal evidence against what would be the major opponent of the 1970s, namely, the nuclear energy industry.

But environmentalism, as it developed, was more than counterexpertise and public information. As it grew, it also built on the broadened notion of conservation that Fairfield Osborn had been one of the first to write about, in which the urban environment and the natural conditions of life in developing countries became central aspects of the environmental agenda. Many of the organizations that developed in the 1970s unwittingly seemed to be following the vision that Osborn had articulated in 1939 when he set up the New York Zoological Society exhibit at the World's Fair—to use zoos or natural parks or museums or nature excursions as educational activities to raise environmental consciousness. Osborn as an individual may have been forgotten, but the role he played and the message that he had been one of the first to spread were themselves sources of inspiration for the environmental movement.

Lewis Mumford, however, keeps growing on us. His influence was there in the 1960s, and, if anything, it continues to expand as the years pass. For now he himself is a part of the history that he tried so hard to implant in his fellow Americans, a history in which individuals make a difference, in which a balanced personality includes a respect for nature, and in which morality itself is to be seen as an awareness of limits and of wholeness. As environmentalism digs deeper into the roots of its own identity, the writings of Lewis Mumford take on an ever-greater importance. Mumford put the contemporary environmentalist cause in its place, by giving it a sense of human history. And that just might be the deepest ecology of all.

4

SHAPING NEW KINDS OF KNOWLEDGE
Leo Szilard, Herbert Marcuse, Margaret Mead

• •

He made an extremely unlikely American hero—an elderly philosopher and disillusioned Communist, peddling a message of negative
thinking in a heavily Germanized and highly abstract English. But for
a few years in the 1960s, Herbert Marcuse was indeed a hero for many
of the alienated young people who took part in the so-called Movement. Like Erich Fromm, he had been associated in Weimar Germany
with the Frankfurt school of critical social theory, and he too had
sought to combine Marxism with psychoanalysis after he came to
America to escape the Nazis. But while Fromm developed a form of
popular psychological social criticism, Marcuse offered the movements
of the 1960s a full-fledged utopian philosophy, putting some meaning
into the mood of liberation that was floating in the air and outlining
the contours of an emancipatory, rather than a repressive, form of
knowledge. During the 1940s and 1950s, Marcuse had tried to rescue
Marxism from Stalinist dogmatism, and he was one of the main contributors to a more humanist or utopian Marxism that seemed to better
suit the postwar era. After leaving the American intelligence service,
which he served during and for some years after the Second World
War, he found a congenial environment for his "dialectical" philoso-
phizing at the newly founded Brandeis University, just outside of
Boston. Brandeis was one of a handful of university campuses, along
with the University of Michigan, the University of Wisconsin, and the
University of California at Berkeley, just a notch below the academic
elite of the time, that provided a breeding ground for radical ideas in
the 1950s. In any case, it was as a professor at Brandeis and then at

the University of California at San Diego, where he moved in 1965, that Marcuse brought a socialist ideal of knowledge into American society. His critique of positivism and scientism, or "one-dimensional thought" as he called it in his most famous book, was extremely influential and opened the door to a general questioning of the way knowledge was used and produced in America.

Margaret Mead's critique was something quite different. Indeed, many would argue that she was not very critical at all, since she tried so hard to be famous and respected and thus accepted so many of the dominant values. But as the most vocal and visible promoter of anthropology in America, Mead sought to teach her countrymen about their own cultural biases; she confronted the positivist ideal of knowledge by practicing and propagating another mode of knowing. Together with her friend and colleague, Ruth Benedict, Mead argued, in book after book and at conference after conference, that modern American ways of doing things were culturally conditioned. Mead's reports from her field trips to the Pacific islands, as well as her extremely active public life as writer and teacher, brought a cross-cultural, comparative perspective into American social science, thus planting some of the seeds for the cultural relativism and eventually "multiculturalism" that have come in the wake of the revolts of the 1960s. By focusing her attention on family and sex roles in different cultures, she also helped to foster an academic interest in childhood and what is now called gender bias, serving as a midwife for much of the contemporary research being done in women's studies departments and in and around the movements for women's liberation. Mead challenged the scientistic positivism of the postwar era through her research practice, while her husband, Gregory Bateson, eventually fashioned a more theoretical challenge out of much the same psychological and anthropological materials. Mead showed in her very person what interdisciplinary knowledge could look like and how one could go about producing it; and in the networks she shaped, as well as the books she wrote, her impact on intellectual life in the United States was substantial. Like Marcuse, however, her contribution has tended to be neglected, at times even vilified, as the years have passed (they both died in 1979). In the meantime, however, the postpositivist conceptions of knowledge to which they both contributed have ever more come to be taken for granted. Perhaps the time has come to give them a second reading.

The significance of the seeds that Leo Szilard planted are perhaps more obvious. He was in many ways a typical, if eccentric, representative of the coterie of émigré physicists who contributed so much to twentieth-century American science. After leaving his native Hungary for Germany, Szilard had been one of the main developers of atomic physics in the 1930s and then, after fleeing to America, played a central role in the actual construction of the atomic bomb. It was Szilard who drafted the letter to President Roosevelt that was signed by Albert Einstein which told of the potential power that was contained in the atomic nucleus and urged a strong American research effort to counteract what the Germans were most likely doing to harness that power. It was Szilard and the Italian physicist Enrico Fermi who first produced the process of atomic fission in a scientific laboratory, which hundreds of scientists under the direction of Berkeley physicist Robert Oppenheimer spent their war years trying to transform into a practicable instrument of destruction. Szilard was one of those atomic scientists, but unlike Oppenheimer, who moved into a position of political authority after the war as a member of the Atomic Energy Commission, Szilard took on the role of expert critic. When Germany had surrendered and it became clear that the bomb was to be used on Japan, Szilard was the one who organized the protest actions, sending letters and petitions to President Harry Truman, urging restraint.

Szilard was one of the most tireless and unrelenting critical experts to emerge out of World War II and also one of the most eccentric; while many of the other atomic scientists who had responded to their guilt over the atomic bomb eventually returned to their laboratories in the 1950s, leaving politics behind, Szilard pressed on with his protest letters, his innovative campaigns, and his projects for peace. At the time when the cold war was intensifying, Szilard was one of those few individuals who helped to keep open within the world of science a space for reflection—and eventually for research and education—about the new relations of science and society. Now a field of its own, with societies and journals and university departments, the study of science, technology, and society could be said to have emerged out of the postwar work of people like Leo Szilard. He helped to articulate the terms of the discourse and to carve out some room in the university environment for raising issues of social responsibility, research ethics, and the political implications of science. It was scientists like Szilard, those who had touched evil, who most effectively developed a countermovement of critical scientists. In the *Bulletin of the Atomic Scientists,* in the Pugwash conferences, and in the demonstrations and activities against nuclear weapons, critical scientists took a stand and outlined a new kind of social role for scientists to play in postwar American society. Even though he was not a particularly effective organizer, Szilard came to play the role of spiritual leader for many of the critical scientist-activists. He went further than many of his colleagues, in that he shifted from physics to biology and played a role in the discovery of DNA, and he also became more and more of a scientific outcast. In his writings and even more in his actions, he planted important seeds for the "radicalization of science" that would come in the 1960s.

From very different directions—and in very different ways—Marcuse, Mead, and Szilard changed the ways we think about science and knowledge. Mead helped to raise the status and influence of the social sciences, offering, almost in spite of herself, a radical challenge to the scientific elite, which for most of the postwar era was dominated by the physicists who had taken part in the wartime research programs. Her challenge was that of the successful insider, practicing a different kind of science, a culturally critical science, using corporate and government funding—the new intellectual institutional contexts—for "progressive" purposes. Both Marcuse and Mead had done wartime government work, and they both benefited from the new institutional arrangements that emerged after the war. Marcuse found work at Russian research centers at Columbia and Harvard, and Mead launched a number of large, interdisciplinary research projects on national character and child development, both under government and United Nations auspices. But their response to the military-industrial state was far more critical than that of the physical scientists—even one as actively outspoken as Szilard. In Marcuse's critical theorizing and in Mead's critical research practice, we see two of the main "humanist" alternatives to scientism, the one abstract and all-encompassing, the other conciliatory and pragmatic. Where Marcuse kept alive the socialist theory that so many of his colleagues disavowed, Mead kept alive the ambition to popularize and be useful, an ambition that had characterized so much of the intellectual activity of the 1930s. Szilard, in contrast, helped to preserve among American scientists something of the partisanship and political commitment that had been widespread during the depression, when scientists had moved out of their laboratories to take part in the political battles of the time. Marcuse, Mead, and Szilard countered the positivism, professionalism, and narrowing of vision of postwar academic life with positive alternatives. It is well worth the effort to try to recapture their contributions.

American Knowledge Traditions

Knowledge in America has traditionally come in two main varieties, usually separated and even antagonistic, which might be termed religious and scientific, or in modern parlance, normative and objective. The religious came first: American thinkers, from the early colonial days, had seen it as their mission to implant the Christian faith in the heathen world, translating the terms of European theological discourse into a language that suited the very different conditions of the new world. The strong religious faith not only inspired the flight to North America among the early settlers, many of whom came to America to escape repression for their beliefs, but colored the way they developed their educational and other knowledge-producing institutions. The American colonial thinker, usually a Puritan and almost always a man, sought to develop a way of living in which the pursuit of knowledge was a part of a deeper moral project. Jonathan Edwards and the other Puritan preachers who tried to put their faith into print pointed to the spiritual challenges confronting modern man rather than the technical or constructive ones; but in the course of the eighteenth century, they were joined by other pioneers, who saw in technology and experimental science the keys to a glorious, somewhat more secular, future.

By the time of the American revolution, experimental science, which had waged its own "scientific" revolution in Europe a century before, had taken hold in the colonies, and at least one American had become renowned throughout Europe for his research results: he had discovered the fact that lightning was electric. Benjamin Franklin, however, was not merely a gifted scientist; like Thomas Jefferson and other revolutionary leaders, he was a new kind of scholar, a man of the people, a politician as well as an active producer of scientific knowledge. He was also an artisan printer and retained all his life a faith in hard work and practicality, providing already in the eighteenth century a democratic ethos and a kind of indigenous commonsense philosophy for scientific endeavor. Knowledge, for Franklin and Jefferson, was to be used for the good of the people and not pursued in relative isolation by a prosperous elite. The democratic ethos, which was so central to many of the activities carried out by American intellectuals in the 1930s, can trace its roots back to the revolutionary period—and to the writings of Franklin, Jefferson, and Thomas Paine. As Puritanism and a more priestly, elitist ideal of knowledge established itself at Harvard and other northeastern colleges and found expression, perhaps most elegantly, in the long-lived and highly influential Adams family, the democratic ideal spread to the countryside and led the long march westward. For some two hundred years, they have competed with one another, at times combining in fruitful syntheses but more often opposing each other in orientations of research, definitions of disciplines, and selection of problems.

During the nineteenth century, the different traditions developed for the most part in different organizational contexts. The Puritan, religious ideal of knowledge as a moral missionary undertaking entered into the range of sects and churches that came to be formed as the country expanded westward. Emerson's transcendentalism—and his notion of the self-reliant scholar as a preacher of the people—had an enormous influence in nineteenth-century America; and as "populism" took on the character of a political movement in the late nineteenth century, a kind of people's knowledge, heavily tinged with moral precepts and based primarily on an experiential relation to reality, gained a strong foothold in American culture. In this tradition, the true producer of knowledge was the independent self-willed individual with his own personal relation to God, and as cities grew and social problems grew with them, a more modern missionary ideal of social work and philanthropy emerged, epitomized, on the one hand, by Jane Addams and her applied sociology and, on the other, by William Jennings Bryan and his conservative moral theology.

Both paths to wisdom came to be transformed by the leaders of the corporations that propelled America into the industrial age. In industry, a practical engineering, commonsensical approach to reality came to dominate; and at the universities, which spread, like the settlers, across the plains and on to California in the course of the nineteenth century, these practical-scientific ideals of knowledge took hold. Here it was utility that governed, a philosophy of means and techniques. The democratic ethos had been transformed into what came to be known as pragmatic philosophy, while the religious spirit was diffused through the popular culture as a newfangled religion of progress. There was an opposition to this secular religion, which eventually would grow into the moral conservatism of the late twentieth century; but even there, science and technology were never viewed as the enemies. It was only when science was seen as opposing the biblical Gospel, as in the Darwinian theory of natural selection, that the religious groups became "anti-intellectual." Whatever else can be said about it, however, American religion, of even the most fundamentalist type, has seldom opposed material and technological progress.

By the early twentieth century, American intellectual life had retained its original duality—into religious and scientific realms—but it had, as well, been increasingly fragmented or compartmentalized into distinct disciplines and specializations. Indeed, this became one of the main contributions of America to the social organization of knowledge, the academic specialist, trained to be effective in both the production and dissemination of knowledge but leaving morality, religion, and even reflection itself to others, to the amorphous popular realm. In the so-called Progressive Era, the expert emerged as a kind of hybrid between the academic specialists and the managers of industry and government, who wanted to transform society itself into a well-oiled machine. A technocratic vision entered into both popular culture and government; and scientific, positivist methods and ideals spread from the natural sciences into the domains of social and human studies.

In the 1920s, many of the frameworks that still govern American intellectual life were put in place: the corporate foundations, the industrial research laboratories, the public interest organizations, and the research university organized around the professional schools of law and medicine and the graduate departments of research training. In the depression, there was a brief moment of oppositional hegemony in the emergence of what we have called populist pragmatism, combining, or at least trying to combine, the disparate worlds of the expert and the common people, of science and morality. For a time, the two traditions of knowledge interacted as the worlds of morality and objectivity met in new patterns of intellectual activity. An important element was the infusion of Freudian psychoanalytic theory into America, with a new terminology of emotions and a new way of integrating the mind and the body, the heart and the soul. Freudianism, which, at the turn of the century, had been a critical force among intellectuals, offered in the interwar period a science of the soul, and it found fertile ground for development in an America beset by soul-searching intellectuals in a society in the midst of economic crisis and a world in the throes of political chaos. The passionate science that emerged for a time, combining the populist traditions of the craftsmen with the pragmatic traditions of the scientific expert, challenged the positivism and the scientism that had been so dominant in the Progressive Era; but the challenge was short-lived. The radical vision would all but disappear during the Second World War, as the experts moved into the secret worlds of intelligence and government consulting.

What Marcuse would come to call technological rationality dominated the postwar universities, as moral or ethical issues were not so much eliminated as banished to the other side of the academic fence, where they could be discussed in splendid isolation from the real world of science and technology. Experts in culture joined with the scientific and technical experts in professionalizing knowledge and in separating what had been combined in the 1930s, namely, an interest in science with a democratic populism. Science itself came to be organized in the manner of the industrial corporation. The so-called Big Science of large laboratories and multidisciplinary teamwork that had proved so successful as a form of research organization in the military projects during the war came to dominate the world of science also in the postwar era. Science became an ever more integral part of big business and a crucial component in what came to be termed the military-industrial complex. In the postwar scientistic age, only a handful of intellectuals tried to keep alive the vision of a democratic and more artisanal knowledge, the "little science" that seemed to have disappeared from view.

Leo Szilard, the Partisan Scientist

Leo Szilard was in many ways an unlikely dissident. He was never a populist; on the contrary, he was the very epitome of an elitist scientist. Born in Budapest in 1898 the son of an engineer, Szilard already at an early age had come to see himself as part of a privileged class, and his political beliefs, such as they were, always put the men of knowledge at the top, in a new position of leadership. He was inspired by the tales of H. G. Wells, which combined futuristic scientific visions with proposals for an "open conspiracy" of scientists and engineers leading the world. Szilard thought that scientists simply knew more than other people, because he certainly did, and he saw no reason why scientists could not solve political problems as successfully as they were able to solve physical and technical problems. He tried to bring the rational ingenuity of the scientific engineer into the resolution of political problems.

Szilard may have been an elitist, but he was also strongly antiauthoritarian, bringing with him to America a distaste for all totalitarianisms, especially for the Nazism that had taken over his homeland and was murdering his fellow Jews across Europe. His activity—both as a scientist and as a political activist—was colored by the anti-Fascist partisanship that formed a common political denominator for many of his generation. Szilard did not subscribe to the populism that was propounded in America with its notion that anyone could be a scientist; his partisanship was more derived from a code of personal ethics and a passionate belief in rationality. What Szilard and a handful of other equally elitist scientists tried to do in the postwar era was to exercise responsibility for their actions. For them, science was not merely a nine-to-five job carried out in the laboratory, a career path like any other. Science was rather a calling, a very special kind of work that carried with it its own kind of responsibilities. Szilard's faith in science was thus both elitist and democratic. On the one hand, science was a democratic mode of practice; on the other hand, it could only flourish in a democratic society that upheld freedom of expression and free debate. Scientific knowledge, for Szilard and many others of his generation, was seen as growing through a kind of collective or at least interactive thinking, and all of Szilard's best work took place when he was theorizing and experimenting with others, freely letting the scientific imagination run wild. The science that Szilard and the other émigrés had been a part of in Europe had been a particularly dynamic and exciting science, in which bold, young geniuses like Szilard had discussed on equal terms with the old established professors.

The ideal of science that Szilard and the others had taken with them to America was of a community of thinkers, bound together by a mutual devotion to critical and free exchange of ideas and not governed by bureaucratic and hierarchical structures and rules. Derived as much from the actual historical legacy of struggling for academic freedom as from the "mandarin" values of nineteenth-century central European intellectuals, the idea of science as a vocation for an elite community of scholars was characteristic of many of the leading scientists during the early part of this century. It was, in many ways, a defensive standpoint against the totalitarianisms of both the Left and the Right. One of Szilard's friends from Hungary, the chemist Michael Polanyi, who helped Szilard establish himself in England after he fled from the Nazis in 1933, later wrote about the importance of protecting the "republic of science" from all kinds of political intervention.

In any case, as it came to be increasingly difficult to practice this democratically elitist science in continental Europe, Szilard came to feel that such a science, indeed science itself, could only survive in a democratic regime, with a free debate and an open discussion about implications and consequences. He opposed from the beginning the secrecy and military style that came to govern the Manhattan Project— the construction of the atomic bomb—which he himself had helped to initiate. There was definitely no love lost between Szilard and General Leslie Groves, the director of the Manhattan Project. During their first meeting at the University of Chicago in 1942, when Groves had just been given responsibility for the project, it was already clear that their approaches to science diverged dramatically. Where Groves sought to impose regimentation, discipline, and strict security measures on the atomic scientists, Szilard affirmed the importance of the free and open exchange of ideas. When most of the atomic scientists, for security reasons, were moved to the desert sands of Los Alamos, New Mexico, to work in guarded isolation, Szilard stayed behind in Chicago, where, it was said, he could continue to eat his beloved pastrami sandwiches but also where he could live and work in greater freedom than was available in the closed and extremely guarded world of Los Alamos. Even the vow of silence that he had taken in order to be able to work on atomic research was hard for Szilard to stomach; but he was loyal to the cause. Groves, however, never trusted Szilard: Szilard's style, his eccentricities, his brilliance, his whole being was unacceptable to the quintessential military man. Groves tried to remove Szilard from the atomic program and even have him thrown into jail as a security risk; but he was never able to prove to his superiors that Szilard actually was a dangerous man. The only danger that Szilard represented was his devotion to freedom of expression and his belief in the importance of what might be called the democracy of science. After the war, that devotion to an open science, free from military control and domination, would make Szilard one of the most outspoken scientific critics of the scientific-technological state.

It was to the democratic debate about the new role of science in the postwar society—and especially in the production of atomic weapons—that Szilard sought to make his contributions felt; and in that respect, even though his opinions were often unacceptable, even naive, he never tired of voicing them and trying to get other scientists to partake of what he saw as their democratic duty to reflect on the social consequences of their work. In his practical activity, which included lobbying politicians, writing letters (he wrote, among others, important open letters both to Stalin and Kruschchev), circulating petitions, taking part in public debates, organizing meetings, and starting organizations as well as writing analytical articles, he helped to carve out a new identity in postwar America: the critical scientist. While many of his former friends and colleagues basked in their newfound fame and fortune and saw the increased status of physics and physicists after the war as the justified reward for their wartime service, Szilard left physics altogether and saw the new challenges that atomic weapons posed for the world more as cause for concern than celebration.

Szilard had particular reasons for feeling the urgency of the tasks he took on. He took responsibility for the atomic bomb; after all, the bomb was his idea in the first place—the idea that electrons could bombard an atomic nucleus and set off a chain reaction of enormous power had come to him while crossing a street in London in 1933—and he had been the first to demonstrate in a laboratory the possibility of atomic fission, the scientific process on which the atomic bomb was based. Unleashing the forces of atomic energy had been a kind of scientific and political obsession for him throughout the 1930s, as he wandered through a Europe on its way to war. He saw his duty as scientist first and foremost to help save the world from destruction, but to do that the forces of nature had to be understood and tamed. Later, it was in large part because of his urging that the American government devoted so much money and manpower to building the atomic bomb during the war. Szilard was convinced that German scientists were far ahead and that America had to develop a bomb of its own. But what he had started he could not stop. After the Nazis were defeated and it became clear that their scientists had not come very far in their atomic research program, Szilard led the fight to keep the bomb from actually being used. He felt responsible, but he was powerless to affect policy. Decisions were taken far over his head, by the military leaders whose prestige and postwar power were to depend on the bomb being dropped. And his scientific influence would also wane, as the times, at least in physics, no longer seemed to call for the mad genius, the brilliant hatcher of ideas and inspired guesses but rather for those who could manage and negotiate, who could organize large-scale research projects and direct mammoth institutions. In such a world of Big Science and scientific politics, Szilard felt an outsider.

He was not alone, and in certain respects, the impact of the organizations that he helped start but then left behind as he moved on to other arenas was greater than his own individual role. The Federation of Atomic Scientists and its journal, *Bulletin of the Atomic Scientists*, continued to provide a forum for debate and discussion of science and politics even after the urgency of the immediate postwar years had passed. One of the founding members and main sources of inspiration for both the journal and the federation, Szilard had little time for organizational work. He was too impatient to work for long in any one organization. Later, when the Pugwash meetings of American and Soviet scientists began to be held in 1957, Szilard kept his distance, his independence. He was critical of the large, formalized meetings that the Pugwash conferences became and continued to work and discuss in smaller, more informal groups. Pugwash was largely his idea, and he took part in the meetings, but he was "typically, both an inspiring and disruptive presence." As Barton Bernstein puts it, "He would sometimes introduce proposals, seem to gain considerable support for them, and then withdraw them. He did not want a vote but a discussion, not a victory but an exploration of ideas" (1987: xiv).

Szilard's significance was more in his personal commitment and his ceaseless suggesting of new ways to carry on the crusade than in any one particular organizational achievement or set of ideas. In his endless letter writing and pestering of presidents and prime ministers, Szilard showed in his very person what a concerned scientist could, and should, do. It was his idea to provide a forum for American and Soviet scientists to meet together, even though it was Bertrand Russell and Albert Einstein who actually organized the first Pugwash meetings. And later, in the early 1960s, when he created the Council for a Liveable World to bring scientists and politicians together to discuss international security issues and to help elect peace candidates to Congress, he left the organizational work to others.

Szilard was not a very good organizer even of his own life; and, indeed, he spent a good deal of the postwar era without a real academic post or, for that matter, a clear academic identity. He had a chair in biophysics at the University of Chicago, but he published little in that field. Later, he had a chair in social science also at Chicago—without ever having studied social science—and, more than once, he tried to start new interdisciplinary research institutes on public health and public policy issues. His proposal for a research institute for fundamental biology and public health in 1957 failed to get the support he needed, but in that proposal, he outlined research projects—in science and public health, in birth control, and in fertility—that twenty years later would be the standard fare of many interdisciplinary studies departments. He tried to fight the dominant specialization trend of academic life through his own person as well as through proposals and ideas that he circulated among foundations and university presidents, without much success. In this respect, he was a forerunner of the academic generalism and interdisciplinary research that would characterize many of the institutional reforms of the 1960s and beyond.

The histories of DNA usually give Szilard some credit for inspiring molecular biologists to think a little harder or to take up some new approach in their experiments; but his own contribution to the burgeoning field of genetics was rather minimal. He published little and rarely followed up on his own ideas, which were in typical Szilard fashion usually brilliant but a step or two ahead of the research front. Except for two or three years of active experimental work in biophysics in the early 1950s, Szilard was mostly occupied, or preoccupied, with the bomb and its political implications, and his writings proposed plans for research and policy measures to deal with those consequences. He was one of the first strategic thinkers, but he thought his unthinkable thoughts not as a technocratic futurologist or strategic analyst for the CIA but as an independent, partisan intellectual. He drafted memorandums on world government and devised any number of proposals for international control of atomic weapons. Through all of these writings, the particular tone of the partisan scientist comes through, expressing sustained concern, investigating the relations between science and society not as a part of a professional social science discourse but as a personal political commitment. Before science and society became a topic for courses and textbooks, it was being pursued by partisan scientists like Leo Szilard.

Nowhere does the particular flavor of his thinking come out better than in the volume of stories that he published in 1961 under the title, *The Voice of the Dolphins.* Trying to reach a wider audience, Szilard camouflaged his beliefs about disarmament and world peace in science fiction and in a light satiric style, and, to his delight, the book was even published in Russian. In these stories, Szilard shows himself as one of the transgressors of the abyss that separated the two cultures. He wrote satirical science fiction not to earn a living as a writer (although the book did sell rather well) but to portray the absurd paradox of the postwar age, when knowledge was produced primarily for destructive purposes and when the greatest minds that ever lived—or so it was claimed— were busily outdoing themselves in trying to devise ways to destroy the world. The stories presented Szilard's ideas about disarmament and control of atomic weapons in a fictionalized setting and succeeded in making his name and perhaps some of his ideas known outside the world of science. There is also a good deal of humor in the stories; in one of them, Szilard has travelers from outer space report on a visit to Grand Central Station in New York, left standing after the earth's population has been wiped out by nuclear war. Why the population had become extinct is explained by one of the visitors on the basis of the coin machines that were found in the toilets at the station. "Xram," we are told by the rapporteur of the alien group, "has a theory of his own which he thinks can explain everything, the disks in the gadgets as well as the uranium explosions which extinguished life. He believes that these disks were given to earth-dwellers as rewards for services. He says that the earth-dwellers were not rational beings and that they would not have collaborated in co-operative enterprises without some special incentive" (Szilard 1961: 120). Xram has thus deduced that the earth-dwellers lived in a state of economic chaos because such a system of disks was inherently unstable and could even lead to war between the same species. The reporter is skeptical, however, but the point has been made, this time with a touch of satire and humor.

The stories were certainly not literary masterpieces, nor were Szilard's political writings particularly effective or influential. Rather, Leo Szilard's significance was as a personal witness, one of the first and definitely most publicly concerned scientists of the postwar era. His criticism was not of science itself but of the confluence of science with power, the postwar alliance between the military and the elite physicists who had been his colleagues and friends. As he broke with them after the war and looked for ways to take responsibility for what they had done, he helped to open up a new kind of platform for intellectual activity. It was at the interface between science and society where Leo Szilard operated. And by operating there for some twenty years on a full-time basis, he opened up, or at least helped to identify, a space for others to populate in the decades to follow. It would be wrong to say that all the university departments of science and technology studies with their courses on science and the military and the social responsibility of scientists were somehow due to the work of Leo Szilard, but he was one of the handful of scientists in the immediate postwar era—one of those who had seen evil—who pointed to some of the social implications of the postwar intellectual regime. The coming of the scientific-technological state changed science and the social role of scientists, but it also led to the emergence of a new social role, that of the critical or partisan scientist. Leo Szilard was one of the first—and still one of the most interesting—practitioners of that role, a kind of unsung hero of the postwar era.

Herbert Marcuse, the Old Dialectician

Central to the scientism of the postwar years was its linear belief in progress, the view that history moved in one direction, forward. In keeping with the notion proclaimed by the General Electric advertisement, "progress is our most important product," postwar thought posited a reality of uniformity, consensus, order, and endless progress. It was the one-dimensionality of both the society and the thought that seemed most typical but also, for some of those who had seen other totalitarian regimes close up in the 1930s, most oppressive. Herbert Marcuse was one of the most successful opponents of this one-dimensional thought, and in resurrecting—or remembering, as he would have said—the Hegelian-Marxian dialectical approach to human history, Marcuse helped to provide the New Left with an alternative ideal of knowledge and science.

Marcuse sought to "negate" contemporary thought, stressing the hidden contradictions, the false assumptions, and the narrowness of vision that characterized postwar American philosophy and scientific thinking more generally. Out of Marx and Freud, Marcuse fashioned a dialectic of liberation, in which truth was derived not from empirical, objective research but from the subjective participation of the observer in shaping reality. In some of his writings, he appeared to portray such a subjective counterpoint to objectivism as an end in itself and glorified what Freud had called the "pleasure principle" as a kind of overriding goal for humanity. His book, *Eros and Civilization* (1955), became popular among the hippies of the counterculture as a philosophical proclamation of the power and importance of subjective experience.

In the course of the postwar era, his message evolved from one of historical recovery and resuscitation into a more offensive program of emancipation or liberation, in which aesthetic, environmental, and even feminine principles were given a pride of place in what might be termed a utopian epistemology. From negating oppression to giving it a name, Marcuse went on to try to educate desire. And the further he progressed in his program of opening up alternative philosophical perspectives, the less acceptable he became for his academic colleagues. In the 1970s, as hippies grew older and the spaces for liberation—the liberated zones—were occupied by drug dealers and terrorists and eventually eliminated with the help of repressive countermeasures, Marcuse tended to lose his audience. But his writings remain important for having inspired among many sixties radicals a search for new approaches to knowledge, which continues—at least for some of us—into the present.

Marcuse reconceptualized a critical theoretical way of thought that had all but disappeared from the American academic landscape in the 1950s. He helped bring the Marxist tradition into the postwar era. Marxism had been one of the sources of inspiration of the movements of the 1930s; literary critics like Edmund Wilson, philosophers like Sidney Hook, and even sociologists like Robert Merton had made use of Marxist categories and frameworks in their writings during the depression. Admittedly, theirs had been a peculiarly American Marxism, pragmatic, even positivist in style, amenable to the empirical and objective methods of science that were so dominant in the United States and rather insensitive, if not downright antagonistic, to more Hegelian or philosophical styles of Marxism that continued, even in the hard times of the 1930s, to be pursued in the homelands of classical humanism in central Europe. Refugees from Nazism, like Marcuse and his Frankfurt school comrades Horkheimer and Adorno, brought a different kind of Marxism with them to America, a continental Marxism, in which Hegel and his so-called dialectical method occupied a position of central importance. The dialectic, which for Wilson and Hook represented a lingering mysticism in the midst of Marxist enlightenment, a metaphysical, even meaningless abstraction that needed to be cleansed from the Marxian legacy, was for the Frankfurt school in exile a central key to understanding. Identify contradictions, and you are on your way to understanding social reality, the dialecticians contended; reduce reality to material conditions, and you have understood everything, the more American-style Marxists responded.

Horkheimer and Adorno, and Ernst Bloch as well, for that matter, all came to America during the war and then went back to Germany; for various reasons none of them could deal with the "vulgar Marxism" and, indeed, the vulgarity in general that America represented to them. Marcuse stayed; and not only did he stay but he put his philosophical learning and his linguistic skills at the disposal of the office of wartime intelligence. He assimilated into his new environment and eventually moved on to universities that were, if not open, at least not directly hostile to his negative thinking, his dialectical way of thought. He found ways to be useful, among other things by applying his understanding of Marxist theory to deciphering the doctrines of Soviet communism; but mostly he stayed in the margins of postwar academic life, weathering the storm, reconnecting Marxism to its philosophical roots, and helping to prepare the way for the new wave of Marxian socialism that emerged in the 1960s. He was not alone, of course, but Marcuse, as person and author, was perhaps the one intellectual in the postwar era who most effectively linked the two radical generations. When his old colleague Erich Fromm grew too successful in his popular psychoanalysis and turned radicalism largely into a personal quest for mental health, Marcuse took him on and questioned whether Marxism was really a humanism at all, as Fromm claimed. Unlike Fromm, Marcuse never ceased being—or at least trying to be—a revolutionary. Marcuse sought to keep the radicalism of Marx from being watered down, from being transformed into a toothless liberalism; but he also resisted the attempts to freeze Marxism in its own past, to reify the writings of Marx as dogmatic truths that were in no need of amendment. Marcuse tried to pass on some of the hard-won lessons of the past to a new radical generation. In the end, he was probably more affected by the sixties than the sixties were by him; but his writings provide an interesting documentation of the ideas, in particular, the ideas about knowledge, that were at the center of the 1960s movements.

Like Hannah Arendt, Marcuse had studied philosophy with Heidegger, and although the direct theoretical influence would wane, he bore with him all his life the style and tenor of German philosophy. He remained, even in America, a classical humanist scholar. But Marcuse had also been influenced as a young student in Germany by the radical uprisings that came in the wake of the First World War. He came from an upper-middle-class Jewish family and lived a rather sheltered nonpolitical life until 1918, when, as a twenty-year-old, he took part in the "worker's council" movement in Berlin. He joined the Social Democratic party but resigned after the murder of Karl Liebknecht and Rosa Luxembourg, who had formed a more radical faction, the so-called Spartacus group. By 1919, as his biographer puts it, "Marcuse's brief period of political activity was over" (Kellner 1984: 18). What Marcuse himself later admitted was that the political conflicts on the Left in the aftermath of the First World War and the Bolshevik revolution in Russia led to a lifelong interest in Marx. In the 1920s, he moved to Freiburg to study with Heidegger and Husserl, and for a time he tried to combine the teachings of Marx with the phenomenology being developed by these philosophers.

Marcuse broke with phenomenology, however, when Heidegger began to support the Nazis, and in 1932, he left Freiburg to work with Horkheimer and eventually Adorno and Fromm and others at the Frankfurt Institute for Social Research. These were formative years for Marcuse, and his interaction with Horkheimer and Adorno and other "critical theorists," as they came to call themselves, colored most of his future writings. The Frankfurt school opposed the dogmatic Marxism of Stalin and his henchmen with a more detached philosophical approach to social theory and revolutionary change; Marxism was first and foremost a radical theory of society for the Frankfurt school, not a political program to be followed literally. If Marcuse had more respect for the writings of Lenin and other Soviet Marxists than many of his Frankfurt colleagues, he nonetheless shared their overriding interest in theory. Perhaps most important, he shared their interest in developing a twentieth-century Marxism, one that was informed by historical experience—and not least the historical experience of Marxist revolutionary movements, both successful and unsuccessful—as well as by other contemporary streams of thought.

What was particularly crucial for the critical theory that Marcuse took part in shaping during the 1930s was the rise of Nazism, the emergence out of capitalist society of an irrational, barbaric movement. This was something that Marx had not foreseen, and its interpretation would be perhaps the most significant element in the "revised" Marxism that emerged from the Frankfurt theorists. The Marxism of the

Frankfurt school was an open-ended enterprise; reflective criticism was viewed as an ongoing, unfinished process that involved academic collaborations as well as creative syntheses of theoretical and empirical research. After the war, when Horkheimer and Adorno returned to Germany, the Frankfurt school would grow even more detached from politics; it would be primarily those members who stayed in America—Marcuse, Lowenthal, Fromm, Franz Neumann—who would most actively keep alive the political motivations that had first given inspiration to "critical theory."

Marcuse's writings for the journal of the Frankfurt school during his years of direct involvement in the 1930s and early 1940s dealt with many themes, but perhaps the most central issue for his early theorizing—and an issue that would sustain his interest throughout his life—was the increased influence of technology in twentieth-century civilization. Like his Frankfurt colleagues, Marcuse was sensitive to the new forms of work organization that had come to establish themselves in the industrialized world: the mass-producing conveyor belts of Henry Ford and the "scientific" management techniques pioneered by Frederick Winslow Taylor. Like the other Frankfurt theorists, Marcuse recognized that, with the coming of Fordism and Taylorism, technology would come to play a far more determinant role in the production process than it had played in the nineteenth century, when Marx was analyzing capitalist society. But perhaps because of his involvement with Heidegger, Marcuse focused somewhat more strongly than the others on the effects of this new technological regime on patterns of thought, in particular, the philosophical effects of twentieth-century technology on knowledge production.

Already in 1941, Marcuse was using the term "technological rationality" to characterize the hegemonic, or dominant, form of knowledge production in industrial society, and in the postwar era, he would continue to focus attention on the social implications of modern technology. As he parted company with his former Frankfurt colleagues, he came increasingly to place technological developments at the center of concern. While Horkheimer and Adorno developed their critical theory in a somewhat more elitist direction, expressing disapproval at the lowering of cultural standards and the commercialization and massification of culture, Marcuse sought instead to define alternatives to technological rationality. Their starting points were similar, but while Adorno and Horkheimer, in different ways, to be sure, returned to classical humanist themes and traditions, Marcuse took what had been a more or less shared critique of the decline of reason in contemporary society in a different, more utopian direction. It was for this reason that he could welcome the revolts of the 1960s, while Horkheimer and Adorno kept their distance. Intriguingly, it would be Marcuse rather than Horkheimer and Adorno who would most stimulate the revived critical theory that emerged in the late 1960s, when Jurgen Habermas replaced Horkheimer as the Frankfurt school's director and main spokesman.

Part of the reason for the differing trajectories of Marcuse and Horkheimer and Adorno is that Marcuse stayed in America and, in some sense, sought to apply the insights of critical theory to the reality around him. Particularly important for Marcuse's postwar development were the changes that were taking place in American academic life: the return to professionalism and the ascendancy within philosophy and science more generally of a positivist ideal and an instrumental approach to knowledge. Marcuse tried to keep alive, in his lectures and his writings, a broader perspective of philosophy and of the relation between philosophy and science than was common at postwar American universities. Rather than follow another group of central European émigrés into what came to be known as logical positivism, with its highly delimited role for philosophy and its very academic approach to scientific truth and morality, Marcuse tried in his writings and lectures to keep the big philosophical questions alive. In this, he resembled John Dewey, who had written his philosophy for a broader public and had always engaged in politics and social change. Rather than withdraw from political debate, as so many American philosophers did after the war, and escape into the expanding world of higher education, singing the praises of science and technology, Marcuse chose to disclose his society's hidden and often uncomfortable assumptions.

Instead of following the postwar fashion of turning philosophy itself into a kind of science, a science of logic, and exploring what Ludwig Wittgenstein called the language games of human existence, Marcuse sought to analyze the relations between philosophy and life. Unlike many American humanist scholars who also rejected the postwar cult of science, Marcuse, in his critique of scientism, made use of the humanist tradition without ever becoming traditionalist; rather than merely call for a return to the past, Marcuse tried to explain why technological rationality had come to dominate academic life, and he tried, in most of his postwar writings, not merely to resuscitate lost traditions but also and more significantly to argue for the contemporary relevance of alternative paths to knowledge.

His first American book, *Reason and Revolution* (1941), was published during the war and served as the first presentation of the Marxism of the Frankfurt school to the English-speaking public. Marcuse's aim was to show the continuing relevance and radicalism of Hegel's philosophy; he emphasized the crucial role that Hegel's thought had played in the formation of the radical social theories of the nineteenth century, especially those of Karl Marx and Friedrich Engels. For Marcuse, Hegel had brought to an end the era of classical philosophy, but in his dialectical method, he pointed the way to social theory, to Marxism. Marcuse's book was an academic history of ideas, but it was also a challenge to the more mechanical or determinist treatments of Marxist theory that were so prevalent in the 1930s. Marcuse provided one of the first sustained treatments of the "early writings" of Marx, which had come to light in the 1930s and which showed the strong influence that Hegel's philosophy had on at least the young Marx. The emphasis that Marx placed on the "alienation of labor" under capitalism was, according to Marcuse, a translation of Hegel's "alienation of reason" into social theory. Marcuse argued that Marx transformed the abstract categories of Hegel into historical concepts and that the Marxian dialectic, while retaining the emphasis on contradiction, differed from the Hegelian in locating contradictions in real life, most especially, in the world of production.

If his first book was an attempt to revive interest in Hegel and the Hegelian roots of Marxism, his next book, *Eros and Civilization,* which appeared in 1955, after he had left government service for academic life, was more contemporary in its concerns. It was nothing less than a radical reinterpretation of Freud, who by then had been adopted by the American middle class as a new kind of prophet. By the mid-1950s, much of the Freudian canon had been taken over by a psychoanalytic establishment, and Freud's later writings, which had been highly critical of contemporary civilization, had tended to be neglected in favor of the more clinical, methodological works. The Americanization of Freud was, in many ways, similar to the Americanization of Marx, and Marcuse argued with Fromm and others about the narrowing of vision, the loss of radical insight that had resulted from this American cultural assimilation. Freud was seen at the time as the founder of a new science and of a new and highly profitable form of psychotherapy; what Marcuse tried to show was that Freud was really a revolutionary critic of contemporary society.

Freud, in Marcuse's reading, was a dialectician, pitting a pleasure principle—eros—against the reality principle, the norms of behavior that governed civilization. From there, Marcuse added his own emancipatory philosophy based on a new idea of reason as eros and a new emphasis on aesthetics and sensuality in human life. Marcuse argued that Freud should be taken seriously and that his insights, which were then applied to the individual, should be applied across society. It was thus both a critique of Freudianism and the psychoanalytic establishment and an original and ambitious liberatory philosophy.

For Marcuse, *Eros and Civilization* was also an attempt to locate sources of revolutionary thought outside of the Marxian corpus. Marcuse had long felt that Marxism lacked an adequate psychology, an appropriate understanding of emotions and feelings. As he read Freud and some of the earlier utopian philosophers, especially the nineteenth-century Frenchman Charles Fourier, who would have a strong influence on Marcuse's later writings, he came to realize that Marxism was not sufficient as a philosophical basis for social change, certainly not in the 1950s. Marxism could no longer provide a way out of the repressive, capitalist society; it did not focus enough on the personal motivations of people, or on the ways in which those motivations and inner drives were manipulated and repressed. Marxism had not been able to oppose the Fascist appeal, because the Fascist appeal was an appeal beyond reason. Marxism, we might say, had remained a prisoner of the reality principle, and it needed to breathe the heady air of liberation, of utopia, of eros.

The revolution—which, for Marcuse, now meant above all else a path beyond the reality principle—needed to be as much cultural as political. In the 1950s, the age of affluence and conformity, when so many Americans had become fat and contented but, of course, also alienated, such a message was both optimistic and naive. It was a hopeful vision of a new realm of human interaction, a resurrection, in modern times, of some of the old utopian visions of the preindustrial past. A society based on the pleasure principle, on libidinal energy unleashed: the path beyond reality was a freeing of eros from the constraints of history. In America, it was possible to envision such a state, but how could it ever come into being? Where would such a revolution come from? Who, in the technological society, when all needs, erotic as well as material, aesthetic as well as economic, had become commercialized and vulgarized, would be the bearers of such a cultural revolution? Marcuse had provided something of the goal; but he, as little as anyone else in the mid-1950s, had no idea about the potential agents of change or the strategy of liberation.

In the late 1950s and early 1960s, Marcuse turned increasingly pessimistic. The efforts that were being made within the affluent society to free eros from the constraints of civilization seemed far too partial, far too limited for the elderly prophet of liberation. In the East, the Hungarian uprising had been brutally suppressed, and it seemed increasingly difficult to see hopeful signs emerging in the Communist world. In the West, repression had taken on new, more ghastly forms, and in both the East and the West, the words of liberation were being used to keep people down. Technological rationality had become the common language of both Soviet Communists and American capitalists; the systems seemed to be converging into a similar state of affairs, and all opposition was tamed and destroyed before it had a chance to express itself. From the vision of *Eros and Civilization,* Marcuse tried to understand the mechanisms of oppression, how the opportunity or the potential for liberation was contained by the holders of power. He wrote *Soviet Marxism* (1958) to indicate how Marxism had been transformed into a dogmatic state philosophy serving a regime of managers and self-serving party bureaucrats. There he focused, as he was to do for America in *One-Dimensional Man,* on the hold that technological rationality had come to exercise over the minds of men and women. It was the transformation of ideas into things, the renunciation of ends for means, the reduction of eros to individual gratification that was at work.

One-Dimensional Man (1964) built on the earlier works, but it surpassed them in several ways. For one thing, it made use of empirical findings of social scientists and journalists to illustrate the abstract arguments and could therefore reach a somewhat broader audience. Even more important, it applied the theory to reality: it was not a reading of other theorists, a restatement of Hegel or Freud or Marx, as his earlier works had largely been; it was a philosophical reading of contemporary American society. What Marcuse did in *One-Dimensional Man* was to show that philosophy, an academic and abstract mode of thought, could be directed with force and power at the thought patterns of contemporary society. America was one-dimensional because there were no longer any permissible alternative ways to behave or to think. Marcuse disclosed something of how that one-dimensionality operated and reproduced itself—he sought to uncover its mechanisms of control and dissemination—both as social practice and as scientific-technical research. His insights became influential partly because they were so all-encompassing but also because they were so contemporary. He took examples from newspapers as well as from philosophy textbooks. And it hung together. The positivist logic that dominated philosophy departments was connected to the reality of bombs and drive-ins, the domination of the American society and economy by the military and the commercial culture. Marcuse analyzed the totality of American society, and although he was abstract and diffuse, he gave examples.

The liberation he called for was as total as the diagnosis. In remaining loyal to the spirit of Hegel, Marcuse called for a negation of reality. He disclosed the totality and argued for the need to transcend a stifling totality, with what? Imagination, theory, art, nature, negative thought: these were the alternatives. What Marcuse offered was a diagnosis of domination, and he pointed to the historical sources of opposition that needed to be remembered, revived, recombined. In the following, heady years of the late 1960s, Marcuse would produce some small guides to help the process along, but his main contribution was the diagnosis. *One-Dimensional Man* remains readable, although largely forgotten, today because so much of our own theorizing is based on its assumptions. Marcuse made it possible once again to conceptualize alternatives, to see that positivism and scientism were not only stifling and repressive but also severely, disastrously limited. Marcuse helped to open a space for critical reflection, and if many were later to find his formulations too vague and too vacuous, it was he who nonetheless pointed the way forward. Marcuse's book showed that philosophy and knowledge could be something far different from the dominant modes being practiced at American universities. And in that respect—as well as in his reinterpretations of Hegel, Marx, and Freud—he planted some important seeds for the postpositivist era, which would be ushered in by the 1960s student revolts.

Margaret Mead, the Eternal Optimist

Margaret Mead's particular blend of optimism and criticism has gone out of fashion, but perhaps it is time for a comeback. She was, unlike Szilard and Marcuse, a bona fide American and proud of it. Indeed, her message during the postwar years was an unabashed Americanism, keeping alive the values of commonsense practicality and idealism that had been characteristic of many of the activities of the movement intellectuals of the 1930s. Mead's own contribution to the populist pragmatism of the 1930s had been a cross-cultural comparative approach to reality and a particular emphasis of subject matter, a focus on "women's issues." By keeping both the approach and the focus alive in the postwar era, she served as a midwife for the flowering of feminist—and anthropological—scholarship that has emerged over the past two decades.

Margaret Mead was born in Pennsylvania into an academic family; her father was an economist, and her mother was a social scientist, but she was most influenced by her grandmother, who told her stories and—at least according to Mead's own recollections—was responsible for that enormous amount of self-confidence and ambition that would most characterize Mead's life and her relations with other people. Mead wanted to be famous, and she wanted to make a difference in people's lives, preferably as many as possible. Her particular way of becoming famous and important to people was to address and make "scientific" the events of everyday life. And in that respect, if in no other, she certainly broadened the contours of what is considered knowledge. She also provided some important examples of how that knowledge could be gathered and disseminated. Like Szilard, she was more important for her practice than for her theory, more worth remembering for her activity than her ideas. But both the ideas and the practical activity were significant presences in the postwar academic world, even though she had made her mark and become the most renowned anthropologist in America before she turned thirty.

Mead had already become famous in the 1920s with the publication of her book, *Coming of Age in Samoa*, which is at the same time one of the most successful and apparently one of the least accurate anthropological books ever written. The extent of its success is reflected in the fact that a best-selling book-length refutation appeared in 1983, fifty-five years after being published and four years after Margaret Mead's death. Derek Freeman's *Margaret Mead and Samoa* led to a vociferous controversy about Mead's research capabilities that was carried out primarily in the mass media and in Mead's absence. In retrospect it seems to have been largely a result of Freeman's pent-up hostilities toward what he termed "cultural determinism" rather than a specific critique of Mead's own anthropological approach. Although Freeman did identify substantial mistakes in Mead's interpretation of Samoan society, he certainly failed to challenge the more general significance of her work as a whole—namely, the propagation of what might be termed an "anthropological imagination" in American society. His book and the controversy it aroused have no doubt helped to weaken the stature and influence of Margaret Mead vis-à-vis American anthropology and social science more generally, but the fact that *Coming of Age* has recently been reprinted indicates that the damage might not be irreparable. Indeed, the Freeman controversy might actually have led more people back to Mead's by then largely forgotten writings than would otherwise have been the case.

Mead was only twenty-three when she went to Samoa as a graduate student, and she constructed her immortal vision of the easygoing Samoan adolescent way of life on the basis of her own limited experience and, not least, her own preconceived notions. What would lead to a public debate of the first order in the 1980s was received with interest and admiration in the 1920s, for here was a young woman who had gone off on her own and found patterns of behavior that were strikingly different from those of her own society. Even though there were undoubtedly mistakes in her observations, due to her limited number of informants and her unfamiliarity with Samoan history, she managed to depict them in such colorful, even provocative language that she could succeed in bringing an anthropological approach into the mainstream of American life. Mead was one of many young American intellectuals who found their own culture confining and limited; and while others went to Paris and Berlin to breathe the rarefied air of high culture, Mead went to the South Seas for the disappearing air of primitive cultures. She had a mission, perhaps more religious than scientific, to preserve ways of life that were rapidly fading from existence. In what would be her characteristic combination of romantic exoticism and down-to-earth pragmatism, she viewed the Samoans as providing a kind of mirror image of the cultural patterns and beliefs of her fellow Americans. And even though she was sometimes wrong, or at least too strongly opinionated, in the ways she interpreted the primitive peoples she studied, she nonetheless brought "primitive behavior" to the attention of Americans. It seems fair to say that Margaret Mead's journey to Samoa brought anthropological or cultural relativism into American society for good.

In the words that now grace the hall devoted to her fieldwork at the American Museum of Natural History in New York, Mead presented her approach in a nutshell: "The last primitive peoples were being contacted, missionized, given new tools and new ideas. Their primitive cultures would soon become changed beyond recovery. . . . The time to do the work was now." There would soon no longer be people who were—or so she thought—fundamentally different from herself. There would soon no longer be mirrors of other realities for Americans to look into and see their own behavior, their own culture, from a distance. Mead was driven by a rather simple belief in the value of such cultural comparisons as well as by a deep-seated conviction that primitive cultures were soon to be gone forever from the face of the earth.

She was apparently surprised at the success of her book, even though she had quite consciously written it in a popular way. Freeman, her latter-day detractor, claims that the book supported ideas that were in the air at the time, ideas about cultural determinism, as he calls it, ideas that anthropologists in America had been promulgating for quite some time. Mead's professor, Franz Boas, was one of the founding fathers of anthropology in America, having studied the Eskimos in Alaska in the 1880s; and he had brought with him to America both the radicalism that had been a part of his family life and the humanism that had been part of his education in Germany. Boas had done battle with the sociobiologists of his day, the eugenicists, who saw all behavior as biologically determined; and he and his more famous students, Mead and Benedict, brought to the intellectual struggle not merely a home-grown American pragmatism but also literary talent and marketing, or public relations, skills. It was Mead and Benedict who made popular an anthropological approach to the world; and it would be Mead and her third husband, Gregory Bateson, who would be the main carriers of that anthropological perspective into other disciplines and other institutional contexts after the war (especially after Benedict died in 1948).

It is no exaggeration to say that it was largely the writings of Mead and Benedict that placed the all-encompassing, anthropological con-cept of culture in the center of the interwar discourse. "Culture" at the time was a term that still meant cultivation or the fine arts: snobby stuff. Mead and Benedict helped to give culture its more contemporary connotation as a total way of life, or pattern of behavior, as Benedict would have put it. From Boas, they received a schooling in classical humanism, to which they added, as women and Americans, a demo-cratic respect for other peoples; and they gave to each other the support that academic women often depend on to be able to compete in a man's world. In their anthropological work, they shared an interest in children and education, but it was especially Mead who would write about such "women's" themes, thus singling herself out for criticism and ultimate neglect when the women's liberation movement came along in the 1960s. For Mead was the woman who made it, a kind of token woman intellectual, whose ideas must have been mistaken, at least according to a more radical and aggressive generation of femi-nists. An entire chapter was devoted to criticizing Mead in Betty Friedan's *The Feminine Mystique* (1963).

Compared to Marcuse, Mead's contributions to the development of knowledge in postwar America were more methodological than conceptual, more organizational and practical than theoretical. Mead was a pioneer in anthropological field observation, and she is still honored for her attention to the details of the cultural lives she observed on her various field trips to the Pacific islands. Mead never tried to check her own impressions, never really sought in any of her writings to contrast her own observational findings with those of others. That would have weakened their utility, their value for comparative reflection. She was not a positivist natural scientist, trying to practice an objective scientific method; following the lead of her mentor, Ruth Benedict, she was rather an innovator in what might be termed personal science, pursuing a kind of subjective research methodology. In many ways her method resembled the fieldwork techniques of other anthropologists, but in significant ways it was different—more open-ended, empathetic, reflective. She went to the South Seas to learn lessons about people, to understand humanity and cast light on her own society and its taken for granted assumptions. The power of her books derive in large measure from the fact that they were based on Mead's personal impressions and reflective observations, however deceptive or imprecise they might have been. "The anthropological approach," she wrote in her most important postwar book, *Male and Female* (1949: 29), "is to go out into primitive societies without any too specific theories and ask open-ended exploratory questions. How do male babies and female babies learn their social roles in different societies? What types of behaviour have some societies classified as male, what as female? What behaviours have they failed to treat as sex-typed?"

Mead viewed primitive societies not as laboratories for social engineering and political experimentation but more as windows into a generalizable human experience. She went to primitive societies to compare the diverse patterns of adapting to universal human needs and challenges. But she was aware of the fact that the anthropological "findings" were also constructed by the anthropologist. "When the anthropologist enters the village of a primitive people either alone or as one of a married couple to set up a household among other households, the situation is also a controlled and conscious one." The environment to be studied was shaped by the anthropologist's own perceptions, but, as opposed to others who wanted to apply anthropological insights to development planning and foreign aid projects,

Mead was quite insistent that the anthropologist's task did not include trying to change the people being studied. The anthropologist, she wrote, "does not want to improve them, convert them, govern them, trade with them, recruit them or heal them. He wants only to understand them, and by understanding them to add to our knowledge of the limitations and potentialities of human beings" (39).

Even though she claimed at times to adhere to a norm of scientific objectivity, she never really followed it in any of her work. Instead, she developed an approach to knowledge that could be said to have combined the objective and the subjective in the immediately perceived; her main concern, from the first book to the last, was to draw on her perceptions of other cultures to raise questions about the dominant patterns of behavior in her own society. What she was so successful at doing was making her own experiences believable, interesting, and, above all, relevant. Margaret Mead's scientific ideal was to make knowledge useful in a process of public self-enlightenment. She and Benedict pursued the populist aims that Dewey and other pragmatic philosophers professed. And in the postwar era, when professionalism and objectivism came to dominate the social sciences, she found herself going against the stream, even in anthropology.

Mead never questioned her own perception of anthropology or her own ideal of social science, nor did she stop using her perceptions of primitive societies to say provocative things about her own society. In this respect, she was one of the very few American intellectuals after the war to continue to reject disciplinary distinctions and traditional modes of academic behavior and forge interdisciplinary networks and ways of thinking. She was not an explicit critic of scientism; in a way, she shared a good deal of the scientistic world view. She too believed in rationality, and she too believed in a form of "pure" observationism. The difference was in her practice, most especially in the different uses that she made of her "scientific" observations. She used anthropological findings to develop her own special brand of moral philosophy. She was a kind of science-based preacher, who linked the scientific mode of knowing to the more spiritual or religious mode that had gone out of academic fashion in the postwar era.

After her first trip to Samoa, she realized that her perspective and insights were limited and that she should never again carry out fieldwork alone; indeed, it can be argued that she sought husbands who could serve as useful collaborators as much as loving companions. Even in matters of the heart she had a strong sense of practicality, inspired, no doubt, by her upbringing and her mother's example as well as by her lifelong devotion to Christianity. She harked back to the earlier religious tradition of knowledge making in America, living her life as a type of missionary activity, bringing the gospel of rationality and common sense to the middle classes, especially to middle-class women. In the work she carried out after the war to reform American schools and to educate Americans about the ways of life of other peoples, Margaret Mead was keeping alive that missionary zeal and idealism that had been so central to the original colonists. But by traveling so far and knowing so much about other cultures, she also could temper that zeal with a kind of relativism, at times even skepticism; and at her best moments, she could make her own habits and those of her countrymen appear odd, amusing, even something less than fully rational. She could make the existence and even more the value of cultural difference meaningful and relevant to a wide range of audiences; and in that, she was not only opposing the main drift of her contented, conformist times but planting some important seeds for the multiculturalism that was to emerge out of the movements of the 1960s.

She took her observation seriously, and she carried it out conscientiously and earnestly, as a kind of role-playing of its own, for she loved all kinds of ritualized theatrical performance, as her writings on Bali indicate; and if she was not quite the theorist that she sometimes thought she was, she was nonetheless able to make effective use of her theoretical friends and husbands, particularly Ruth Benedict and Gregory Bateson. Benedict's writings are, in some ways, more substantial in their references to history and literature, but Mead's have almost a journalistic freshness that gives them a documentary appeal. Bateson, of course, was always theorizing, even though his years with Mead did leave a remarkable exercise in photographic ethnography, *Balinese Character: A Photographic Analysis* (1942), with its intriguing combination of text and picture and of observation and reflection. The joint work that the three carried out in bringing psychology into anthropology remains important, even though the particular ecologies of mind that were articulated by each of them after the Second

World War pointed in different directions—Benedict to history and "area studies," Bateson to therapy and philosophy, and Mead to practical reform work and institution building in "mental health" and education.

Mead developed, with a good deal of help from Benedict and Bateson, a comparative approach in anthropology, and she combined her field observations with psychological and sociological insights to try to address what she often called the fundamental questions of the time. After the war, however, Mead was no longer merely the ethnographer, describing patterns of other cultures; she became instead a kind of moral philosopher, using her experience to challenge educational, scientific, technological, and developmental policies. In many ways, she was one of the first action researchers, concerned more with using knowledge to improve things than with developing some fundamental truths. Even more important, she was a popularizer of knowledge; like Rachel Carson, Mead wrote for a mass audience about difficult things, and she wrote well and colorfully. She enlightened her countrymen perhaps more than she actually presented them with "facts." As her daughter, Mary Catherine Bateson, puts it, "When I look over her work today, it seems to me that she was both right and wrong, above all right in knowing that there is a range within which communities can choose their future. Such choices will always be mixed and success will never be complete, but the affirmation of the possible is surely the place to begin" (Bateson 1984: 193–194). She educated the American public by contrasting their lives, their values, and their visions with those of other peoples half a world and many centuries away.

Mead's importance to the movements that would almost unknowingly draw on her writings for their cognitive development was primarily in her intrinsic interdisciplinariness, a result, among other things, of her endless meanderings through intellectual territories. Margaret Mead can be considered a pioneer in shaping academic networks and in devoting energy and enthusiasm—often too much for her colleagues (and husbands) to take—to bringing people together, temporarily at conferences and meetings and more permanently in the various centers and programs that she worked within. Mead gloried in conference going and was most often the center of attention;

she considered conferences and interdisciplinary centers to be the places where new ideas were generated. Knowledge making was always a kind of performing for Mead; her practice consisted primarily of thinking on her feet, in front of audiences of students or women's groups or at smaller conferences or meetings. She and Bateson were active participants at the Macy conferences during and immediately after the war, where a cybernetic perspective was brought into social science as well as into natural sciences like ecology; and she was also a central figure in bringing scientists together to address social and political problems, from nuclear weapons to racial unrest to the war in Vietnam.

She was also a project maker, the kind of academic who is now a commonplace in the social sciences but in the 1940s and 1950s was still something rare. With and then without Benedict (her friend and mentor died in 1948), Mead established a number of innovative interdisciplinary research projects, drawing on her wartime experience, when she had been called on to provide cross-cultural behavioral comparisons for the military intelligence services. Comparative studies became her special academic territory in the late 1940s and 1950s, as she worked with other, most often female, researchers in psychology and the humanities to compare character structures, styles of parenting and education, and attitudes toward childhood in different cultures.

Mead was able to make use of some of the new intellectual opportunities for funding and for organizational reform and innovation, and she was at home in the new world of corporate finance and bureaucratic management, creating her own highly feminine institute cum consulting firm in the tower of the Museum of Natural History. In that respect, Mead was one of those who made social science "useful," but, in her case, the clients were not so much the rich and powerful as the more amorphous general public. Her audiences, like everything else about her, were mixed: she wrote for academic journals as well as for popular women's magazines. But she was, perhaps more energetically than any other single person in the United States during the 1950s, a scientist for the people, one who tried to orient scientific knowledge to public debates and concerns and also one who sincerely tried to put her knowledge to use to make normal people's lives more meaningful. She studied the customs and mores of other cultures not so much for their intrinsic interest as for the light they cast on normal human beings, their potentialities, their hidden talents, but also their "basic needs." If she had a tendency to overrate her own importance and the importance of her insights concerning how other people should live their lives, she nonetheless tried to be helpful. And it is the ambition, the desire to be useful and relevant, rather than the particular substance of any of her works, that seems most important to remember. Margaret Mead wanted knowledge to be used for the improvement of the situation of normal people; and if she did not accomplish all that much, at the very least she carved out some spaces and provided some possible roles for other social and human scientists to try to fill and follow.

She was, from school days to the end of her life, unusually open to new ideas, and her writings display a unique ability to combine perspectives from different subjects. Her daughter, who has probably given us the best appraisal of Mead's life and works, has said,

> The greatest part of her originality lay in the invention of ways of listening and synthesizing ideas. By her peripatetic life, she created a kind of multilogue to which individuals contributed who would otherwise have been in isolation, their ideas never juxtaposed in fruitful ways. . . . She was at her best as a visitor in other people's intellectual territory or tasting their experience, not demanding that they share in the breadth of her own. (Bateson 1984: 248)

In terms of subject matter, Margaret Mead's contribution to American thought was to focus attention on some of the neglected areas of social life, the behavioral patterns of women, children, families, and, of course, "primitive" peoples. She took an interest in the commonplace features of social reality, which she would attribute at times to the fact that she was a woman and at other times to a particular anthropological mode of analysis that she was at pains to describe for her fellow Americans. In the words of her biographer,

> In all the career that began with Mead's work in Samoa, she focused, more intensely than any anthropologist ever had before her, on matters of gender and women and children. The average child interested her more than the average adult did, and the average

woman more than the average man. Wherever she went in her nearly seventy-seven years she called attention to the ordinary, the previously unsung, and sanctified the mundane. (Howard 1984: 14)

• • •

Margaret Mead, Herbert Marcuse, and Leo Szilard were among the most publicly visible, certainly among the most vocal, of the intellectuals who chose to challenge, rather than accept, the coming of the scientific-technological state. In their different ways, they questioned the ideals of knowledge that became so dominant in the years after the Second World War; and, even more important, in their writings as well as in their broader intellectual activity, they pursued other paths to knowledge that would serve as sources of inspiration for many of the student rebels of the 1960s and beyond. Even though the movements of the 1960s would, in many ways, leave each of our critics behind, their role in helping to form the consciousness of those movements was significant. Szilard contributed both to the struggle to control the spread of atomic weapons and to the broader work of discussing and trying to change the "social relations of science." As those activities became more organized and radical in the course of the 1960s, Szilard's own efforts tended to be seen as limited and all too liberal and elitist; and he himself had little patience for the extremisms and amateurisms that characterized so much of the peace movement and the science and society programs. But he was one of the few scientists in the 1950s who continued to play the role of the partisan scientist, and if his contributions tended to be forgotten as the movement heated up, he should nonetheless be remembered as one of those who helped to construct a public space in which the relations between science and society could be debated, discussed, and even reformed. He helped to invent a new subject, or set of subjects, and his writings still provide important insights and sources of inspiration for those who would try to make a more responsible science.

Marcuse's utopianism was a much more central ingredient in the 1960s movements. Indeed, in the mid-1960s, Marcuse was often identified as the main philosopher of liberation and the major intellectual guide to the rebellious young. His critique of one-dimensional thought provided some of the conceptual scaffolding on which the counter-culture of the 1960s was eventually constructed, and even if the moment was brief, there was definitely a time, in the mid-1960s, when Marcuse's ideas provided for many a radical student a philosophical grounding for the more intuitive and emotional revolt. But as push turned to shove and the American aggression in Southeast Asia led to frustration among the rebels, Marcuse came to be vilified by a "New Left" that all too quickly grew old. His work for the intelligence service was publicized and questioned, and his calls for liberation and erotic behavior were rejected by Marxists who wanted to close the doors that he had opened. The elderly Marcuse, meanwhile, spent his later years reading and writing and lecturing much as he had done earlier; and while the New Left largely disintegrated in internecine battles and sectarianism, reifying the nineteenth-century Marx whom Marcuse had tried so hard to bring up to date, Marcuse himself continued to explore the paths to a liberatory knowledge, where ethics, aesthetics, and utopian visions had an important pride of place.

Mead spoke out against the war in Vietnam, but the deeper currents of anti-Americanism that came to the surface in the late 1960s distressed her. As one of the few women intellectuals who had suc-ceeded in postwar America, she also found herself criticized by radical feminists for having played too much according to men's rules. Mead's seeds for the sixties were more indirect than those planted by Szilard and Marcuse; her writings made anthropology visible and present and perhaps contributed something to the idealism and internationalism that remained alive even after the spirit of the 1960s had waned. No doubt, her books had been read by many a student rebel, and they opened other worlds and other cultures to American consciousness. Most certainly, her interest in women's issues and in sex roles in different cultures inspired anthropologists and other social scientists to explore subjects and areas that until then had been too little in-vestigated. She carved out some space in the academic world for the cross-cultural investigation of children's and women's lives, and that space continues to be filled by important research, even though most of Margaret Mead's own findings and theories are no longer as pop-ular—or treated as seriously—as they once were.

Important as they were as individuals, however, Szilard, Marcuse, and Mead can also be seen as intellectual types; their critiques of the scientific-technological regime that dominated so much of American postwar intellectual life are representative of broader critical streams. Szilard typified what might be called the "internal" revolt from within science, a revolt that challenged the militarization of science and the confluence of the state with the production of knowledge. For Szilard, the ideal was always the autonomous scientist of interwar Europe, communicating with colleagues throughout the world, combining theory and practice, and trying to take some responsibility for his discoveries. Social responsibility is still a concern within the scientific community, now challenged not merely by an active military state but by an active entrepreneurial culture as well. The groups of socially responsible scientists can well be seen as having grown from seeds that were once planted by Leo Szilard and other critical atomic scientists.

Marcuse and Mead are also representative figures. Marcuse was one of the central European émigrés who brought a more reflective Marxism to postwar America. While most American intellectuals gave up their youthful interest in Marxist theory, Marcuse and other critical theorists, mostly from Europe, brought Marxism into the contemporary society. They formed a generation, shaped by the Bolshevik revolution and the rise of fascism in Europe and living on the margins of their adopted homeland until a new generation arose in the 1960s to read their books and learn from their experiences. Mead was also read in the 1950s and 1960s by a generation of students looking for nonpositivist, more culturally relative ways to develop knowledge and understanding. Both Marcuse and Mead were pioneers in outlining a cultural perspective on knowledge, in producing a kind of knowledge that combines the subject and object and, for that matter, passions and facts in new combinations and permutations. If those postpositivist paths to the truth continue to exist at American universities today, at least part of the credit or blame should be given to Margaret Mead and Herbert Marcuse.

5

THE RECONCEPTUALIZATION OF CULTURE
Allen Ginsberg, James Baldwin, Mary McCarthy

· ·

On a cold day in early spring 1943, Irwin Allen Ginsberg, the son of Russian immigrants who had settled in Paterson, stood on a New Jersey dock awaiting the ferry to New York. Not yet seventeen, he was on his way to take the entry examination at Columbia University. In a rush of youthful emotion, he solemnly vowed to himself that if accepted to that great institution he would study labor law and devote his life to helping the working class. This was a vow not taken lightly, since Ginsberg's parents were both active in the socialist movement and his early life had been colored by heated debates concerning the relative virtues of Joseph Stalin and Leon Trotsky and the importance of class solidarity. Although he would never receive a law degree, completing a degree in English instead, the categories that defined politics in the 1930s would remain important to him throughout his life, and through the poetry he created and the life-styles he experimented with, he would build a bridge from the cultural politics of the 1930s to the politics of the 1960s.

Mary McCarthy learned about Trotsky in quite another fashion. The daughter of devout Irish Catholic parents, McCarthy never heard the word "socialism" until she went to college. Her acquaintance with Trotsky came at the time of the Moscow trials in 1936, when James T. Farrell, celebrating the publication of his classic proletarian novel *Studs Lonigan* at a cocktail party, loudly asked the room, "Do you think Trotsky is entitled to a fair hearing?" Like most everyone else at the party, Mary McCarthy answered, "Yes." Four days later, she discovered her name on the letterhead of the Committee for the Defense of Leon Trotsky. This anecdote comes from McCarthy's own fiction-alized account and is reflective of both the style and aim of the writing that would make her famous. She wrote, for the most part, semiau-tobiographical tales about well-known people and places. Her style was ironic and biting; people hated her for it. They were always afraid to turn up in one of her stories. This sort of self-ironizing pleased neither friends nor enemies, for in exposing her own foibles, she also exposed theirs. What McCarthy created, however, was much more than in-teresting social satire; her writing developed a stance and a perspective that would help a new generation of women interpret their own place in society.

James Baldwin entered the American literary scene from Paris. He needed the distance permitted by the Atlantic Ocean to give him a clearer view of the country of his birth. In 1949, he published in the first number of a small Parisian magazine "Everybody's Protest Novel," a review of American protest fiction from *Uncle Tom's Cabin* to Richard Wright's *Native Son*. In painting the world in simple black and white, with the normal meaning of these terms reversed, protest fiction, he wrote, created cardboard characters, who moved about with neither passion nor reason in acting out the author's moral message. Such fiction, even when it attempted to do good, was only sentimental and dishonest and left unanswered the only important question, What moves people to do what they do?

This essay at once announced the arrival of a new man on the scene and identified a literary project. By including Wright in his attack, the only black American novelist then acceptable to the white literary world, Baldwin was making room for himself. At the same time, he set himself squarely in the realist tradition in American literature. The realist program, of attempting to bear witness to the experience of real people, would color Baldwin's literary work until the early 1960s, when the civil rights movement again brought him home from Paris. His engagement in politics would change both his writing style and, for a time, his life-style as well. Throughout the 1960s, Baldwin approached literature more as spokesman for a cause than as a disinterested witness. His penchant for self-description found new expression in the essay form, where he combined personal reflection with moral message. Baldwin moved from being the white eye in the Negro world and the sexual avant-garde to giving voice to the unarticulated, from novelist to movement intellectual.

Allen Ginsberg, Mary McCarthy, and James Baldwin were central actors in the reconceptualization of American culture that was taking place in the postwar period and, more important, in planting seeds that would sprout in the 1960s. This reconceptualization can be understood in two interrelated ways. On the one hand, new frameworks for interpreting and evaluating culture were debated and developed. One outcome of this process was the idea of mass culture itself and the elaboration of criteria for its evaluation. Here, as with the development of the idea of mass society, small journals like the *Partisan Review, Dissent,* and *Commentary* and intellectuals like Dwight Macdonald, Irving Howe, and Phillip Rahv played a central part. Most studies of American intellectuals in this period focus on just these actors and issues. At another level and involving a different set of actors there occurred another reconceptualization.

On the other hand, rather than developing new criteria of critical judgment, a handful of writers and artists developed new forms of cultural practice, new ways of seeing, acting, and communicating thoughts. Ginsberg, McCarthy, and Baldwin were central to cultural reconceptualization at this level in postwar America. Through their writing, all three challenged the universal claims of the "official" American culture that was being packaged and distributed by a new culture industry, whose basic aim seemed to be the standardization of taste at the lowest possible level.

Allen Ginsberg, who helped shape the Beat alternative and then took active part in the counterculture of the 1960s, was a key actor in the process of creating an alternative to both high and mass culture. Like other radical artists before him—the sensualists, dadaists, and surrealists—Ginsberg turned the images and traditions of high culture against itself, and like the marketing man he trained to be, he used the tools of mass culture to spread the alternative he and his fellow Beats, William Burroughs and Jack Kerouac, were creating. As the official representative of an unofficial culture of resistance, Ginsberg helped to carve a path between the commercial products of the culture industry and the snobby elitism of high culture. In reaching out to the mass paperback audience, both Mary McCarthy and James Baldwin also participated in this process of cultural transformation. But it was more the content of their message and their style of writing that was important. McCarthy helped to identify a masculine way of seeing and being and, in the process, paved the way for the new feminism that would emerge a decade later. Similarly, Baldwin helped to identify a white way of seeing and thus contributed to the development of an explicit black way of seeing. All three made use of the mass media and mass distribution to spread their message. They refused to retreat into the moral high ground provided by the critics of mass culture and the ghetto that formed around serious journals. As such, they too took sides—in their case, for a popular culture, an alternative to the established modes of literary expression. In this way, they also brought the democratic American cultural tradition, which had been so influential in the 1930s, into the postwar era.

Culture in America

Despite a short-lived dream of some early pioneers that a distinctly American way of life could be carved out of the wilderness, Americans have had difficulty replacing the European ideals about culture they inherited. The notion that culture was serious business came over on the *Mayflower* as part of the Puritan intellectual heritage and was associated with cultivation as such: that which symbolized the anointed and separated the civilized from the savage. The notion that culture implied work and discipline was given all the more force in the new world, where a new way of life had physically and visibly to be carved out of nature.

This particular conception of culture was eventually systematized and institutionalized in regimes of education that focused on uplifting the innocent and the fallen, whether children, natives, or newly arrived immigrants, into the spiritual realm of culture. Because it required discipline and practice, culture was approached with a seriousness and decorum that sharply distinguished it from the "natural" and spontaneous behavior of primitive peoples as well as from activities deemed

144

playful or entertaining. These latter were considered common, even decadent, while culture was deemed the proper region of an elite, the civilized few rather than the masses.

Well into the nineteenth century the struggle over the transplantation, development, and distribution of culture in the new world raged among American intellectuals. On the one side were those who saw themselves as part of a genteel tradition, a cultured class, who took it as their task to uphold and defend a European—and in their eyes universal—tradition against degradation from all that was vulgar and commercial in America. This class and its idea of culture was seen as continually under threat by the territorial expansion of the country and by the waves of immigrants that arrived on its shores, each bringing with them their own culture. Lawrence W. Levine puts it this way, "These attitudes were part of a development that saw the very word 'culture' becoming synonymous with the Eurocentric products of the symphonic hall, the opera house, the museum, and the library, all of which, the American people were taught, must be approached with a disciplined, knowledgeable seriousness of purpose, and—most important of all—with feelings of reverence" (1988: 145–146). In this view, culture was an autonomous aesthetic realm of literature and art, which, although forced to pay attention to the material world of commerce, constituted a realm apart. On the other side were those who believed that a uniquely American, democratic culture could be constructed out of the waves of immigrants. After various, rather limited movements among intellectuals to develop more popular alternatives to elite culture in the nineteenth century, major challenges to the idea that culture existed only in bourgeois drawing rooms appeared in Greenwich Village and Harlem in the early years of the twentieth century.

The Making of a Mass Culture

The concept of the masses is an old battle-ax in the struggle to define cultural experience in America. One of the earliest organs to promote it was a journal of cultural radicalism called, appropriately enough, *The Masses*, started in 1910 by a Dutch immigrant, Piet

Vlaag. *The Masses* set out to undermine the elitist, or genteel, notion of culture as uplifting and refined. Quoting William Morris, Vlaag expressed his aesthetic philosophy thus: "Sure, we need art. But not art that's for the few—not art that lives in pretty ivory towers built on golden quick sands. . . . Art must live with people—in the streets, in the slums" (quoted in Green 1988: 32). Reorganized in 1912 under the editorship of Max Eastman, with the help of a young Harvard graduate named John Reed, *The Masses* became the voice of Greenwich Village radicalism and the first American avant-garde in the period prior to World War I. Reed wrote its opening manifesto: "The broad purpose of *The Masses* is a social one; to everlastingly attack old systems, old morals, old prejudices—the whole weight of outworn thought that dead men have settled upon us. . . . We intend to be arrogant, impertinent, in bad taste" (quoted in Green 1988: 94). As the voice of American cultural radicalism, the journal attempted to combine a political and moral perspective with artistic innovation. The great silent majority of Americans were supposed to be its audience, not the cultural elite. Unfortunately, this was not to be the case. Like other small journals, before and after, *The Masses* was read by a very select few.

In the debates concerning culture and politics in the 1930s, heavily influenced by Marxism and socialism, the concept of the masses, and by implication the culture of the masses, carried positive connotations. The masses were seen by many writers as the bearers of the future and the hope of mankind. Social realism and proletarian literature aimed at portraying the life of the masses, a neglected object of artistic interest and imagination. European ideologies, rejuvenated first in the new Soviet Union under the banner of Bolshevism and later by the struggles between various factions of Stalinists and Trotskyists, also affected America's view of culture through the influence of such popular and innovative writers as Theodore Dreiser, Steinbeck, and Dos Passos, all of whom were drawn to left-wing causes and organizations. In the 1930s, debates about a particular proletarian literature would both inspire and divide intellectual circles, along aesthetic as well as political lines. Here again, the struggle between European culture and American particularism was reinvented in radical circles.

The European idea of culture as a realm apart was challenged, in the 1920s, from another direction by rapid developments in mass-produced popular entertainment. The development of a new industry, producing a commercialized, prepackaged culture for the masses, appeared to threaten the imported, European ideals of culture as well as the bohemian alternative. Up until the 1920s, the printed word dominated the distribution of culture in the United States. Newspapers were the prime source of information and books and magazines the source of more serious intellectual debate.

Around the turn of the century, for example, magazines like *The Nation* and *Harper's* were the main vehicles for defending the genteel ideal of culture against the growing influence of the masses. Even in the fields where the genteel mixed with more popular cultural practices, the printed word dominated. Popular as well as serious music was spread through sheet music up until the First World War, when advances in technology underwrote a great expansion in the production and sale of records. It was the perfection and mass production of a new invention, however, that radically changed the way culture was transmitted and experienced and brought about a new compromise between serious and popular forms of culture. For the first time, terms previously restricted to the sphere of commerce, terms like "packaging," "production," and "distribution," could now be applied to culture as well.

In 1916, a visionary radio engineer, David Sarnoff, who had achieved considerable fame through spending three days and nights at the telegraph key decoding messages during the *Titanic* disaster, sent a now-famous memorandum to his superiors in the American Marconi Company. He wrote,

I have in mind a plan of development which would make radio a "household utility" in the same sense as the piano or phonograph. The idea is to bring music into the house by wireless. . . . The receiver can be designed in the form of a simple "Radio Music Box" and arranged for several different wavelengths, which should be changeable with the throwing of a single switch or button. . . . The box can be placed on a table in the parlor or living room, the switch set accordingly and transmitted music received. (Quoted by Melvin L. De Fleur, "The Development of Radio," in Wells 1972: 40)

Within ten years, Sarnoff's Radio Music Box would be found in over 27,540,000 American households. This was an almost unbelievable growth considering that between only 500 and 1,000 people heard the news over the air that Warren G. Harding had been elected president six years earlier, in 1920. After short-lived and feeble attempts to establish governmental control over the new mass medium, radio was defined as "an arena of business competition," and by 1919, a new corporation, the Radio Corporation of America (RCA), had gained control over almost the entire industry. That same year, Sarnoff was made its first commercial manager.

The 1930s and 1940s have been dubbed the golden age of radio. By the end of the 1930s, despite economic depression, there was more than one radio in every household in America; by 1950, this figure had doubled. Radio, it seemed, fit the needs of a nation pressed for time; its effortless way of producing sound and carefully planned programming made it possible to listen to music and work at the same time. The boundaries between work and play, between culture and production, were thus blurred. For those who believed in the distinctiveness of culture as a realm of human activity and the seriousness of cultural practices, this was a troublesome development.

Another troublesome development was the use made of radio for propaganda purposes during the war. Radio proved to be an effective way of spreading news to a dispersed population as well as a powerful means of influencing opinion. For critics and proponents alike, it did not go unnoticed that the spread of fascism in Europe had been greatly aided by the radio and other mass media. In the United States, the radio industry made itself available to the war effort, for everything from spreading information to selling war bonds.

The year 1939 marked not only the beginning of World War II in Europe but also the year that a new company called Pocket Books was founded in the United States. First plans called for the publication of ten books—complete and unabridged—in a cheap (25 cents) and small (4¼ × 6½ in.) edition. The books sold more than 100,000 copies in the first three weeks in New York City alone (Davis 1984: 15). A cultural revolution had begun. The classics of serious literature were now available in cheap mass-produced editions and sold alongside the most popular crime and western pulp fiction.

Between 1905, when the first "nickelodeon" opened in Pittsburgh, showing movies to small groups of people, and 1947, when an estimated 80,000 motion picture theaters were serving a weekly audience of about 235,000,000 around the world, the cinema grew into a major source of popular entertainment. In the beginning, the cheap price and the silent pictures served a largely immigrant audience, as both price and silence suited the conditions of poor workers in search of relaxation after a long day of dull labor. From the nickelodeons in immigrant neighborhoods, the movies soon moved to more comfortable settings in middle-class neighborhoods. And movie houses began to compete with the stage for its public as well as its actors. One of the early innovators in motion pictures was an old stage actor named Larry Griffith, who would gain fame as D. W. Griffith, the director of the first feature film, *The Birth of a Nation,* in 1915. With the closing of European film production during World War I, the movies became an American art. By the time talking pictures were introduced in 1926, American companies and American "stars," like Charlie Chaplin, were known the world over. American culture had found a new weapon in the struggle against European ideals.

The use of culture, particularly radio, as a tool in the war and the development of film and paperback books and other media for the masses gave new meaning to the relations between culture and society as well as the relations between intellectuals and the masses. Rationalization and standardization seemed now to be as applicable to the cultural realm as to the productive world of industry.

Dwight Macdonald's essay, "A Theory of Popular Culture," in the first issue of his short-lived wartime journal, *Politics,* helped name the new phenomena. For Macdonald, popular culture, which he would later term "mass culture," was something dangerous, a threat to civilization and indeed to thought itself. The distinguishing characteristic of mass culture was that it was "manufactured wholesale for the market" (Macdonald 1957: 59). It was "a parasitic, a cancerous growth on High Culture" (59) and was dangerous because it could be so easily consumed, without much effort from the reader or the viewer. It was produced in standardized packaged form and overwhelmed the market through its sheer quantity. It was everywhere, leaving no escape. "It absolutely refuses to discriminate against, or between, anything or anybody" and thus it "destroys all values, since value judgments imply discrimination" (62). And he went on,

> There are theoretical reasons why Mass Culture is not and can never be any good. I take it as axiomatic that culture can only be produced by and for human beings. But in so far as people are organized (more strictly, disorganized) as masses, they lose their human identity and quality. For the masses are in historical time what a crowd is in space: a large quantity of people unable to express themselves as human beings because they are related to one another neither as individuals nor as members of communities—indeed, they are not related to each other at all, but only to something distant, abstract, nonhuman: a football game or bargain sale in the case of a crowd, a system of industrial production, a party or a State in the case of the masses. The mass man is the solitary atom, uniform with and undifferentiated from thousands and millions of other atoms who go to make up "the lonely crowd," as David Riesman well calls American society. (69).

One can easily understand how the postwar world looked entirely different to intellectuals whose categories of interpretation and action had been formed in the interwar years. All the assumptions and institutions around which their world revolved had been transformed. The great narratives of historical development, like socialism and communism, and even more modest ideologies, like liberalism, no longer seemed to make sense. More to the point, simple categorizations like high culture and popular culture no longer fit the complexity of the postwar world. The alternative to mass culture—a truly popular, or democratic, culture—would come from other voices than those that had been active in the thirties.

The Making of a Counterculture: The Beat Alternative

In the midst of the Second World War, three pilgrims from as different social backgrounds as one could probably find among white Americans met by chance in a Manhattan apartment. What drew William S. Burroughs, Jr., Irwin Allen Ginsberg, and Jean Louis (Jack) Kerouac together was a feeling of being outside the main drift of American society. All three were sitting out a popular war while their fellows rushed to participate; all three were alienated from the careers their families and American society had planned for them. In addition, they all shared a love of literature and a taste for life on the social margins.

The scion of a wealthy Protestant, St. Louis family and many years older than Ginsberg and Kerouac, Burroughs had already gathered a range of life and literary experience and a sophistication that enraptured the two younger men. He had taken a degree in English literature at Harvard and studied medicine in Vienna, before finding his way to the shadowy underworld of drug dealers and small-time thieves around Times Square in midtown Manhattan and in the bohemian community in Greenwich Village. These two sides of Burroughs—the educated snob and the low-life deviant—fascinated the middle-class Ginsberg more than the working-class Kerouac, who had come to Columbia on a football scholarship. Ginsberg came to Columbia and to New York City from nearby Paterson, New Jersey, where his father, a moderately well-known poet, worked as a high school English teacher. Ginsberg's mother moved in and out of mental hospitals. Both of his parents were first-generation immigrants, the children of Russian Jews who were also active in radical politics. Louis Ginsberg, Allen's father, had been a socialist and a supporter of Eugene Debs, while his mother, Naomi, attended Communist party meetings and defended Stalin against Louis's criticisms. The young Ginsberg grew up amid constant political squabbles as well as the anxiety surrounding his mother's mental health. In typical street socialist fashion, he mixed the immigrant desire for respectability and social mobility with political conscience, entering Columbia as a prelaw student. It was his older brother, however, who became the lawyer; Allen Ginsberg gravitated to the English department.

Located near Harlem in upper Manhattan, Columbia University and the promise of higher education provided the justification for the move into New York City for Ginsberg and thousands like him, including Kerouac and, for that matter, a young musician named Miles Davis. New York offered, as well, a variety of subcultures that could nourish the development of an alternative vision. Besides the Greenwich Village environment, the traditional home of cultural radicalism, where Burroughs and Ginsberg first met and to whose gay community they both continually returned, the proximity of Columbia to Harlem provided another essential linkage. Columbia students in search of adventure and a lively experience outside their normal, middle-class upbringing did not have to look very far. Both Kerouac and Ginsberg were soon under the spell of Harlem nightlife and especially its music.

Columbia's English department was at that time one of the most respected in the country. Ginsberg's first criticisms of American culture were formulated against the background of what he learned there, especially from faculty members Lionel Trilling and Mark Van Doren. Like C. Wright Mills, Ginsberg found both a source of inspiration and criticism in Trilling's work. Trilling's defense of American liberalism and support for the formalism of the so-called New Criticism provided a foil against which Ginsberg formulated his own views. Both Ginsberg and Kerouac took the formalism of the New Criticism as their main enemy, as they developed the spontaneous style of writing that was to become the characteristic trademark of the Beats. In their articulation of what they came to call the "New Vision," they drew inspiration from romantic poets, especially Baudelaire and Rimbaud. Like Mills, Ginsberg opposed Trilling's political liberalism and cultural conservatism from the Left.

The New Vision set out to challenge the traditional view of American literature being taught at Columbia, taking its cue from the culture found on the streets of New York as interpreted through the spontaneous energy of the young artist. In his notebooks from the time, Ginsberg recorded the intended meaning of this vision: "Since art is merely and ultimately self-expressive, we conclude that the fullest art, the most individual, uninfluenced, unrepressed, uninhibited expression of art is true expression and the true art" (quoted in Miles 1990: 47). The attempt to seek refuge in art was, of course, not new. What was distinct about the New Vision was not only that it was formulated by dissidents in a time of national celebration rather than defeat but also that the emphasis was put on individual spontaneity and the rejection of all inhibition and repression.

Like their European predecessors, art was seen to express an entire form of life and thus should offer a guide to living. Their art was confessional as well as expressive: what they sought was not a pure art of sensuality but more nearly the very opposite, a raw art of an almost primitive nature, to be found among the outsiders and the outcasts of the mass society. Unconstrained by the elitist notions of their European predecessors, they could introduce a form of playfulness to their writings.

> Pull my daisy
> tip my cup
> all my doors are open
> Cut my thoughts
> for coconuts
> all my eggs are broken
> Jack my Arden
> gate my shades
> woe my road is spoken
> Silk my garden
> rose my days
> now my prayers awaken . . .
>
> (Ginsberg, Kerouac, and Cassady,
> "Pull My Daisy," 1949)

In rebellion against middle-class respectability, they could open new areas of life to poetic expression.

> What do I want in these rooms papered
> with visions of money?
> How much can I make by cutting my hair?
> If I put new heels on my shoes,
> bathe my body reeking of masturbation and
> sweat, layer upon layer of excretement
> dried in employment bureaus, magazine
> hallways, statistical cubical, factory
> stairways, . . .
> what war I enter and for what prize! . . .
>
> (Ginsberg, "Paterson," 1949)

For the first time in its history, America seemed on the way toward developing a uniform national identity, an official culture based on middle-class notions of propriety and success. During the war, deviance in terms of ideas or life-style was little tolerated for fear of threatening the war effort. Now, with the organizational means of ensuring conformity still in place, a new threat was being discovered in communism, as the former ally against fascism, the Soviet Union, was now seen as the new menace to freedom.

The side streets and bars of New York City, with their ethnic subcultures and small-time criminals, kept the Beats in touch with another America, permitting the sense of being outside the mainstream and its drift to conformity. In this respect, too, the New Vision could trace its roots back to earlier periods of American cultural radicalism: Henry Miller and Ernest Hemingway in the 1920s and the proletarian writers of the 1930s rejected middle-class life-styles and sought out the downtrodden and the outsiders in a quest for authenticity and experience. By the 1940s, the political aspects of the quest had largely disappeared; what was left was the existential search for meaning and escape from the ever-growing encroachment of the official culture. Out of this search would eventually emerge the counterculture of the sixties.

A new sense of energy—as well as alienation—was expressed in Ginsberg's poems and Kerouac's novels. In Ginsberg's *After Dead Souls* (1951) and Kerouac's more famous *On the Road* (1957) the American mythology of the open road and the western frontier were reinvented for a new generation.

> Where O America are you
> going in your glorious
> automobile, careening
> down the highway
> toward what crash
> in the deep canyon
> of the Western Rockies,
> or racing the sunset
> over Golden Gate
> toward what wild city
> jumping with jazz
> on the Pacific Ocean!
>
> (Ginsberg, "After Dead
> Souls," 1951)

One of the cornerstones of the New Vision was that poetry should not only deal with the everyday experience of common people but should also speak in their language. Living alone in New York and working as a free-lance market researcher, Ginsberg began in 1951 to compose the poem that was to become the anthem of a new generation. The other central subterraneans, Kerouac and Burroughs, were each on their separate roads in search of new experience. Ginsberg was thus free to return to one of his earlier sources of inspiration, namely, William Carlos Williams, one of America's most famous poets who was from a neighboring New Jersey town. He also drew on his own outsider experience, both his mother's mental illness and his own meanderings through the streets of New York. He had also, through a chance encounter with a Chinese painting at the New York Public Library, become interested in Buddhism. As already noted, the nearness of Columbia to Harlem had put Ginsberg in touch with black culture, especially jazz. Eventually all these influences would congeal into *Howl*, which combined these various strands with a powerful sense of rhythm. It was poetry that was best heard, rather than read. It seemed to require a collective presence to be fully experienced. It began with the famous lines,

I saw the best minds of my generation destroyed by madness,
    starving hysterical naked,
dragging themselves through the negro streets at dawn looking
    for an angry fix,
angelheaded hipsters burning for the ancient heavenly connection
    to the starry dynamo in the machinery of night,
who poverty and tatters and hollow-eyed and high sat up smoking
    in the supernatural darkness of cold-water flats floating
    across the tops of cities contemplating jazz . . .

Howl was first read publicly in San Francisco in 1955, in an event that has since taken on mythical proportions. In a room packed with all the notables of the West Coast poetry revival, Ginsberg read to the cheers and shouts of an audience of about one hundred. He filled the room with the sounds and symbols of the New Vision. As Barry Miles describes it,

[Ginsberg] was nervous and had drunk a great deal of wine. He read with a small, intense voice, but the alcohol and the emotional intensity of the poem quickly took over, and he was soon swaying to its powerful rhythm, chanting like a Jewish cantor, sustaining his long breath length, savoring the outrageous language. Kerouac began cheering him on, yelling "Go!" at the end of each line, and soon the audience joined in. Allen was completely transported. At each line he took a deep breath, glanced at the manuscript, then delivered it, arms outstretched, eyes gleaming, swaying from one foot to the other with the rhythm of the words. . . . Allen continued to the last sob, the audience cheering him wildly at every line. (Miles 1990: 196)

As Kenneth Rexroth, a well-known critic and central figure in San Francisco poetry circles, said directly afterward, the poem would make Ginsberg "famous from bridge to bridge." The reading, as well as the poem itself, helped to catalyze the subterranean literary communities in New York and San Francisco. Something was indeed happening to counter the main drift in American culture. The mass media would soon help make it into a movement.

The Beats moved and drew inspiration from the marginal urban subcultural pockets and linked art and life-style together in a creative way. The underbelly of the consumer society sustained them in a material as well as a spiritual sense. But San Francisco and northern California added something else, a rural, pastoral sensibility that would connect the Beats to the ecology movement of the 1970s. Rexroth's ties with Western populism and anarchism provided an essential link to this intellectual and geographic side of America: the self-reliant frontier tradition, which was also threatened by the new mass society and its culture. While Rexroth kept his distance from the Beats, acting more as a benevolent elder statesman than participant, one of his younger followers, Gary Snyder, was both influenced by and came to exercise an influence on Allen Ginsberg.

Snyder read his poem, "A Berry Feast," directly after *Howl* that October night in 1955. The stylistic contrast could not have been greater, yet both represented aspects of the same impulse. In quiet, somber tones Snyder's poem invoked the tale of the first-fruits festival of the Indians of Oregon, where Snyder had grown up. While Ginsberg excited and drew together the public with powerful rhythms and chants, Snyder's images encouraged quiet self-reflection and withdrawal. This was not surprising, as Snyder was to spend much of the next twelve years of his life at a Zen monastery in Japan.

Remarking on the religious references in Beat poetry, Michael Davidson has distinguished between the East Coast (Ginsberg, Kerouac) and the West Coast (Snyder, Philip Whalen) variants.

> Using two concepts from Buddhism, we could divide the poets of the Beat movement into two camps; those who take the direction of *karuna* (compassion) and those who follow the direction of *prajna* (wisdom). . . . In more familiar terms, this division could be seen as that between Emersonian idealism with its belief in an unmediated relationship between phenomenal reality and spiritual life, and a more solitary, speculative form of transcendentalism like that practiced by Thoreau. (Davidson 1989: 97)

In the former, the individual poet or writer attempts to become an empty vehicle through which "the currents of the universe" (Emerson) may flow. The musical rhythm of the poem, especially when read as a chant, is communal, aimed at bringing its audience into this universal current. Here the poet serves more as medium than midwife, in a process, common to oral cultures, in which community is re-created as the audience is drawn together under its spell. The second tradition is more intellectual, where self-reflection through meditation is the primary aim of the poem and its reading.

It was more than two techniques or paths to enlightenment that were united when East met West in San Francisco in the midfifties, however. The tensions that had been inherent in the Beat program from the outset, between the demand for extreme individual freedom of expression and the desire, at first unstated, to create a new sense of community in a society moving more and more in the opposite direction, were here brought out and, for the moment at least, resolved.

The New Vision formulated in a New York apartment in 1947 may have given first voice to an emerging subculture, but for many years it was an unheard cry in the wilderness. The more lasting name, "the beat generation," would be anointed by the mass media. An article in the *New York Times* in 1952 with the headline "This Is the Beat Generation" gave them not only a name but visibility. Their new vision for the arts came more and more to stand for a whole style of life, a culture in the wider, rather than narrower, sense of the term. What had begun as a program of individual redemption and artistic creation was transformed by the media attention into an alternative way of life. As opposed to many more politically oriented intellectuals, the Beats did not resist this attention from the mass media. On the contrary, Ginsberg, who worked part-time in various advertising agencies, actively used the mass media to further the Beat program.

Ginsberg was especially active in seeking out the popular magazines, such as *Time, Life, Esquire,* and the *New Yorker,* to review or comment on their work. Their work was also popularized through the greatly expanding paperback book trade. The publisher of *Howl,* Lawrence Ferlinghetti, was also the owner of the first paperback bookstore in America, City Lights, and the poem still remains under the imprint of City Lights Books. The great appeal of the Beats is unthinkable without the cheap paperback editions in which their works appeared and the mass-distribution newspapers and magazines that gave them both their name and their visibility. These were an essential part of the link between the coasts; like the new mass culture itself, the alternative went national.

The Beat culture for Ginsberg was essentially urban. It depended on the sights, the sounds, and the living conditions provided by city life. While the attempt to expand consciousness and the realms of personal experience demanded being on the road in search of new frontiers, the Beat writing and reflection was sustained in the city, amid the noise, the crowds, and, most important, the clubs and bars that brought the likes of Ginsberg, Kerouac, and Burroughs together in the first place. The road may have been the source of new experience, but the city was the crucible of creation. The city was where thoughts could be collected and where the small but sophisticated audiences could be found. San Francisco and New York, with stopovers in Denver and Tangiers, were the urban environments that cradled the Beat alternative to the mass culture. The San Francisco Poetry Renaissance, the West Coast link that gave the Beat alternative national recognition, is usually dated with that 1955 public reading of *Howl.* But it was New York's streets and bars, from Greenwich Village to Times Square to Harlem, that were the essential sources for Ginsberg's reconceptualization of culture. Drawing on the jazz rhythms of the small Harlem clubs and the pulsating sound of the streets, Ginsberg and his coconspirators helped shift the meaning of culture from its civilizing and rationalizing connotations to the more communal notion of collective experience. Ginsberg's poetry, as revealed in that reading of *Howl*, drew on premodern oral traditions, in which public performance was as important as, if not more important than, the meaning of the words or the representations they invoked. Rhythm, self-expression, and confession were central elements in the linking of the individual to the collective through the shared experience of poetry. This was something learned not only from Walt Whitman and American populism but also from black music, from blues and jazz, and from Eastern religion. It was not only the openness to mass culture and the alleged "destruction of the important barrier between mass culture and high art" (Davidson 1989: x) that worried critics of the Beat writers and poets; it was more that they threatened the very idea of culture that had dominated American intellectual life since the mid-nineteenth century.

As combination advance man and poet laureate, Allen Ginsberg carried the message of the Beat experience beyond the boundaries, both natural and artificially erected, of postwar American society. He carried the message of alternative culture and altered experience on the back roads of America from Boston to Tacoma and outside America from Havana to Prague. In 1965, in the midst of cold war tensions, Ginsberg was kicked out of Cuba for promoting "decadent" values. Put on a plane to Prague, he was greeted not by soldiers but by representatives of the Beat underground. And in a rollicking, alternative, May Day festival, he was elected Allen Kral Majalis, the King of May, by no less than 100,000 supporters. Back in the United States, Ginsberg was an important link across the generations, between the Beats and the hippies, and, less obviously, between the vague pacifism and antipolitics expressed in Beat culture and the new, directaction politics of the 1960s. In 1963, Ginsberg took part in his first political demonstration, protesting against an appearance of Madame Nhu, the infamous Dragon Lady of Vietnam, whose fierce Catholicism and religious repression had contributed, among other things, to the self-immolation of Buddhist monks. In protest, Ginsberg sang mantras for fourteen hours on the streets of San Francisco. Later in the 1960s, he acted as the forty-year-old "elder-statesman" of the political wing of the counterculture. He spoke on "Consciousness and Practical Action" at a conference on the "dialectics of liberation" on a program that included black power spokesman Stokely Carmichael, Paul Goodman, and Gregory Bateson, and the Marxist theorists Paul Sweezy and Ernest Mandel. While the other key figures of the Beat generation followed a more nonpolitical road, Ginsberg helped to facilitate the transition to the new politics of the sixties. Allen Ginsberg was more than a seed of the 1960s: he was one of the most colorful flowers of the new generation.

James Baldwin, Manchild in the Not-So-Promised Land

The Harlem that inspired the Beats was a long way from the one that produced James Baldwin, one of the greatest black writers of the postwar period. In fact, Baldwin was extremely critical of Beat writers, making a point of chastising passages of Jack Kerouac's *On the Road* as "absolute nonsense . . . and offensive nonsense at that," for its romantic view of blacks and Mexicans. Although they moved through some of the same New York streets and frequented the same Village bars and Harlem jazz clubs, Baldwin's path and the Beat road seldom crossed.

Born in 1924 into a family that would eventually include ten children, James Arthur Jones, as he was first called, grew up in dire poverty. He never knew his biological father but was given his stepfather's name when his mother married David Baldwin some years after he was born. James Baldwin was raised in a harsh atmosphere dominated not only by poverty but also by his stepfather's fire and brimstone Christianity and hatred for whites. It was an atmosphere softened only by the fact that his stepfather was forced to commute every day to a factory on faraway Long Island, leaving the child care to Baldwin's mother, a warm and loving person who protected him throughout his life. But David Baldwin's presence was always felt. His weekend activity as a preacher in storefront churches shaped not only his own identity but that of the household as well. He ruled over his family with an iron hand on the Bible. "As for me and my house, we will serve the Lord," was the motto he both preached and practiced.

In such a strict religious household, in the grip of poverty, it is not surprising that a quick and gifted child should move early to the pulpit himself. At fourteen, James Baldwin was making his mark as a Holy Roller preacher, and in his own modest assessment, he was "a great preacher" at that (Campbell 1991: 10).

After his writing talents were discovered and encouraged by various teachers, Baldwin received his first break as a professional on the smaller reviews and journals that flourished in New York in the 1940s. Like other precocious and persistent street kids before him, Baldwin got his chance by hanging around editorial offices and having a book thrown at him by a benevolent editor, with the accompanying gruff words, "See what you can do with this." Baldwin's particular book was thrown by Saul Levitas of *The New Leader* (where C. Wright Mills also got his start), a journal where political opinion mattered almost as much as personal contact. Baldwin describes the encounter and his own politics in this way: a close friend

> was a Socialist—a member of the Young People's Socialist League (YPSL) and urged me to join, and I did. I, then, outdistanced him by becoming a Trotskyite—so that I was in the interesting position (at the age of nineteen) of being an anti-Stalinist when America and Russia were allies. My life on the Left is of absolutely no interest. It did not last long. . . . But it was during this period that I met the people who were to take me to Saul Levitas, of *The New Leader,* Randall Jarrell, of *The Nation,* Elliot Cohen and Robert Warshow, of *Commentary,* and Philip Rahv, of *Partisan Review.* (Baldwin 1985: xii–xiii)

Baldwin's first novels were written in the tradition of American realism, with a particular nod to Henry James and John Dos Passos. He defined his role as author as being "white America's inside-eye on the closed families and locked churches of Harlem, the discreet observer of homosexual scenes in Paris, above all the sensitive recorder of the human heart in conflict with itself," as one biographer put it (Campbell 1991:117). From this "I am a camera" perspective, with its commitment to telling the cold truth at whatever cost, Baldwin wrote novels about growing up poor in Harlem (*Go Tell It on the Mountain,* 1953) and homosexual relationships (*Giovanni's Room,* 1956) at a time when most writers were dealing with less controversial topics. Written as first-person narratives, these books told their tale from the inside, exposing the public not only to unknown mysterious worlds but also to the author. The opening lines of *Go Tell It on the Mountain* makes the autobiographical reference clear: "Everyone had always said that John would be a preacher when he grew up, just like his father. . . . Not until the morning of his fourteenth birthday did he really begin to think about it, and by then it was already too late."

It was in essays rather than novels that Baldwin would be most effective and most influential. He supplemented writing in smaller intellectual journals like the *Partisan Review* and *Commentary* with better paying assignments in more widely distributed magazines like *Harper's, Esquire,* and *Mademoiselle*. "Notes of a Native Son," which first appeared in *Harper's* in 1955, marked Baldwin's entry to a literary field in which he could combine autobiography and politics in a more explicit and powerful way. This was the form and the format that suited him best and in which he would further develop in the role of the committed artist. Here are the first lines:

> On the twenty-ninth of July, in 1943, my father died. On the same day, a few hours later, his last child was born. Over a month before this, while all our energies were concentrated in waiting for these events, there had been, in Detroit, one of the bloodiest race riots of the century. A few hours after my father's funeral, while he lay in state in the undertaker's chapel, a race riot broke out in Harlem. On the morning of the third of August, we drove my father to the graveyard through a wilderness of smashed plate glass. (1985: 127)

"Notes of a Native Son" was still written in the realist mode, describing events in the first person in a rather dispassionate way, reporting on a seldom seen reality for a white middle-class readership. The juxtaposition of biography and history used so effectively here, recounting not only portions of his father's life but also some of his own encounters with racism, would later be developed to give the reader both the sense of being there with the author and "being white," that is, of being at least in part responsible for the terrible events described. The camera is thus revealed to contain a moral point of view.

Baldwin's life took on new dimensions with the emergence of the civil rights movement in the late 1950s. The great display of protest and hope in the early days of this essentially religious movement struck deep chords in Baldwin, deep enough to draw him home from Europe. He returned to the United States from France in July 1957, after nine years in exile. In September, Baldwin was commissioned by *Harper's* to cover the struggle for school integration in Little Rock, Arkansas, and Charlotte, North Carolina. This trip resulted in several essays and in a new perspective on the relationship between the writer and his public.

This was Baldwin's first time in the South and in addition to reporting on the events at hand, he found occasion for personal reflection. "The South had always frightened me. How deeply it had frightened me—though I had never seen it—and how soon, was one of the things my dreams revealed to me while I was there. And this made me think of the privacy and mystery of childhood all over again, in a new way. I wondered where children got their strength—the strength, in this case, to walk through mobs to get to school" (161).

Although he could never leave this self-reflective mode, finding in all experience cause for personal reflection, Baldwin now placed self-reflection in a wider historical context. From being a Negro writer carving out a place in the white world through faithfully describing seldom seen worlds, Baldwin was becoming black. Without realizing it, he was slowly developing a black perspective, both of himself and of the world around him. He was trading in his camera and about to take on the role of spokesman.

Baldwin's prime audience for these new reflections was still the white middle class, but now he was offering that audience not only insight but education as well. Through his voyage of self-discovery in the American South, Baldwin carried his northern white audience along for the ride. They were, after all, paying for the trip. In this period of self-reflection and reeducation, all the roles were reversed: the young taught the old, students taught teachers, and, most important, blacks taught whites. "Americans keep wondering what has 'got into' the students. What has 'got into' them is their history in this country. They are not the first Negroes to face mobs: they are merely the first Negroes to frighten the mob more than the mob frightens them" (228).

The Fire Next Time was the name the publishers gave to two of the most powerful essays Baldwin wrote; indeed, they were two of the most powerful essays written in postwar America. "A Letter to my Nephew," the first of these, originally appeared in *The Progressive* in 1962, where it was read, presumably, by a small number of liberal, mostly white, readers. When it was collected together with "Letter from a Region in My Mind," originally published as "Down at the Cross" in the *New Yorker* and released in 1963 as a small book by Dial Press, it became an instant best-seller. Even the FBI took enough interest to obtain prepublication proofs, predicting—and dreading—the book's wide public appeal.

Addressing himself to his "nephew" allowed Baldwin to weave the strands of personal history and the history of black America in an even more powerful way than he had previously done. With familial intimacy, he talked to his nephew about his father, his own "brother," with the wider meaning given the term in the new black idiom and through him to all black people: "Other people cannot see what I see whenever I look into your father's face, for behind your father's face as it is today are all those other faces which were his" (334).

Here we have the artist on fire; for James Baldwin, after the bombings and the riots, after walking with Martin Luther King, Jr., and Malcolm X, the fire was not next time but now. Baldwin's eyes are no longer those of the objective camera recording events or silently witnessing the experience of black America; the writer is now giving voice, not only articulating what was unspoken but amplifying it to a new level of awareness for all to hear. James Baldwin, who had previously taken Henry James as his artistic model, had been transformed into the midwife of an emerging black consciousness.

The second essay in *The Fire Next Time* had already caused a great stir when it appeared in the *New Yorker*. This probably had more to do with the topic, the Black Muslims, than with any developing black awareness. Again Baldwin was taking curious white eyes with him into an unknown region of black America, into the home of Elijah Muhammad and the Nation of Islam. White interest had recently been aroused not only through the fiery speeches of Malcolm X, the movement's most prolific spokesman, but also through the conversion of Cassius Clay, the heavyweight boxing champion, who would soon be stripped of his title in part for insisting on being called Muhammad Ali and refusing, on religious grounds, to register for the military draft.

The white world was curious about this newly visible black world, and, based on past performance, Baldwin was the man to tell them about it. But Baldwin was less interested in white curiosity than in reflecting on the history of black-white relations. The essay is a remarkable performance of weaving personal and collective history in which baring one's soul reveals a collective soul as well—and of leading an audience along a path it is reluctant to tread.

To his surprise, Elijah Muhammad reminded Baldwin of his own father and the Nation of Islam of the Harlem where he had grown up. "I had heard a great deal, long before I finally met him, of the Honorable Elijah Muhammad, and of the Nation of Islam movement, of which he is the leader. I paid very little attention to what I heard, because the burden of the message did not strike me as being very original; I had been hearing variations of it all my life" (352). Baldwin retold the story of his Harlem life through the newfound perspective, placing his own development in the light of the collective. Rather than telling a tale of personal suffering or triumph, he recounted the emergence of a new awareness.

When we finally arrive on the Chicago doorstep of the Honorable Elijah Muhammad, we have been well prepared for the role the church and its ministers play in ghetto life. Baldwin's portrait of the man and his movement is sympathetic after all this prehistory. White America had reaped what it had sown, and the Black Muslims, with their inherent threat of violence, were only the outgrowth of the long history of repression and invisibility accorded black Americans.

> The brutality with which Negroes are treated in this country simply cannot be overstated, however unwilling white men may be to hear it. In the beginning—and neither can this be overstated—a Negro just cannot *believe* that white people are treating him as they do; he does not know what he has done to merit it. And when he realizes that the treatment accorded him has nothing to do with anything he has done, that the attempt of white people to destroy him—for that is what it is—is utterly gratuitous, it is not hard for him to think of white people as devils. (362)

Elijah Muhammad and the temples of the Nation of Islam have succeeded in what "generations of welfare workers and committees and resolutions and reports and housing projects and playgrounds have failed to do: to heal and redeem drunkards and junkies, to convert people who have come out of prison and to keep them out, to make men chaste and women virtuous, and to invest both the male and the female with a pride and with a serenity that hang about them like an unfailing light" (354).

The Black Muslims were portrayed as being as much the products of white failure and indifference as the outcome of black experience. But Baldwin was not merely telling his white audience what to expect; more important, he was lending his voice to the growing tide of black consciousness. "For the horrors of the American Negro's life there has been almost no language. The privacy of his experience, which is only beginning to be recognized in language, and which is denied or ignored in official and popular speech—hence the Negro idiom—lends credibility to any system that pretends to clarify it" (362).

The civil rights movement had given the writer a new role, a purpose in life that he could find only in America. As he told an interviewer a year after his first trip South, "I realized what tremendous things were happening and that I did have a role to play. I can't be happy here, but I can work here" (quoted in Campbell 1991: 125). This new role, however, of giving voice where there had been only silent suffering, turned out to be a thankless task. Baldwin was attacked on many fronts. His former allies among white liberals attacked his new stance as articulator of black consciousness, preferring the objective camera to the spokesman. It depreciated his art, they said. He was also attacked from a more unexpected source, one that hurt him much more, in part because it was so unexpected. In a wide-ranging review of Baldwin's corpus, Eldridge Cleaver, the minister of information of the newly formed Black Panther Party, castigated him for "antipathy towards the black race" and found in his homosexuality a "racial death-wish." This hurt not only because it came from blacks but also because it came from a young black militant and seemed to represent the feelings of the new generation in whom Baldwin placed so much of his hope for the future.

A committed integrationist and supporter of Martin Luther King, Jr., Baldwin was open for this attack, but that did not make the accusations any easier to swallow. The black nationalist movement was not only northern but also urban and, like the members of the Student Non-Violent Coordinating Committee (SNCC) who challenged the older, more conservative integrationists in the National Association for the Advancement of Colored People (NAACP) and the Southern Christian Leadership Council (SCLC), mostly young. The new black nationalists criticized Baldwin for being a white nigger, not in Mailer's meaning, which they (Cleaver, in any case) approved of, but in the older sense of Uncle Tom. This attack shook Baldwin and caused him to rethink his role as artist and intellectual in a movement that, from his point of view, had made a turn for the worse.

The news of King's death reached Baldwin in Hollywood, where he was busy writing the screenplay of *The Autobiography of Malcolm X*. The coincidence of terrible news with the task he was engaged in, occurrences that linked together strands of his life as well as of the history of black America, proved to be too much. He became convinced that he was next. "Medger [Evers], Malcolm, Martin" became his often-repeated refrain, with the assumption that Jimmy would soon follow. What may appear as self-aggrandizement to an objective observer had real consequences for Baldwin. Combined with the criticism he received from black nationalists and white liberals, the fear that he would be the next to be assassinated drove Baldwin into exile once more and back to writing novels.

James Baldwin's contribution to the reconceptualization of culture in postwar America was not so much in the setting of new artistic standards, or in the discovery of new forms of expression, as was the case with Allen Ginsberg. Rather, his role lay in lending voice to a rising black consciousness, contributing not only to its constitution as a historical force but also to white self-understanding. This contribution was made all the more significant because it appeared in mass circulation magazines as well as intellectual journals. Through his powerful prose, Baldwin not only gave witness to the events he described but also revealed through his practice that morally based criticism still had a place in American mass society and that the engaged and enraged artist had a role in a society dominated by mass culture. Like Allen Ginsberg, whom we have already discussed, and Mary McCarthy, to whom we will now turn, Baldwin was one of a handful of writers who transformed the models and traditions inherited from the 1930s and successfully navigated the rough waters of transition in the 1950s to inspire the more committed popular authors that emerged in the 1960s.

Mary McCarthy, and the Company She Kept

Like James Baldwin, whom she would meet in midlife, Mary McCarthy got her literary start in the small journals centered in New York City. From an entirely different social background, however, her path to the center of American intellectual life was much shorter and more direct than Baldwin's. Born in Seattle, Washington, in 1912, McCarthy was raised by her grandparents in solid middle-class surroundings after both her parents died, along with a half million other Americans, in the flu epidemic of 1918. She attended private boarding schools and then Vassar College in Poughkeepsie, New York, where she studied English. From there, the trip to New York City and to a literary career was only a short fifty miles down the Hudson River.

Her first husband, Harold Johnsrud, an actor, director, and playwright, introduced her to New York's bohemian circles. His tutelage and the friends she met at Vassar, as well as the critical skills and interest in literature that she cultivated there, all prepared her to enter New York's literary world. This sort of accumulated social and cultural capital put her much nearer that scene than James Baldwin's Harlem. Harlem may only have been a subway ride away, but it was millions of miles away measured in social distance.

Even with these advantages, McCarthy had to prove her worth in this competitive, man's world. She got her first chance at the *New Republic,* submitting book reviews to Malcolm Cowley, one of its famed editors, while still at college. At Vassar she had been told that her talent lay in criticism, not creative writing. She took this judgment seriously. *The Nation,* another of New York's liberal weeklies, provided her with the space to display these critical talents. After publishing several witty and biting book reviews in their pages, she was given the task of writing a series of articles on newspaper book review critics. By the young age of twenty-two, she had published three major series of critical essays in this national magazine and had made her mark on the intellectual battlefield.

Her first published fiction revealed another talent, however, an ability for self-irony and for coolly observing the manners and mores of the middle class. "Cruel and Barbarous Treatment" appeared in the *Southern Review* in 1939, the year she graduated from Vassar, and later as the first chapter of *The Company She Keeps* (1942), her first novel. Here she recounted in fictional terms her own extramarital affair and recent divorce. Her flair for observation through ironic distance offered more than social satire; she also put into print what were, for the middle class, revolutionary attitudes concerning male-female relations.

In the following passage, she paints a (fictional) scene involving herself, her husband, and her lover expressing her (real) need for the public display of deviance from mainstream mores.

> The Public Appearances were not exclusively duets. They sometimes took the form of a trio. On these occasions the studied and benevolent carefulness which she always showed for her husband's feelings served a double purpose. She would affect a conspicuous domesticity, an affectionate conjugal demonstrativeness, would sprinkle her conversation with "Darlings," and punctuate it with pats and squeezes till her husband would visibly expand and her lover plainly and painfully shrink. For the Young Man no retaliation was possible. These endearments of hers were sanctioned by law, usage and habit; they belonged to her role as wife and could not be condemned or paralleled by a young man who was himself unmarried. They were clear provocations, but they could not be called so, and the Young Man preferred not to speak of them. *But she knew.* (1942: 4)

On the real train to Reno, to get that divorce, she had a few drinks with a man in the club car and woke up the next morning to find herself in his coupe. This incident formed the basis for the third chapter of *The Company She Keeps* (the second chapter was based on a description of a close friend). It was a pattern that would hold throughout her life, writing fictionalized accounts of very real events, using irony to create a distance between herself and the female role her middle-class upbringing and education had prepared her for.

McCarthy moved in left-wing New York literary circles throughout the 1930s and 1940s. The incident with Farrell mentioned above changed her life, as she later put it. Her unintended participation on the Committee for the Defense of Leon Trotsky was followed by the decision to continue after the initial anger at the way it occurred had worn off. She stayed on, she said, in another expression of self-irony, because others urged her to get off. This decision forced her to read up on the Moscow trials and on the Russian revolution. Such reading and the contacts made through the committee automatically placed McCarthy within the newly forming anti-Stalinist Left that emerged in intellectual circles after the Moscow trials. It was in this context that she met Philip Rahv, who together with William Phillips started the *Partisan Review* in 1934. McCarthy moved in with Rahv and at the same time onto the editorial board of this Trotskyist and modernist journal. Everything seemed to happen as if by accident, so easily and so naturally. In a way, writing satire was a defensive reaction, a means of reflecting, of making the judgments and choices that seemed impossible for her in everyday life, where she seemed to float along, taking her attitudes from her social background and her opinions from those around her.

As the only woman on the editorial board of what was to become the single most important intellectual journal in America, Mary Mc-Carthy always felt herself "among the boys." The other editors, including Rahv, never fully trusted her because of her "bourgeois" appearance and demeanor. She was made to feel the outsider, a "bourgeois throwback" and a "good-time girl from the 1920s," an accusation and an attitude that only reinforced her already developed talent for ironic distance. She was to write a book about her experience on the *Partisan Review* (*The Oasis*, 1949), adding her own intellectual coterie to the list of topics that were subjected to satirical treatment. This did nothing to endear her to her friends and colleagues. It was all right to expose liberal circles, as she had done in "Portrait of the Intellectual as a Yale Man," the fifth chapter of *The Company She Keeps,* but it was quite another thing to apply the same cool observations to her own intimate group. This only further proved, to those in that circle, that one could not take Mary McCarthy or her political commitments seriously.

Like McCarthy's sense of moving in uncertain territory, of being continually among the boys, the *Partisan Review* as a whole felt itself surrounded by Communists. Its offices, first on Union Square and then on Astor Place in downtown Manhattan, shared building space with journals dominated by Stalinists, like the *New Masses;* in their eyes, this whole section of New York City was a Communist party stronghold. Never absent, factional infighting began in earnest among left-wing groups in the mid-1930s. The smaller magazines, like the *Partisan Review* and the *New Masses,* were the main public venues for this conflict, but even the larger journals, like *The Nation* and the *New Republic,* got involved. The intellectual Left was beginning a process of fragmentation that would only accelerate during the war and the triumphant peace that followed.

In this atmosphere of political conflict and intellectual competition, the smaller journals like the *Partisan Review* were in constant search of new recruits, especially of the well-known kind. Edmund Wilson, perhaps America's best-known critic at the time, was one of the most sought after. Printing an article by Wilson was a great prize for any journal but even greater for one that felt itself struggling to survive, economically and politically, in such a hostile environment. When Wilson expressed interest, McCarthy was sent as an envoy to woo him onto the *Partisan Review's* pages. She prepared herself by dressing up and drinking too much. Much to her own surprise, the wooing turned out to be of another sort. Wilson eventually published in the *Partisan Review,* and Mary McCarthy left Philip Rahv to marry him. In 1938 at the age of twenty-five, McCarthy arrived at the center of American letters.

The seven-year marriage to Wilson turned out to be a mixed blessing. On the plus side was his extreme loyalty and encouragement of her writing. It was Wilson who convinced McCarthy she could write fiction, and it was through his insistence that *The Company She Keeps* was written. But Wilson, seventeen years older than McCarthy and into his third marriage, was also an alcoholic who beat her, sending her to the hospital and into psychoanalysis. It was a strange marriage by any standards. Even after their angry divorce in 1945, Wilson never ceased to encourage and defend her writing, publicly and privately.

One of the least recognized effects of the Second World War on the United States was the contribution to American culture made by European refugees. New York was flooded, and as McCarthy noted in a later interview, "The whole character of New York was changed by the appearance of these refugees who had a certain wisdom that was totally lacking in the crude society that was described in *The Group*" (quoted in Gelderman 1988: 118). Hannah Arendt, one of those influential refugees, was to become an intimate friend of McCarthy.

From McCarthy's point of view, the most central contribution of this wave of intellectual immigrants from Europe was the introduction of what she called a "moral core," previously lacking in American culture. By this she meant that these European intellectuals revealed a major flaw in the work of their American counterparts: a connection between what they "read and wrote and their own lives, how they were living and what they believed in" (119). This had also been something that stood, perhaps unconsciously, behind her own satirical representations. The attempt to make visible this disconnection was the impulse behind *The Oasis* and would lie more consciously in *The Group*. While the former satirized the attempt of intellectuals to construct a utopian community, the latter described another sort of community, the graduates of Vassar College, class of 1933.

The Group was a best-seller even before it was published in 1963. By this time McCarthy's status as a critic and satirist of contemporary mores was well established. She had produced two novels since *The Oasis, The Groves of Academe* (1952) and *A Charmed Life* (1955), as well as a book of short stories and two travelogues. Her childhood recollections, *Memories of a Catholic Girlhood* (1957), had been hailed as one of the finest literary accomplishments of the postwar period. She was known for a sharpness of eye and tongue and for frankness in describing the relations between the sexes. Elizabeth Hardwick has written that Mary McCarthy's descriptions of sexual encounters were in stark contrast to "the hot prose of male writers" and that part of her original contribution was "to have written, from the woman's point of view, the comedy of Sex" (quoted in MacKenzie 1966: 92). Bits and pieces of what was to be *The Group* had already appeared in the *Partisan Review* and the *New Yorker,* and the publisher's publicity machine was already in full motion before publication. The public was thus well prepared for what was coming.

The Group covers the lives of eight Vassar classmates from the end of their college days to the beginning of World War II. It differs from McCarthy's early works in that the voice of the author is almost entirely absent. Rather, this is a tale told by the subjects themselves, and thus eight different voices and interpretations of the same events are presented. Only in the first and last chapters does the singular author's viewpoint, that which had dominated her previous works, reveal itself. By choosing this approach, McCarthy is more able to let the characters speak for themselves, making the feeling of real documentary even stronger. The characters speak through the clichés of their time, as they have learned them from their upbringing and their college education. They are thus meant to represent types, women of a particular social background and age, rather than to stand for real individuals. But the two ways of writing were intertwined, and many readers were confused, looking for the real persons behind the character. Some Vassar alumni wanted her expelled from their ranks, for what they interpreted as her slander of the school and its graduates.

It had not been McCarthy's intention to write the kind of satire she had done previously, which had depended on a fine blending of concreteness of description and caricature. Instead, *The Group* was meant to be "a kind of mock-chronicle . . . about the idea of progress . . . seen in the female sphere, the feminine sphere. You know, home economics, architecture, domestic technology, contraception, childbearing; the study of technology in the home, in the play-pen, in the bed" (135). To show this, this gradual loss of faith in progress, she had the characters mouth all the popular phrases and all the popular theories, from psychoanalysis to scientific child-rearing, that dominated the perceptions of people of their backgrounds.

Mary McCarthy's original plan for the novel, which she outlined already in 1953, had been to cover a longer period, a full twenty years, up to Eisenhower's inaugural address in 1953. But since this was satire, it proved impossible to cover such a long period, because, as she later explained, "the girls are all essentially comic figures, and its awfully hard to make anything happen to them" (135). Comic characters cannot learn, cannot develop, making it difficult for an author to cover longer periods of their lives in anything but a shallow and repetitive way. As it was, some critics were to make these claims about the seven years actually covered in the published version.

The book was successful not only because of its satire and its frank discussions of female sexuality but also because it articulated what were still only vague feelings about the changes that were taking place in American society. McCarthy recorded faithfully, one assumes, the conversations, tastes, and dispositions not only of college women of a certain background but also of some of those on the Left at the time. Witness the following recollections made by Kay, one of the "group," whom some commentators mistakenly thought represented the author.

> What she [Kay] could not remember, though Harald [her playwright husband] kept drilling into her, was that she and her friends did not count anymore, except as individuals, in the wider picture of American society. . . . The transfer of power, he showed, from Threadneedle Street to Wall Street was an event in world history comparable to the defeat of the Spanish Armada, which had ushered in the era of capitalism. When Roosevelt, just now, had gone off the gold standard, it was a declaration of independence from Europe and an announcement of a new, flexible epoch. The NRA and the eagle were symbols of the arrival of a new class to power. Their class, the upper middle, he told the two girls [Kay and another member of the group], was finished politically and economically; its best elements would merge with the rising elements of workers and farmers and technicians, of which he, as a stage technician, was one. (McCarthy 1963: 59)

This is good comedy, the pompous stage technician including himself as a member of the rising knowledge class, but it is also insightful reporting of opinions held in the 1930s. Like James Baldwin, McCarthy used the I am a camera technique to make a moral, and political, point: revealing the foibles of her characters to help her readers reflect on their own situation. The fact that this moralistic message was couched in humor and satire only adds to its appeal.

McCarthy's moralism became even clearer in her later nonfiction. In 1967, in the midst of the Vietnam War, while married to an American diplomat to boot, McCarthy went to Vietnam to report on the war for a voice of intellectual opposition, the *New York Review of Books*. In her report, she focused not on military strategy or politics but on the effects on the country of the American military and civilian presence, what could be called the mass culturation of the country.

> As we drove into downtown Saigon, through a traffic jam, I had the fresh shock of being in what looked like an American city, a very

shoddy West Coast one, with a Chinatown and a slant-eyed Asiatic minority. Not only military vehicles of every description, but Chevrolets, Chryslers, Mercedes-Benz, Volkswagens, Triumphs, and white men everywhere in sports shirts and drip-dry pants. The civilian take-over is even more astonishing than the military. (Quoted in Gelderman 1988: 281)

It was not only the Westernization of Vietnam that shocked Mary McCarthy but also the language that made this possible. For her, Americans were able to act with such cultural and physical brutality toward the Vietnamese people because of the language they had constructed to filter out what they inflicted. "The worst of all is the terrible removal of morality from the whole affair by this separation of words from their meaning." With the entire United States government and its "experts" and media behind the construction and diffusion of this language, it was difficult to counter. But a moral standpoint offered at least the possibility of maintaining credibility and defending the dignity of language and the sovereignty of culture. McCarthy was to travel to North Vietnam as well, into the heart of enemy territory in the midst of war. Through her reporting, published in the *New Yorker* as well as the *New York Review*, McCarthy became a direct link to the antiwar movement then nearing its height. In this way she connected the social movements of the 1930s to those of the 1960s. But it is another, subtler linkage that we have been attempting to uncover here: the way her writings prepared the way for the new wave of feminism that emerged in America in the wake of both the civil rights and the antiwar movements.

Here the linkage was not only subtler but unintended as well. McCarthy never would have called herself or her literature feminist. Like her good friend and compatriot, Hannah Arendt, as well as many of her Old Left colleagues, she distanced herself from the emerging women's movement and from what it considered women's issues.

As for Women's Lib, it bores me. Of course I believe in equal pay and equality before the law and so on, but this whole myth about how different the world would be if it had been female-dominated, about how there would have been no wars—and Women's-Lib extremists actually believe these things—seems a complete fantasy to me. I've never noticed that women were less warlike then men. And in marriage, or for that matter between a woman and her lover or between two lesbians or any other couple, an equal division of tasks is impossible—it's a judgment of Solomon. You really have to slice the baby down the middle. (307)

In her own life, Mary McCarthy was happy in her domesticity, and as her biographer points out, "there [was] no 'woman' problem in the circles she move[d] in" (307). So it was not her intention to contribute to any emerging feminist consciousness. Our argument is that she did so nevertheless. The early and frank discussion of female sexuality and contraception is one obvious and well-acknowledged contribution. While not feminist, the actions and, perhaps most of all, the reflections of the heroine in *The Company She Keeps* opened new ground for awareness among women. Most important, her style of writing, the ironic distance she created between herself as author and the characters she portrayed, male and female, contributed to the process of feminist consciousness raising.

Along with Baldwin and Ginsberg, McCarthy provided a literary bridge between the social movements of the 1930s and the 1960s. Her role was to help make visible the subtle forms of conformity that were being reproduced in gender relations in the postwar period. She brought a feminist sensibility into literature almost in spite of herself. And she gave voice to the concerns and perspectives of women's liberation even before there was a movement. Indeed, when the movement did develop, the fiercely independent McCarthy would have little to do with it.

• • •

James Baldwin, Allen Ginsberg, and Mary McCarthy all brought previously excluded cultural perceptions and experiences into mainstream American literature. They broadened high culture without lowering its standards to a mass level. At the same time, they brought the masses out of their anonymity and homogenized "vulgarity" that was attributed to them by the defenders of "serious" culture; in so doing, they carved out spaces for new forms of cultural expression. Victims of oppression themselves—subtle or otherwise—they could better un-

176

derstand and articulate the victimization of the sexually deviant as well as of the racially or sexually oppressed.

In carefully mixing their own biographies in their artistic representations, each revealed the changes occurring in themselves as well as in society. This kind of public self-reflection or exposure, the kind that Mary McCarthy's friend Hannah Arendt identified as the essential characteristic of human action, would help others to reflect on their own lives and the changes that were possible to contemplate. In this way, their writings, as well as their lives, provided seeds for the social and cultural movements of the sixties and beyond.

6

MAKING POLITICS PERSONAL
Saul Alinsky, Dorothy Day, Martin Luther King, Jr.

• •

In 1930, a young graduate student at the University of Chicago's famed department of sociology began his fieldwork for a planned doctoral dissertation on local gangsters. Being a brash young man, he decided to go right to the top, to Al Capone's mob. Here is his later recollection about how he first made the necessary contact.

> My reception was pretty chilly at first. I went over to the old Lexington Hotel, which was the gang's headquarters, and I hung around the lobby and the restaurant. I'd spot one of the mobsters whose picture I'd seen in the papers and go up to him and say, "I'm Saul Alinsky, I'm studying criminology, do you mind if I hang around with you?" And he'd look me over and say, "Get lost, punk." This happened again and again, and I began to feel I'd never get anywhere. Then one night I was sitting in the restaurant and at the next table was Big Ed Stash, a professional assassin who was the Capone mob's top executioner. He was drinking with a bunch of his pals and he was saying, "Hey, you guys, did I ever tell you about the time I picked up that redhead in Detroit?" and he was cut off by a chorus of moans. "My God," one guy said, "do we have to hear that one again?" I saw Big Ed's face fall. . . . And I reached over and plucked his sleeve. "Mr. Stash," I said, "I'd love to hear that story." His face lit up. "You would, kid?" He slapped me on the shoulder. "Here, pull up a chair."
> . . . And that's how it started. (Quoted in Horwitt 1992: 20)

Saul Alinsky never did finish his doctoral dissertation; too many things got in the way. But he never lost his brashness, and it was to serve him well. He soon gave up his professional orientation to community work,

178

since he did not really feel at home in the role of criminologist or social worker, and turned to political activism instead. Alinsky was to invent a new style of doing politics in the 1930s, a form of community organizing that would fit both his own personality and the changing conditions of American society. It was a form of direct-action politics that rejected Marxist class analysis by focusing on the community, where people lived rather than where they worked.

Alinsky believed that politics was about power, not ideology, and that it should be done with style and flair. He invented means for getting things accomplished that infuriated and embarrassed his opponents, like dumping garbage on the lawn of a city councilman during a garbage strike. The press became a major ally in his fight against the political establishment, as the brashness of his tactics made good copy. One should beat city hall, he was fond of saying, but have fun doing it. This approach to politics would resonate well in the 1960s.

Dorothy Day was also interested in organizing at the local level. But she was far from brash, and her approach was based on premises very different from those that guided Alinsky. Perhaps that is why she tends to be neglected in most historical accounts of postwar American radicalism. Although she began her career as a journalist on a socialist newspaper called the 'Call and would later call her own paper the Catholic Worker, Day's audience was not the working class, as was Alinsky's. Rather, it was the poor and the homeless who were her community. Her organizing was done on the skid rows of American cities, and her motivations were neither ideological nor material but moral and religious. At a time when America's cities are lined with homeless, Day's unique contribution—what Garry Wills has termed the "quiet witness of the resister"—deserves to be remembered (Wills 1990: 324).

Day spent a good deal of her early adult life on the streets of New York and in its cafés and bars, as a quintessential Greenwich Village bohemian radical. When she converted to Catholicism in the 1930s, she wanted to erase from public memory the times she and Eugene O'Neill spent drinking among the small-time gangsters in the Hell Hole and other hangouts in Greenwich Village. In later life, she preferred to be remembered for her postconversion activities, for her work for peace among the poor in the Catholic Worker Movement she founded. But the two lives were connected. Her early cultural radicalism and her later immersion in moral causes—both absolute pacifism and good works for the downtrodden—were rooted in the same sense of commitment and defiance of authority. It was this commitment and, in particular, the spaces she created for its expression within the Catholic Worker Movement and the peace movement more generally that made her a source of inspiration for many of the moral witnesses who came on the scene in the 1960s in yet another radical era. By bringing religion and spirituality back into politics, she was one of those who connected the postwar era to a long tradition of American moral politics.

Martin Luther King, Jr.'s motivations for his political activity were also moral and religiously based. The son of a Southern Baptist minister, he grew up in the church. Like James Baldwin, he began preaching at an early age, and also like Baldwin, he fostered ambitions even as a youngster which most of his contemporaries would never have dreamed of. King had wider visions that led him out of the South, to New York City and then to Boston University, where, in the early 1950s, he studied philosophy as well as theology. There he came in contact with people and ideas that would help him become a principal actor in the first stirring of the civil rights movement and in the politicization of the black community that was one of the main prerequisites of its success. It was particularly the radical theology of Reinhold Niebuhr and the moral politics of Mahatma Gandhi that would be central components in the critical process that King—perhaps more than any other single individual—brought into the black community and, eventually, the larger white community as well.

The civil rights movement did much more than point to a dreadful sore in American society: the second-class citizenship of its principal minority. It articulated a striving for social and political recognition on the part of American blacks. But it also provided a space for social learning for all Americans to recall the ideals of democracy and political participation on which the nation had been founded. The oratorical skill of King along with the philosophy of nonviolent confrontational politics that he came to express and embody were central to the carving of these new public spaces. The Emersonian intellectual as priest came into the postwar era in the person of a black man, who did not manage to move mountains but certainly did move the political culture of the country into more spiritual and virtuous directions. Most important, he, along with Day, Alinsky, and a handful of other intellectuals in the 1950s, started the process that brought politics down to the personal level. Along with the organizational and tactical innovations that the civil rights movement contributed to the restoration of American democracy in the postwar period, King's partisan intellectual presence helped reconstitute American politics.

A Tradition Reinvented

Although there is a reluctance among many historical commentators to recognize the role of religion in American politics, there can be no denying the strong moral tone of much of American political life. In earlier chapters, we have identified an intellectual tradition that can be traced back to the New England colonists, in which knowledge, ideas, and intellectual activity in general were embedded in various kinds of religious practices. From Jonathan Edwards to Ralph Waldo Emerson, the spiritual or moral witness has vied with secular experts over intellectual authority and legitimacy. In politics, there has almost been a wavelike process through the centuries, as secular values and programs have replaced spiritual or religious periods with cyclical regularity.

In the twentieth century, the early progressive movement mixed politics and religion to address some of the problems of an industrializing, increasingly urban society; both Jane Addams and Lincoln Steffens—as well as Woodrow Wilson himself—saw politics as a kind of missionary work, an extension of Christian values into the public realm. After the First World War, however, and the general revolt against traditional values and morality that came to characterize the Roaring Twenties, a more secular era ensued, in which material concerns and ideologies dominated the political agenda. During the depression, religion was not so much ignored as marginalized by the followers of John Dewey and Franklin Roosevelt, confined to the private sphere, while public discourse revolved around pragmatic and largely economic issues. At the same time, politics grew more programmatic, and, for a brief period, the class struggle and socialist ideas exercised a hegemonic influence over many American intellectuals. For some, secularization was a personal rebellion, as the sons and daughters of ministers and rabbis escaped from the religious beliefs and Old World values of their parents into a new modern and modernist America. Partisan politics in the 1930s was both abstract and material and rather impersonal. Religion, which Marx had called the "opium of the people," was seen by many as a hindrance to rather than a resource for radical change.

There were influential critics, like Niebuhr and Mumford, who challenged liberals and radicals alike for their rationalism and naive views of human nature. Niebuhr, who would be an important influence on the young Martin Luther King, emphasized the importance that sin and evil continued to play in human civilization even in the modern epoch. Like Mumford, he criticized those liberals who were slow to see the seriousness of the Fascist danger with its conscious manipulation of emotion and spirituality. Both Niebuhr and Mumford saw the ways in which a new aggressive collective identity could serve as a surrogate for the religious experience that remained a central aspect of modern life. They argued that education and pragmatic reformism were not enough to achieve justice; it was also necessary to exercise a kind of moral persuasion and moral example. In short, politics had to be personal and spiritual. But even the critics tended to be swept along in the struggle—first against unemployment and then against fascism. Day was one of the few intellectuals who acted on her moral beliefs to oppose the war.

One effect of the marginalization of religion from liberal politics was to leave the field open to the more fundamentalist and anti-intellectual streams in American religion. In the postwar era, while the "moral majority" was creating itself among an uprooted and alienated citizenry, morality itself largely disappeared from mainstream American politics. Politics became the realm of the expert adviser and the professional politician, either the old war hero or the brash young liberal. The men in the gray flannel suits, with their opinion surveys and their television advertisements, separated politics from the people, as they transformed politics into tactics and manipulation. There were exceptions, of course, the good hardworking politicians who took personal responsibility for their actions and tried to stay in tune with the shifting tenor of popular consciousness. But after Harry Truman turned defeat into victory on that magical day in 1948, the good guys tended to be losers, epitomized by Adlai Stevenson's hopeless presidential campaigns of 1952 and 1956. At least a few disenchanted intellectuals, however, in the margins of American political life, were reinventing the moral tradition and preparing the way for the rebirth of participatory politics in the 1960s.

Restoring Democracy

American politics changed dramatically after the Second World War. If resolving the economic depression required the active participation of the federal government and a change of attitude on the part of the average citizen about the proper role of the state, fighting a war on two fronts expanded the dimensions of these changes. Winning the war had required a great national effort, an effort in which individual priorities had to be subordinated to the collective. This meant that capital and labor, which previously had been at war with each other, agreed not to disrupt the war effort. Unions agreed not to strike, workers agreed not to demand wage increases, and the corporations agreed to turn some of their industrial capacity into the production of military goods, for a profit, of course.

In the 1930s, the labor question had defined much of American politics, at least for many intellectuals. But the class struggle was postponed for the duration of the war. To the surprise and eventually frustration of many intellectuals, it never really got going again. Instead, due to a number of different factors, American politics had lost its defining domestic tension. American Communists, in the aftermath of the Hitler-Stalin pact and the partitioning of Europe, were excluded from the labor movement, while the American Communist party showed both inconsistency and dogmatism in the face of the coming cold war. At the same time, the American Socialist party, whose prospects should have improved with the growing power of the labor movement, failed to attract more than 140,000 votes in the 1948 election, when they had expected to draw over a million. The dream of the golden mountain that had inspired so many leftward-leaning intellectuals in the 1930s came to a definitive end with the defeat of Henry Wallace's third-party campaign the same year. Afterward, what was left was the working out of major compromises between capital and labor in a series of postwar agreements. With the passing of the Taft-Hartley Act of 1947, the power of the labor movement was greatly curbed. By the early 1950s, the labor movement was one of the pillars on which a newly constituted Democratic party rested. Coupled with the ideological softening of the Republicans, American politics was firmly in the hands of the two large mass—and ideologically converging—parties.

Winning the war also marked the emergence of America as a superpower, giving international issues a new significance in American politics. Not only was the economy growing more and more integrated with the rest of the world but the status of responsible victor gave new impetus to the development of a more internationalist outlook among politicians. The Marshall Plan reinvigorated war-damaged Europe, by funneling millions of dollars of aid, while the American occupation fostered the reconstruction of Japanese capitalism. American participation in the newly founded United Nations and the location of its headquarters in New York was another symbolic expression of the new internationalism in American politics. After entering the war to prevent the spread of fascism, America took on the task of stopping Communist expansion and making the world safe for democracy. It was on the domestic political scene, however, that the changes brought about by the end of the war were most apparent.

The decline in importance of the conflict between capital and labor as the defining factor in domestic politics helped to encourage the perspective that political action was motivated by individual choices and the economic interests of loosely related groups, as we discussed earlier. This belief was underscored by the vast demographic, as well as economic, changes that had occurred since the early 1930s. Much of the old politics had been based on coalitions that no longer existed with the same strength. The war had indeed revitalized the heavy industries of the Northeast and Midwest, but this proved to be short-lived. The war had also encouraged the development of new technologies and the formation of new industries in other parts of the country, most particularly in the Southwest. Workers in these new industries, whether they were newly arrived from other parts of the country or locals, lacked the same political traditions and loyalties that defined the older industrial communities. Many were individuals cut loose from older ties, in search of new identities, social as well as political. Postwar prosperity encouraged social and physical mobility. The more clearly class-based communities that characterized America in the 1930s disintegrated as the mass society took shape.

By the mid-1950s, the new prosperity was being heralded as the defining characteristic of American political culture, just as "hard times" had been in the 1930s. It was now loosely formed interest groups—as opposed to classes—that were the focal point of political action as well as analysis. Political parties redefined themselves as mass parties, designed to appeal to the widest possible range of voters. Ideology as well as class-rooted orientations were thus played down.

While all seemed to agree that things had changed, not everyone was encouraged. Daniel Bell, whose phrase "the end of ideology" would later put into words what everyone wanted to believe, announced already in 1955 that a "new framework" was necessary to understand American politics in the new postwar prosperity. "Contrary to the somewhat simple notion that prosperity dissolves all social problems, we see that prosperity brings in its wake new social groups, new social strains and new social anxieties. Conventional political analysis, drawn largely from eighteenth- and nineteenth-century American experience, cannot fathom these new social anxieties nor explain their political consequences" (Bell et al. 1955: 4). While mainstream social scientists went on to legitimate this new "industrial society" and its anti-ideological politics, a handful of partisan intellectuals left the ivory towers to reinvent politics.

Saul Alinsky: "In Conflict You're Alive"

Saul Alinsky may have studied sociology at the prestigious University of Chicago, but he was a man of the streets. Although he was a Jew, he spent much of his time with working-class Catholics. He was more at home roaming the Back of the Yards neighborhood around the packinghouses of the big-shouldered city of Chicago than the clean and safe middle-class surroundings in which he grew up. A man of the people, he loved bridging gaps across ethnic and class lines to form a popular front against the Establishment.

Paradoxically, it was academic study that helped him discover his talent for organizing and for bringing together disparate groups. It was a stroke of luck that he landed at the University of Chicago in the midst of one of the great controversies in American social science and one of its profoundest turning points. The 1930s were a time when the fieldwork-oriented case study approach to social reality was being challenged by the more positivistic statistical approach. Had Alinsky entered the field of sociology a few years later, he might never have stayed on. As it was, he landed in the classroom of E. W. Burgess, one of the founders of the Chicago school of human urban ecology, the community-oriented approach to the study of social problems. With Burgess's prodding, the young Alinsky took his sociological interests out of the classroom and into the streets. The city was his laboratory. He did his fieldwork in Chicago's dance halls and with its teenage gangs, before beginning his graduate study with Al Capone. This was heady stuff, and he was good at it.

Alinsky thought of turning his newly discovered skills with people into a career as a criminologist and spent three years at Joliet Prison working on prison reform. But in 1936, he returned to the Chicago streets, working with Clifford Shaw from the University of Chicago at the Institute for Juvenile Research's Chicago Area Project on juvenile delinquency. When it turned out that he was more interested in organizing reform programs than in the academic work of gathering data, Alinsky left Shaw's project to start out on his own. Through the contacts he made during his academic fieldwork, Alinsky was able to put together private support for a community organizing drive in the Back of the Yards neighborhood he had become familiar with. The year was 1938, and his efforts to help the community clean itself up co-incided with an organizing drive among packinghouse workers by the newly constituted Congress of Industrial Organizations (CIO). Alinsky immediately saw to it that the two processes coalesced.

This mutually beneficial coalition with the radical arm of the labor movement was not only important to the eventual success of the Back of the Yards project. Bringing together two different approaches to organizing, one work centered and the other community centered, proved to be a major political innovation with long-term consequences. As a Left-leaning liberal, Alinsky had been wary of Communists, but his chief labor ally turned out to be a card-carrying party member. Despite this, Alinsky was able to elicit the active support of the local Catholic clergy, including one of Chicago's most famous bishops and some of its most important businessmen. This pattern of weaving together ethnic, religious, and class alliances to support a local community was one that Alinsky would develop into an art.

Organizing the Back of the Yards resulted in the formation of a local council that took charge of the problems that emerged in the community, from neighborhood cleanups to delinquency prevention and health care and nutritional instruction for children. It was staffed with local residents, not social work professionals, and aimed at involving the participation of as many people as possible in the problem-solving process. Just as his ideas about the aims of community work rubbed against the academic grain, so did they anger—and alienate—the helping professions. Alinsky believed not only in working locally but, more important, in engaging ordinary people in decision-making processes. If experts were to be involved, it was only in an advisory capacity. This he had learned from his academic work with Shaw and from the local branch of the CIO.

The success of the Back of the Yards Council led to the formation of a private foundation, the Industrial Areas Foundation (IAF), that would allow the model to be tried out in other neighborhoods across the country. Alinsky became a full-time community organizer, a professional radical and one of the first politicians without any ideology other than the desire to return "power to the people." He espoused a new kind of urban populism, guided by an overpowering belief in the virtues of participatory democracy. It was this that permitted him to accept support from like-minded capitalists as well as socialists and Communists.

Alinsky was a shrewd tactician. He believed that power, not reason, was fundamental to social change. With this belief he developed a method of dealing with power that sometimes lacked the niceties of polite society. He delighted in mischief-making, like when he advised student activists in 1972 who planned to picket an address by George Bush, then American representative to the United Nations, to attend the speech dressed as members of the Klu Klux Klan and carry placards reading "The KKK supports Bush." His books *Reveille for Radicals* (1946) and *Rules for Radicals* (1971) were full of practical advice on the disruptive approach to political action. But he was also an intellectual. He reflected on and wrote about the value of the ends toward which his tactics aimed. And he couched even his tactical considerations in a theoretical framework. The tension between these two roles, the organizer and the intellectual, was one that guided—or misguided, according to some critics—his life.

> Morality is largely a rationalization of the point you happen to occupy in the power pattern at a given time. If you're a *Have-Not* you're out *to get*, and your morality is an appeal to a law higher than man-made laws—the noblest ideals of justice and equality. When you become a *Have* then you are out *to keep* and your morality is one of law, order, and the rights of property over other rights.

So wrote Alinsky in the reflective preface to the 1969 edition of *Reveille for Radicals*. As in *Rules for Radicals*, published two years later, he was reflecting on his experiences for a new generation of radicals in the midst of what many thought was a revolutionary period. But in spite of his instrumentalist-sounding approach to morality, he was himself a moralist. He both studied the morals of others, especially his opponents, and believed in their regulation.

Alinsky, the intellectual, was the author of a play and several books, including a biography of the labor leader John L. Lewis, one of his early heroes and a close friend. At the same time, his process-oriented organizing aimed at creating spaces in which individuals could begin to reflect on the conditions that determined their lives. The statement of purpose justifying the necessity of the Back of the Yards organizing drive contained words reminiscent of ones C. Wright Mills would write years later.

> In our modern urban civilization, multitudes of people have been condemned to urban anonymity—to living the kind of life where many of them neither know nor care for their own neighbors. This

course of urban anonymity, of individual divorce from the general social life, is one of eroding destruction to the foundations of democracy. (Quoted in Horwitt 1992: 105)

While to the consternation of some critics (Bell, for example), he never did work out a full-blown theory both to account for and to resolve the problems he identified in industrial America, his books—as well as his actions—were major steps in that direction. Besides being a combination call to action and handbook for would-be radicals, *Reveille for Radicals* contained an argument for revitalizing American democracy through a series of hierarchically connected people's organizations. Similar to the alternative democratic institutional structure later worked out by Arendt and implicit also in Mills's analysis of mass society, Alinsky argued that it was possible to steer complex, modern society through an "orderly revolution" based in local organizations that were interwoven on up to the national level:

> The dynamic character of a People's Organization is such that its members recognize the functional relationships that exist between issues, and between their community and the general social structure. They know that their problems are not peculiar to themselves and that their communities do not comprise little isolated worlds. They realize that their local People's Organization has two major objectives: first, to organize and do what can be done on the local scene, and second, to utilize the organization as a springboard for the development of other People's Organizations throughout the nation. They recognize that only through engaging in a national organizational program can they ever hope to break loose from their shackles and their misery. (1989: 62)

Reveille for Radicals was a best-seller when it was published by the University of Chicago Press in 1946. In the years immediately after the war, Americans were still interested in alternative modes of social development. The political atmosphere had not yet hardened into the cold war freeze, and Alinsky's orderly revolution and third way between free market capitalism and ideological communism could still be discussed. A few years later this had all changed. It became, as Dwight Macdonald wrote in a popular essay, a matter of "choosing sides," not of discussing alternative solutions. Red-baited, but never called before any investigating committees, Alinsky struggled through the early 1950s, under the watchful eye of the FBI. His plans for a nationwide organizing drive in 1950, to involve "between twelve and sixteen million" people including the black communities in Atlanta, Birmingham, and New Orleans, never got off the ground. The big foundations were no longer interested.

After working with Mexican-Americans in Los Angeles throughout the early 1950s, where one of his staff was the young Cesar Chavez, later to gain fame as the leader of the Farm Worker's Union, Alinsky returned to his native ground, Chicago, where he started the first major civil rights effort in modern times in a northern city. Inspired by the bus boycott in Montgomery, Alabama, led by Martin Luther King, Jr., in 1955, Alinsky discussed plans to attack housing segregation in Chicago. It was not until 1961, however, that the project got started in the Woodlawn section of the city. Again, he returned to the local church, Catholic and Protestant this time, and to Chicago businessmen for funding.

The project was to be a major success but one achieved largely by his staff. Alinsky retreated, for the most part, to his new home in Carmel, California, to write and to reflect, to again take on the more traditional role of the intellectual. Nicholas von Hoffman, Alinsky's protégé in Chicago, described the Alinsky-style organizer as a sort of magician:

> It's a very strange thing. You go somewhere, and you know nobody, and you've got to organize it into something that it's never been before. You know, you're not a Democrat or a Republican. You don't have much going for you. You don't have prestige, you don't have muscle, you've got no money to give away. All you have are your wits. You've got your wits, charm, and whatever you can put together. So you had better form a very accurate picture of what's going on, and you had better not bring in too many a priori maps [because] if you do, you're just not going to get anywhere. (Quoted in Horwitt 1992: 397)

Alinsky's organizers had even less than usual going for them in Woodlawn. Their usual strategy, of creating an umbrella organization to unite whatever local groups already existed, failed. And, as whites, they were moving in uncharted waters. They desperately needed—and found—the help of black organizers, with knowledge of the local community and not afraid to use "vigorous democratic action," like hiring local toughs to handle dissidents, including some diehard Communists, at meetings.

The Woodlawn project was moving along only slowly when in May 1961, von Hoffman received a call from New Orleans. The Freedom Rides, one of the most dramatic events of the civil rights movement, had just occurred, and one of the riders was calling to ask if Woodlawn would like to host their first public appearance. The meeting was a huge success and gave the Alinsky project a major lift. Two movements were joined at the end of the meeting. One of the Freedom Riders said, "We have a song to sing. It's called 'We Shall Overcome.' How many of you know it?" Only a few hands went up. 'We shall teach it to you,' one of the Freedom Riders said, and they did" (400).

The Alinsky team realized then that a change of tactics was in order. They were no longer organizing around "specific, immediate, and realizable issues" but guiding a social movement. The identities of northern and southern blacks were beginning to merge, and they could be a catalyst in the process. Reflecting this new awareness, their first move was to organize their own version of the Freedom Rides, by busing local residents to city hall to register to vote. This was further solidified—and symbolized—when in 1962, the organization Alinsky helped to set up, the Temporary Woodlawn Organization (TWO), invited Dr. Ralph Abernathy to give the keynote address at a convention to establish its more permanent status. At least in Chicago, the two movements, the people's organizations that flowed from Alinsky's urban populism with a coalition of labor, church, and business support and the civil rights movement, which eventually drew similar sources of support, moved as one.

The paths of the newly emerging student movement and Alinsky's community organizing crossed as well but not with the same confluence. One early focus of Students for a Democratic Society (SDS) was community organizing. In 1964, some of the leaders of the new organization, Todd Gitlin, Paul Booth, and Tom Hayden, met with Alinsky to share some of his expertise. But the meeting did not go well: Alinsky was quick to see a basic difference in their approaches. From his point of view, SDS suffered from hopelessly romantic illusions concerning the poor and participatory democracy, which differed dramatically from his own more realistic approach. But the SDS leaders had read Alinsky's books and one, Booth, would later become chairman of the Campaign Against Pollution (CAP), one of the organizations that grew out of Alinsky's Chicago training school for organizers. One of the three permanent staff members of this training school was another important figure in the New Left, Staughton Lynd. Others, like Hayden and Gitlin, remained critical, the latter even writing a review of *Rules for Radicals* in which he castigated Alinsky for the lack of an overriding ideology, in much the same fashion as Bell had done in 1946, when *Reveille for Radicals* was first published.

The links between Alinsky and the 1960s were clear and direct, even if they were not always smooth. The form of community organizing that Alinsky invented along with his refusal to be forced into a ready-made ideological package were things the new movements were eager to learn from. Alinsky's wake-up call to radicals, his notion of power to the people, and even his appeal to the founding fathers of American society found receptive ears in the new generation. Alinsky was one of those who helped connect the 1930s action-oriented politics to the new politics of the 1960s. His community organizing and his notion of people's democracy kept alive the critical process throughout the 1950s.

Dorothy Day, the Not-So-Quiet Witness

Dorothy Day was also an organizer and a moralist. She too believed in working locally, among the people. Her people, however, were different from those Alinsky moved among; they were even more disorganized and possessed much fewer resources. And the principles that motivated her were not directly political and most certainly not pragmatic. She followed the higher morality of orthodox Catholicism. Hers was an unusual orthodoxy, however, in that she followed her beliefs with unstinting stubbornness to reach radical political conclusions.

Day was not always a Catholic and not always so consistent in her beliefs, especially not in the eyes of her family and many of the contemporaries of her youth. Her father was a sports writer and an Irish

Protestant very concerned with the probity of his family's behavior, if not always his own. Born in Brooklyn, Day grew up in pleasant, middle-class surroundings in New York and Chicago in the early years of the twentieth century. In 1916, she set out on a career in journalism and ended up taking the only newspaper job she could find, writing for the socialist *Call*, with offices on the Lower East Side of Manhattan. She was to write about the daily activities of young single women in the harsh capitalist city. She was, in other words, to write about herself. Partly to fulfill the requirements of her new job and partly out of her own desires, she took up residence among the immigrant Jews in the neighborhood near where she worked. Even on the meager salary she earned at the *Call*, Day found it fascinating to be on her own and live among her poor but exotic neighbors.

At the newspaper, she met another young reporter by the name of Mike Gold, who was to be very significant in shaping the political consciousness that would come to guide her life. Gold, whose real name was Irving Granich, would become editor of the Communist *Daily Worker* and the main defender of proletarian literature in the 1930s. The son of Russian immigrants and a committed socialist, Gold quickly took the younger Day under his ideological wing. Day sympathized with the plight of her poor neighbors and wrote about them in the *Call*, but she never joined any political organizations. Even when, in 1917, two days after her twentieth birthday, she was arrested with suffragettes demonstrating outside the White House, it was more a sympathetic reporter who went to jail then a dedicated political activist.

Day's political attachments became more explicit when she came in contact with Greenwich Village radicalism. Having lost her job when the *Call* could no longer afford to keep her, she found work at *The Masses*. She became assistant to Floyd Dell, one of its editors, and when he and Max Eastman, the other editor, were out of town, which happened often, Day took over editorial responsibility for the journal. In fact, it was Day who presided over the final issues before *The Masses* folded, in part due to censorship imposed through the postal service, in December 1917. Like Gold, Dell was an important influence on the young Dorothy Day. Dell was a main exponent of the new morality, which chided middle-class mores and extolled sexual freedom. The budding moralist Day was swept along by the new morality, at least at the level of idea and attitude. Just as she had done earlier, Day moved her residence to suit her new job, becoming an active Greenwich Village radical.

In addition to her editorial work, she wrote articles and reviews for *The Masses* and hung around with the Village crowd, becoming a regular at the Hell Hole and a drinking companion to Eugene O'Neill. Her exploits were made famous when Malcolm Cowley recorded in *Exile's Return* (1934) how "the gangsters admired Dorothy Day because she could drink them under the table; but they felt more at home with Eugene O'Neill who listened to their troubles and never criticized" (quoted in Miller 1982: 103). Whatever other impressions Dorothy Day made, she always retained her critical distance, even as active participant—no matter what the activity. This form of notoriety would cause her great embarrassment in later life, and she was forced to tell her own side of the story in her autobiography, *The Long Loneliness*, published in 1952.

Like every other American who lived through it, the depression had a profound effect on Day's life. The sight of the jobless and the bread lines inspired her to change the direction of her work. But it was the birth of her first child in 1927, an event she faithfully chronicled in the pages of the recently revived *New Masses*, that was the source of her conversion to Catholicism. This was but another paradox in a life filled with them. The *New Masses* had been revived under the control of the American Communist party, and Dorothy Day was writing a firsthand account of an event that would lead her down a very different path. Awaiting the birth of her daughter had given Day time to reflect over the course of her life and to decide that she did not want her child to drift along as she had. She resolved to give her daughter firm direction by having her baptized in the Catholic church. In the process, she converted herself.

In 1933, with the help of friends and some financial support from the church, she began publishing the *Catholic Worker*. The first issue came out, with intended symbolism, on May Day and aimed at countering the *Daily Worker*'s influence among working-class Catholics. Day herself retained mixed feelings about Communists, with a capital "C," as many of her former friends, like Mike Gold, were ardent supporters. This was an ambivalence that she, like Saul Alinsky and, later, Martin Luther King, was to retain even during the splits that followed the Moscow trials and the emotional fissures brought about by the cold war. Never an anti-Communist, she was never an active sympathizer. Like the others, she carved out her political positions between the dogmas of the Left and the Right.

Whatever the social standing of the *Catholic Worker*'s reading public—and it grew quite large, the circulation reaching 60,000 by the end of 1934 and 110,000 in 1935—the audience she most directly concerned herself with was not workers but the underclass, what Marx had called the *lumpenproletariat*. The ranks of the unemployed, the homeless, and other rejects of capitalist society swelled enormously during the depression. If any group needed organized help, it was this one. The *lumpen,* however, fell outside the normal boundaries drawn by the labor movement and the political Left in general.

This was not a particularly "Catholic" audience, but the church did have traditions that could be called on, and Day, like Alinsky, could appeal to the idealism that still existed among the nuns and priests, especially those younger and at the lower end of the church hierarchy. The first issue of the *Catholic Worker* was printed in 2,500 copies and distributed by hand. It contained a statement of purpose written by Day's main collaborator, Peter Maurin, which outlined their plan of action. They argued that creative work was necessary to the human soul and that this need could best be fulfilled on agrarian worker cooperatives. Besides feeding the poor and housing the homeless in hospitality houses, the Catholic Worker Movement, as it came to be called, sought to initiate a back to the land green revolution, a form of "utopian Christian communism," where "standards of loving" would take precedence over standards of living.

The Catholic Worker Movement aimed a two-pronged attack at the "inhuman effects of industrialization," as evidenced by the depression. Under Day's guidance, and her constant hunting for financial support, hospitality houses were set up in depressed areas of cities around the country (30 existed at the outbreak of World War II), and worker farms were started. A worker's school was also begun in New York which combined night courses with speakers from local universities and colleges, including the poet Hilaire Belloc and the philosopher Jacques Maritain, who also helped Alinsky in raising funds. This was a sort of radical Catholic answer not only to the Communists but also to the settlement house movement a few decades earlier. In 1935, an "agronomic university" opened in the fields of Staten Island, across the bay from the Lower Manhattan office of the newspaper. All this rested on Day's resourcefulness and dynamic energy. She seemed almost single-handedly bent on restoring the tradition of moral witness to American politics.

Like Alinsky's people's organizations, Dorothy Day's hospitality houses had much in common with the settlement house movement that was central to early progressivism. The hospitality houses and the farms and schools that, along with the newspaper, were the basic institutions of the Catholic movement served as spaces for social mixing as well as intellectual stimulation and personal development. Here, the downtrodden and idealistic members of the middle class could meet. In this respect, the settlement house and the Catholic Worker Movement organizations were similar. They were also similar in creating spaces in which new ideas were introduced and debated. But there were important differences. While encouraging the free flow of debate, the settlement houses tended to serve as training grounds for professional social workers, a place to give voice to youthful idealism or part-time activism, before or alongside a professional career. The Catholic Worker Movement asked more of its volunteers; it expected total commitment and adherence to a sort of utopianism that was foreign to the more reformist settlement house movement.

The *Catholic Worker* was a voice of radical Catholicism at a time when conservatism was on the rise in the church and fighting communism was the primary interest of the mainstream Catholic media. Public curiosity about communism was great in the 1930s, even among Catholics who, like the rest of the public, were interested to hear what the fuss was all about. This was probably one reason for the explosive growth of the newspaper's circulation as well as the flood of volunteers who filled the hospitality houses and their courses. On the pages of the *Catholic Worker* and in the courses and seminars the movement sponsored, sensitive issues were openly discussed and debated. This openness included taking a stand on race relations as well as more directly political issues. During the Scottsboro trial in 1933, when nine black men were charged with rape in Alabama and threatened with execution, the *Catholic Worker* proclaimed that "the poor whites and the poor blacks" were "victims of the industrialists who grind the faces of the poor" (quoted in Miller 1982: 266). And its editorial policy, as well as the movement itself, was outspoken in its criticism of racism and anti-Semitism.

The Catholic Worker Movement was fueled by Dorothy Day's application of the new personalism in religious theology. From the same sources that would inspire Martin Luther King, Jr., Day interpreted personalism more as a call to direct, personal engagement in the injustices of the world than as a doctrine about the relation between man and God. The force of her engagement was a source of great inspiration and attracted a large number of young, primarily Catholic, students to the movement. Like Saul Alinsky's people's organizations, the Catholic Worker Movement offered an alternative to the charity approach of the church and the good works philanthropy of private and public agencies as well as to the professionalism of the social workers. The movement valued personal commitment instead of professional expertise. Needless to say, just as Alinsky's community organizing, the movement drew the critical wrath of the professionals and their or-ganizations. It also had the conservative forces in the church to contend with. As a condition of further funding, the *Catholic Worker* was assigned a spiritual adviser by the church to watch over its own morality.

Against the dominant church position, which supported the Loy-alists, and the radical Left, which supported the Republicans, the *Catholic Worker* remained neutral during the Spanish Civil War, adhering to a vaguely defined pacifism. This turned into an all-out morally grounded pacifism when war broke out in the rest of Europe. In June 1940, Day wrote in the lead article in the *Catholic Worker,*

> For eight years we have been opposing the use of force in the labor movement, in the class struggle, as well as in the struggles between countries. . . . We consider that we have inherited the Beatitude and that our duty is clear. . . . We say again that we are opposed to all but the use of non-violent means to resist. (Quoted in Miller 1982: 331)

This outspoken stance was to have a dramatic effect and immediate consequences. Mike Gold criticized his "old friend Dorothy Day" from the editorial pages of the *Daily Worker* for naively "refusing to hate Nazis." Her absolute pacifism in the face of the Nazi threat also alienated many of the movement's own activists and supporters. The war split the movement in half, and, as Day reflected in the 1950s, during the war 80 percent of the young workers betrayed the movement. This loss of support resulted in the closing of at least half of the hospitality houses and a decline in circulation of the *Catholic Worker* to 50,000.

This loss of interest had apparently nothing to do with the newspaper's quality; the writing and reportage had, if anything, improved, and the readers, though smaller in number, had become more committed. The principal reason for this enthusiasm and for the subsequent rise in circulation after the war was Dorothy Day herself. She wrote a daily diary in the paper, in which she spoke in everyday language about everyday things, as if she were sitting face to face with her readers. This form of "personalism" had great appeal, especially at a time when the world seemed all the more complex.

Behind the personal approach stood a strong and principled pacifism and what can be described as a form of religious anarchism. The Catholic Worker Movement based itself on small, self-sufficient voluntary groups, evolving outward from the center in New York: a sort of concentric circle of liberated zones in the new mass society. It was the newspaper and Day's not-so-silent witness, as expressed through both her active example and her daily column, that held it all together. In terms very similar to those expressed by Saul Alinsky—the two met only once and spent the time discussing anarchism—she wrote, "It is our firm belief that we need to decentralize. . . . We need to be getting into regional groups or communities so that the local community would deal with the problems of that community or that region" (quoted in Miller 1982: 382).

By the 1950s, the wider experiments in agrarian communism and alternative education had largely failed. What remained was the Hospitality House on New York's Lower East Side and the newspaper and Dorothy Day's pacifism. This was enough, however, to provide a strong link to the 1960s. In 1955, in what was the first act of collective civil disobedience of the decade, Day was arrested along with A. J. Muste, Bayard Rustin (who the following year would become adviser to King), and David Dellinger (who as editor of the journal *Liberation* would be an important force in the antiwar movement of the 1960s) for refusing to participate in civil defense drills. This was an event that Bob Dylan would include in his early protest songs. In a similar protest in 1960, Day was interviewed on WBAI in New York, one of the early underground listener-sponsored radio stations that would flourish in the new age of the 1960s. Michael Harrington, future leader of American social democracy and author of *The Other America,* came to New York in the 1950s to work at the Hospitality House, as did Robert Coles, social critic and anti-Vietnam War activist.

Day was directly linked to the new political activism that emerged in the 1960s through her influence on Daniel and Philip Berrigan, brothers and Catholic priests, whose dramatic, direct-action tactics led them underground and eventually to jail. "Without Dorothy," Daniel Berrigan wrote in 1981, on trial again for destroying nuclear warheads in King of Prussia, Pennsylvania, "without that exemplary patience, courage, moral modesty, without this woman pounding at the locked door behind which the powerful mock the powerless with games of triage, without her, the resistance we offered would have been simply unthinkable" (Day 1981: xxiii). The pages of the *Catholic Worker* were open in the 1960s to peace activists like Dellinger, whose enthusiastic reportage on the Cuban revolution did not sit well with the Catholic establishment. Like C. Wright Mills but with an altogether different approach, Day was moved to defend Castro as a person with good intentions. He was, she said, "after all a Catholic." Day visited Cuba in September 1962 and reported on it in her column, "taking the readers with her," as she put it. Such reportage was unusual not only for a Catholic newspaper but for the entire mass media of the period. One month later, the Cuban missile crisis would break out, putting the world on the brink of nuclear war.

Through the space it created outside the mainstream and the possibilities for direct engagement in social activism, the Catholic Worker Movement offered a kind of training ground for many of the political movements that would flower in the 1960s. Through her not-so-quiet witness, Dorothy Day provided a personal example for combating the tendency toward massification in American politics and American society in general. In recalling earlier traditions, she added a moral dimension to politics that would resonate with the new generation of radicals.

The Beloved Community of Martin Luther King, Jr.

Dorothy Day's Catholic Worker Movement made religion practical by drawing a social consciousness out of Catholic traditions, even though the absolutism of her approach did not permit the necessary degree of tactical reasoning necessary to a broader and more all-encompassing social movement. Martin Luther King, Jr.'s personal presence and intellectual articulation did something similar with other religious traditions, helping to realize the political potential in the black church. But King was also a tactician—one of the best—and he succeeded in building a movement that dramatically altered the political culture of America.

Martin Luther King, Jr., was born on January 15, 1929, too young to be shaped by the political turmoil of the 1930s—although he would recall the bread lines in Atlanta, where two-thirds of the black male population was unemployed, as a source of his later criticism of capitalism—and too young even to be greatly affected by the Second World War. The major effect of the war on King was that a lack of students due to the war caused Morehouse College to lower its age requirements enough to admit him as a fifteen-year-old freshman in 1944. As a southern black, he would have experienced the 1930s differently, in any case, from the other persons we have discussed, even from James Baldwin, who was born just four years earlier but who grew up in Harlem under very different conditions. Yet King was a child of the 1930s in one very important sense: his vision of America as an integrated society was rooted in a notion of community that combined many of the moral and political ideas articulated in that period. Like Dorothy Day, King transformed an essentially religious notion of community into a source of social criticism and a force for social change. In this respect, he mixed together aspects of the pragmatic and the spiritual traditions in American politics that would prove potent not only in mobilizing the civil rights movement but also in transforming an entire society's ways of thinking about itself.

King was raised with all the comforts of the southern black bourgeoisie: a large home with an extended family in a well-to-do neighborhood, concerts and music lessons, education at a preparatory school, the University of Atlanta Laboratory School, with the early assurance of both a college education and a future career. He was only nineteen when he graduated from Morehouse College and left Atlanta. He set off in 1948 to attend the predominantly white Crozer Theological Seminary in Chester, Pennsylvania, outside Philadelphia, knowing he could return to the pulpit of his father's church any time he wished. The secure and insular environment in which he grew up distinguished him not only from someone like the young James Baldwin but probably from the majority of his contemporaries, black or white.

Crozer Theological Seminary broke this insularity by expanding his horizons in both a social and an intellectual sense. Socially, he was exposed to an unorthodox education in a racially mixed school: of the thirty-one students who entered with King in 1948, one-third were black and several others came from foreign countries. For a young man raised in the strict confines of the Atlanta black bourgeoisie and in the principles of the Baptist church, where dancing was seen as a sign of decadent modernism, this was an eye-opener. He was learning "the ways of white folks" in a rather unusual but still protected setting. Intellectually, King was exposed to the liberal tenets of the social gospel and the new theology. Besides the specifics of these doctrines, what he learned was a different perspective on religion, a scholarly, historical, and even skeptical approach to theological questions, which later would help make it easier for him to apply practical and tactical reasoning in his preaching and give him a way of dealing with the dominant white culture that would prove indispensable.

It was a combination of an emotionally based Christian faith, rooted in the black church, and the more intellectual approach to religion he learned in the northern schools that permitted King to lead the transformation of the black church into perhaps the most potent political force of the postwar era. King believed not only in the American dream of an integrated society in which "all men are created equal" but also in the personal God of the black church, a God capable of intervening in the world to ensure that justice prevailed. This was a belief he could draw on again and again, to move himself as well as the masses of others.

Without such faith, the civil rights movement could not have been the powerful force it was. According to James Cone, the political potential of the black religious culture was already present in the theological tradition that interpreted Christian ideas and symbols as having worldly significance. What King did was to give the black ministry the courage to draw on this tradition, to make it conscious and active. What he learned through his formal schooling in the North was the possibility to use this effectively, to combine the power of faith with practical and tactical reasoning.

The combination of faith and intellect was also the basis for King's adherence to nonviolence. As opposed to others in the SCLC leadership who saw nonviolence as a tactical weapon, necessary to a small minority fighting a much more powerful majority, King came to believe in nonviolence as a moral principle, an end in itself.

At the same time, however, he was capable of viewing nonviolence through the skeptical eyes of the intellectual, as a more or less successful technique in a wider strategic operation. This combination separated King from Dorothy Day, who in many ways drew strength from similar sources. Day's absolute pacifism gave her great personal strength and drew others to her as did King's belief in nonviolence, but Day's absolutism allowed little space for tactical or strategic thinking. In spite of its name, the Catholic Worker Movement was never a social movement in the sense that the civil rights movement was. In fact, this was one of the reasons that drew many of Day's volunteers, in search of a more political outlet for their idealism, into the civil rights movement when it emerged in the late 1950s.

King graduated from Crozer in 1951 and decided against returning to Atlanta and the church and to continue his theological studies. He went on to Boston University, where he began graduate education in the fall of 1951, completing his Ph.D. in 1955, the same year Day was arrested for protesting the air raid drills in New York. By the time he completed his doctorate, King had already decided against a career as a scholar and returned South to become pastor of the Dexter Avenue Baptist Church in Montgomery, Alabama. He could easily have chosen an academic life. After all, he was described by his thesis adviser as "one of the best five or six graduate students he had taught in his thirty-one years at Boston University" (quoted in Cone 1991: 33).

King had several opportunities, but he chose Dexter Avenue primarily because of its educated middle-class membership and because it was far enough away from his father to offer a sense of independence. Even though he had chosen to return to his roots, King wanted to maintain sufficient intellectual as well as familial distance. Martin Luther King had by now learned to move in several worlds, black and white, religious and scholarly, and was starting to become a master at combining or recombining them. Dexter Avenue's parishioners were primarily college graduates and employees of the local black establishment. In their company, he reasoned, it would be easier to mediate these worlds. He began immediately the process of raising both the degree of its education and, more important, its politicization. He set up a social and political action committee, as well as a cultural committee, and preached the social gospel he had learned. He justified its necessity in his statement to the church board in the following way:

> Since the gospel of Jesus is a social gospel as well as a personal gospel seeking to save the whole of man, a Social and Political Action Committee shall be established for the purpose of keeping the congregation intelligently informed concerning the social, political and economic situation. (34)

King may have drawn on a social consciousness potentially present in the black church, but he expanded and reformulated it. His main enemies in this process of reformulation were what he saw as middle-class complacency and the otherworldly views of many blacks. To the former, he addressed his harshest words, attacking privileged blacks for "devoting themselves to the pursuit of liquor and luxury" and daring them to make alliances with their less fortunate brothers (Branch 1988: 207). To the latter, he used biblical references in attempting to turn their eyes from the world beyond to the glories of this world.

If he chose the relatively well-to-do congregation at Dexter Avenue because it would allow him to develop both himself and his beloved community, the congregation chose him because he could move comfortably in both black and white worlds. It was essentially this recognized ability and his own confidence in it that thrust him into a leadership role when the bus boycott began in Montgomery, just one year after his arrival. The success of the Montgomery boycott transformed King from a sophisticated minister in a middle-class southern black church into a partisan intellectual. Instead of simply addressing his congregation, King was now speaking to the entire southern black community. And due to the interest from the national mass media, he soon spoke to America as a whole. At the same time, the importance of this new role as spokesman and witness forced him into a more reflective mode concerning not only his role as leader of a movement but, perhaps even more important, the meaning of his own life.

The boycott's success and the coverage received in the mass media made King into a celebrity, and he was flooded with invitations to speak and to make public appearances of all kinds. While he might have hoped that the power of his speech could induce a mass conversion, he learned through the experience of the boycott that something more material, like power and organization, was required. He thus spent time reflecting on the strategy and tactics of moving people. It was in this context that he reencountered Gandhi.

> At the beginning of the protest the people called on me to serve as their spokesman. In accepting this responsibility my mind, consciously or unconsciously, was driven back to the Sermon on the Mount and the Gandhian method of nonviolent resistance. This principle became the guiding light of our movement. Christ furnished the spirit and motivation while Gandhi furnished the method. . . . The experience in Montgomery did more to clarify my thinking on the question of nonviolence than all the books that I had read. . . . Living through the actual experience of protest, nonviolence became more a method to which I gave intellectual assent; it became a commitment to a way of life. Many issues I had not cleared up intellectually concerning nonviolence were now solved in the sphere of political action. (King 1986: 38)

King had first encountered Gandhi through reading Niebuhr while a student at Crozer. Niebuhr's book, *Moral Man and Immoral Society* (1932), was already nearly twenty years old when King read it in 1950. By that time the shock waves the book had caused in the intellectual world had more or less been covered over by the horrible events of the war, but for the young Martin Luther King, Jr., reading it for the first time it retained its powerful effect. What affected King more than the criticism of liberal theology Niebuhr offered was his focus on morality and what he called "the overridding tragedy" of the age: "modern man's loss of confidence in moral forces." Niebuhr's understanding of morality as a form of justice that combined "love and politics, spiritualism and realism" (Branch 1988: 84), was just what King was searching for. This interpretation of morality—and of justice—would fit well with traditions in black theology he was already familiar with.

It was in this context that Niebuhr presented a discussion of Gandhi. For Niebuhr, Gandhi was an example of someone who managed to synthesize moral and rational factors into a powerful political force. Gandhi, in other words, mediated between the religious and the secular in a way that could easily be transferred to the American Negro. In fact, Niebuhr made the transference himself, offering examples of how Gandhi's teachings could be adopted in the Negro struggle for justice in America, concluding that "there is no problem of political life to which religious imagination can make a larger contribution" (quoted in Branch 1988: 86).

What the *black* religious imagination offered King was a notion of love that was rooted in a sense of community, the beloved community, which included all of mankind. Niebuhr's criticism of liberalism, based on a realistic approach to human evil, and Gandhi's example presented King with a way of transforming love into a moral force, through nonviolent direct action. Reflecting on his trip "to the land of Gandhi" in 1956, King wrote, "True nonviolent resistance is not unrealistic submission to evil power. It is rather a courageous confrontation of evil by the power of love. . . . Nonviolent resistance does call for love, but it is not a sentimental love. It is a very stern love that would organize itself into collective action to right a wrong by taking on itself suffering" (1986: 26).

King was able, as are most American blacks, to speak two languages to two audiences. Where he was unique as well as greatly gifted was not only in the skills he displayed with each but also in the way he could combine them. To whites, he spoke in the language of Protestant liberalism, appealing to their Christian morality and the ideals of the American society. His renowned "Letter from Birmingham City Jail" (1963), for example, was addressed to white ministers, "My dear Fellow

Clergymen," in the belief that as fellow Christians they would support the aims of the civil rights movement for equality and justice, since they shared a common Christian history. Justifying his presence in Birmingham away from his flock, he wrote,

> I am in Birmingham because injustice is here. Just as the eighth century prophets left their little villages and carried their 'thus saith the Lord' far beyond the boundaries of their hometowns; and just as the Apostle Paul left his little village of Tarsus and carried the gospel of Jesus Christ to practically every hamlet and city of the Greco-Roman world, I too am compelled to carry the gospel of freedom beyond my particular hometown. Like Paul, I must constantly respond to the Macedonian call for aid. (1986: 290)

His mass media speeches drew on symbols and myths recognizable to most whites. He spoke to the black community in another language, however, the language of the black church, shaped by the experience of living as an oppressed minority in a hostile society. This was the language of the interventionist God, the language of truth and justice, and by the very nature of its being formed in conditions of oppression, the language of social and political action. At the end of the Selma march in 1965, on the steps of the state capitol building in Montgomery, King spoke these powerful words:

> I know you are asking today, "How long will it take?" I come to say to you this afternoon, however difficult the moment, however frustrating the hour, it will not be long, because truth pressed to earth will rise again.
> How long? Not long, because no lie can live forever.
> How long? Not long, because you still reap what you sow.
> How long? Not long, because the arm of the moral universe is long but it bends toward justice.
> How long? Not long, 'cause mine eyes have seen the glory of the coming of the Lord, trampling out the vintage where the grapes of wrath are stored. He has loosed the fateful lightning of his terrible swift sword. His truth is marching on. (1986: 230)

King was forced to invent a new vocabulary when he confronted the dire conditions and absolute devastation he met when the civil rights movement moved into the ghettos of the northern cities. The liberal social gospel of the black church did not fit the conditions of despair and devastation he met. In addition, those who had experienced such conditions were not prepared to interpret their reality through its precepts. Cone argues that when confronted with this new reality, the positions of Martin Luther King, the great believer in the American dream of an integrated society and in the tactics of nonviolence, and Malcolm X, the black nationalist and advocate of "by any means necessary," began to converge. The shots that killed them make it impossible to say. It is clear, however, that King's analysis of the causes of black oppression and the possibilities of whites to change took a new turn in the late 1960s.

As we noted earlier, black culture provided an alternative space to the new mass society, by the very force of its exclusion. Black Americans did participate to some extent, it is true, in the sense that a number of blacks did experience an increase in their standards of living. But the trickle-down effects of the new prosperity, which allowed many workers to move from city to suburb, from apartment living to home ownership, and which so troubled those whose intellectual frameworks were formed in the 1930s, did not reach black Americans to anywhere near the degree it did white Americans.

Black religion was one of the prime resources of a culture formed or, depending on one's point of view, misformed in this context of always being last or left out, of always being trickled down to. Black religion was the religion of hope and justice as much as the religion of escape, and the black church was its central retainer. King drew on both in the 1950s. With the impetus provided by the budding civil rights movement and his own role in it, he helped to transform this religion of hope and justice into an extremely powerful political force.

The notion of the beloved community, a phrase taken from black religion, in which all of mankind formed one community in the eyes of God and which summarized the utopian aims of the civil rights movement, became also a direct source of inspiration for whites, especially white students in the 1960s. The Freedom Summer campaign initiated by SNCC in 1963 drew a young graduate student from the University of California at Berkeley by the name of Mario Savio to Mississippi and into political action, leading the free speech movement when he returned to the University of California that fall. Tom Hayden, one of the founders of SDS, went to Alabama. Mary King and Casey Hayden, who were central actors in the early stirring of the women's movement, were both products of SNCC and the civil rights movement. And, of course, the influence of King's rhetoric and moral presence only grew, as he took the civil rights movement to the north—in 1963 in the March on Washington and then into the urban ghettos.

· · ·

Saul Alinsky, Dorothy Day, and Martin Luther King, Jr., three very different people drawing on different traditions, all planted important seeds of the 1960s. They each were important to the reconstitution of politics in America in the postwar period; they brought the people—all the people—back into politics. In their lives and in their writings and speeches, politics was made personal and moral in an age when the main drift was in quite a different direction. In a wider sense, they were each part of a small group of partisan intellectuals who built bridges through the 1950s between generations of American radicals.

7

CONCLUSION

Taking Sides in the Fifties

· ·

We have described the efforts of fifteen individuals to challenge the dominant ideas of their times. They were radical witnesses to the consolidation of the scientific-technological state, critics of the wasteland that took shape in postwar American society. While most of their contemporaries celebrated what Henry Luce of *Time* magazine called the American century, they were dissidents, who tried to keep alive radical ideas, traditions, and intellectual practices. For all their differences, and there were many, they shared a commitment to the right to have different opinions at a time when conformity, allegiance, and loyalty reigned supreme.

As Americans were being actively brought in line in the battle for global supremacy, these people broke ranks. They were partisan intellectuals, who identified new problems and developed new conceptual understandings but, most important, struggled for that special kind of intellectual freedom that is so necessary if democracies are to survive. In their actions and in their ideas, that is, in both theory and practice, they sought to redefine the role of the intellectual in postwar America. Doggedly individualistic, they nonetheless shared a collective commitment to the preservation of public spaces for reflection, criticism, and thought itself.

To be partisan is to adopt a particular kind of stance toward reality; it is to be engaged in what happens around you and to take sides. In the 1950s, partisanship for most Americans took the form of a patriotic national chauvinism, a taking of sides for the United States in the cold, sometimes hot, war with Soviet communism. Partisanship, which earlier had been concrete, specific, and highly personal, became abstract, ideological, and ever so distant; for many intellectuals, partisanship became the rather distasteful option of choosing the lesser of two evils. That kind of partisanship bred alienation, deviance, and escape for many of the disenchanted young people who grew up in the suburbs and urban ghettos of postwar America. While it provided jobs and prosperity for those who could take its aggressive message to heart, it fostered hopelessness and despair among those who could only see the visible signs of its curious progress: the arms race, environmental deterioration, and the vulgarity of mass culture.

Making partisanship personal and potentially meaningful once again is what united the people discussed in this book. What made them special and worthy of remembrance is that they consciously sought to preserve their autonomy and freedom of expression even while they took political stands and spoke out on the issues of their day. They refused to accept the main drift of the times. But their partisanship was of a new type. Their commitment was not to any one idea or ideology, or even to a political party or party program. It was Martin Luther King, Jr., among them who became a political leader, but even in his case, the leadership was exercised more through moral example and eloquence than through any will to power.

These radical witnesses were rather partisans of critical process, seeing their task, indeed, the main task of intellectuals, not to formulate truths but to help others to share in the collective construction of truth. Their ambition was to catalyze dialogic understanding in the general public; in the words of Mary Catherine Bateson, her mother, Margaret Mead, "created a kind of multilogue to which individuals contributed who would otherwise have been in isolation." Encouraging such multilogical cognition, a kind of generalized intersubjectivity, was, for most of our subjects, the main aim of their intellectual work. Theirs was a commitment to arguing in public, to opening up and keeping open spaces for what has been called "critical discourse." Such spaces seemed to be threatened in the mass society of the 1950s, and their preservation had to be fought for. These people exemplified the will to resist.

The people in this book drew on traditions of partisanship from earlier periods, without reducing their own commitment to movements that had become historically passé. They drew on history, while insisting on retaining their own personal and creative relation to it. They were never dogmatists. Even in the 1930s, when so many of their contemporaries joined Communist or socialist parties and followed what was then the dominant fashion, the involvement of our subjects in the movements of the time had been different. Even then, they had sought to uphold their personal integrity, keeping a kind of critical distance from the enthusiasms of many of their fellow intellectuals. There is a fine line between sectarian dogmatism and idealistic partisanship, a line that is all too easy to cross over. C. Wright Mills in his praise of Castro's revolution in Cuba and Herbert Marcuse's support for the Black Panther party can perhaps be considered transgressions. But even then, the ideological commitment was temporary and qualified, born more from overexuberance and desperation than from anything else. The struggle for personal autonomy and the commitment to critical process remained central in both cases, as it did for all of the other people in these pages.

That commitment was usually displayed in public, either in direct encounters with students or citizen groups or through the more surrogate public of the mass media. Academic colleagues were of little concern to the people in this book unless they were to be recruited to one or another cause—whether the disarmament campaigns of Leo Szilard, the social activism of Dorothy Day, the educational reforming of Margaret Mead, or the socialist humanism of Erich Fromm. Indeed, fellow scientists and other intellectuals were most often seen as the main targets of criticism, their subservience, accommodation, and disinterested professionalism the subject of some of the most vehement attacks. It was the very disavowal of commitment and engagement—and of intellectual passion itself—on the part of so many postwar thinkers that most seemed to irritate our partisan intellectuals. The people Mills called NATO intellectuals had sold out; they had, for all intents and purposes, sold their souls to the devil and that was why it was so important for some intellectuals to stay honest. And while Mills and the others often displayed their independence in extreme and eccentric ways, it was nonetheless necessary to show it, even show it off, at a time when intellectual dependence had become hegemonic.

This shared attitude of dissent in relation to their academic colleagues did not make the people in this book very popular in intellectual circles. Although some of them managed to carve out niches for themselves and their ideas within academic settings, most of them spent most of their time communicating directly with nonacademic popular audiences. They were, in that sense, public intellectuals—but not always popular in their mode of presentation. No one can say that Marcuse and Arendt are easy to read, but the amazing thing was that their books were read—and not, for the most part, by fellow academics. In contrast, Fromm and Carson, Baldwin and Mead, and perhaps especially Mary McCarthy were readable and accessible to a mass audience, at the same time that their books were not the usual popular fare; they put demands on their readers and, in the best sense of the word, provided enlightenment. They used the opportunities afforded by the mass media—the large circulation magazines, the pocket books, and even television—to inform, educate, and activate the public mind.

While some of them stepped outside of the rat race that the cities had become and made their own liberated spaces in the countryside, most of them conducted their intellectual work in traditional urban settings. What set them apart, however, was their refusal to accommodate to the institutional imperatives of the multiversity and the mass circulation magazine. Some of them created new institutions, like Fairfield Osborn whose Conservation Foundation sponsored some of the key research behind the environmental awakening of the 1960s and, of course, Martin Luther King, Jr., whose Southern Christian Leadership Conference brought the moral tradition of the black church into the struggle for civil rights. Others, like Margaret Mead and Leo Szilard, carved out spaces for interdisciplinary critical work within universities, organizing forums for debate as well as for innovative research and education. Others—Lewis Mumford, Erich Fromm, Hannah Arendt—kept their independence and critical distance, while teaching at universities as a sideline to their main activity, writing. Still others, like Allen Ginsberg and Saul Alinsky, worked more informally, creating underground networks of communication that would blossom in the 1960s into alternative communities and community organizations, the liberated zones of the counterculture and the New Left.

All of the people in this book were successful in what they did; but they were neither heroic nor tragic figures. They were able to move between the established and the not yet established. In the ways they lived their lives, they prefigured an alternative society while remaining passionately involved in their own times. They were utopian realists, in the sense that they all envisioned something beyond or outside the wasteland, while firmly realizing and living within the bounds and limitations of their society. While they sometimes sought escape, they never dropped out. They channeled their spiritual energy, which in other eras most likely would have taken more philanthropic or idealist expression, into shaping the real utopias of an alternative practice: in their writings and sometimes in their activities as well, they brought to life a not-yet-existent reality. But even for Dorothy Day and Martin Luther King, the most religiously committed of the group, their utopianism was tempered; it was focused on addressing the real problems of the age and on providing realistic alternatives.

They were realists but not opportunists. Their ideas were not for sale, although they certainly did not mind making a living—and for some of them, a comfortable one at that—on the basis of their intellectual work. The important point, however, is that money was never the prime consideration for reaching out to wider audiences. Mead's and Ginsberg's wealth was spent on friends and good causes, while Fromm, Baldwin, and Carson used their fortunes to gain some private space for critical reflection. Baldwin, the black homosexual, was perhaps the one who needed to escape the most; but even he continually returned from his self-imposed exiles to take on the struggle once again. He could live in France, he once said, but only work in America. It was only in America that he could act as a partisan intellectual.

In an increasingly commercialized environment, the people in this book tried to keep intellectual options open. They made use of the opportunities offered by mass circulation magazines to explore new themes and to raise the standards of popular culture. Indeed, in their hands, popular culture was turned on its head, as Baldwin's powerful prose met head-on the pinup pictures in *Playboy,* and Mead's columns on cultural patterns followed the makeup advice and recipes in *Redbook.* The less commercial magazines also benefited from the contributions of our public intellectuals; Mumford and Carson wrote of the destruction of the landscape in the *New Yorker,* and Arendt and Fromm contributed to *Commentary,* and almost all wrote, at one time, in Irving Howe's *Dissent.*

Even more important than the individual articles was the role being articulated, the dissenting voice of the partisan intellectual. It was, in most of the cases taken up here, a double-sided role that was being constructed. On the one hand, it was future oriented, pointing to ways out of the current situation, identifying new problems and providing new kinds of intellectual tools for their solution. On the other hand, it was rooted in the past, in previous generations of intellectuals, who had constructed the ideals of commitment and engagement that the partisan intellectuals of the 1950s reinterpreted and, in a very real sense, reinvented. While planting seeds of the sixties, they themselves were harvesting the fruits of intellectual activity of previous decades.

The Roots of Partisanship

The kind of commitment that characterized the lives of our subjects built on many sources, but for most of them, two precursors were especially significant: the resistance intellectuals of Europe who fought against fascism and Nazism, and the pragmatic populist intellectuals of the New Deal era in America. Both were themselves the products of history, but they had added, each in their own way, an important new dimension to the self-conception of the intellectual, an egalitarian or democratic ethos. Previously, throughout history, in both Europe and America, intellectuals had been a conscious or unconscious elite: their ideals had been derived from class societies, and their roles in society had been stratified. In Europe, they had emerged as part of the bourgeoisie, and their struggle for intellectual freedom had accompanied the capitalist's struggle for economic freedom. The idea of the intellectual had, at least until the First World War, been a privileged one: the intellectual was supported by the privileged classes, and the work of the intellect was itself a source of privilege. In America, the situation was somewhat different, but even there intellectuals had tried to create special conditions for themselves, as priests, scientists, or men of letters.

In this respect, the 1930s were a time when new kinds of intellectuals came to the fore. There were, of course, many factors at work
far too familiar to be discussed in any detail here. Suffice it to say that
the economic collapse made it seem to many that capitalism had
outlived its usefulness, and ideas that had given inspiration and hope
for a better world suddenly seemed inadequate and insufficient. The
depression marked the end of a certain vision of progress in America,
while the rise of fascism and Nazism marked the end of reason and
reasonability in Europe. Those who resisted fascism could no longer
take the genteel rationality of Western civilization for granted; they
needed to construct a new, more militant and collective vision of
intellectual activity to carry on their struggle. And in that vision, the
"masses," whom many intellectuals had previously looked down on as
the great scourge of civilized values, were central actors. They had to
become historical subjects if subjectivity itself was to survive the
barbarian onslaught of fascism. From being the enemies of reason, the
masses needed to become its new carriers. And the partisan intellectual
was called on to educate the desires of the masses.

In America, a different kind of partisanship grew out of the New
Deal reform program. Many intellectuals—from Lewis Mumford to
Rachel Carson, from Dorothy Day to Saul Alinsky—took part in those
efforts, which served to revive an earlier tradition of progressive social
reform that had all but disappeared in the course of the 1920s. For
academics, the political movements of the times fostered the combination of Marxism with the reform-oriented American pragmatism of
John Dewey. These two traditions were creatively synthesized in the
writings of street socialists like Sidney Hook, who, in their social
climbing from the immigrant ghettos to the university, carried with
them their radical political heritage. Hook and many other children of
working-class immigrants moved between the academy and the
street, facilitated by the labor movement that was so influential in the
1930s, especially in New York. Hook, like the literary critic Edmund
Wilson and the theologian Reinhold Niebuhr, combined intellectual
contexts that had previously been separate. Perhaps more than anything else, the 1930s were a time when boundaries were broken down
and new kinds of hybrid or synthetic intellectual identities were being
formed.

These pragmatic populists were very different from the European partisans who came to America, but they shared a commitment to social change and improvement that, each in their own way, redefined enlightenment in the context of the twentieth century. With the end of the Second World War and the coming of the postwar era of prosperity, those experiences tended to fade into the past and be forgotten. The nightmare of the 1930s grew dim as the consumerist daydreams of the postwar era took hold on ever more Americans, intellectuals included.

For a certain handful of intellectuals, however, the lessons of the 1930s remained central, formative experiences that served to define their lives, or at least their lives as intellectuals. Arendt, Fromm, Marcuse, and Szilard brought the ideal of enlightened partisanship with them from Europe to America. They had been forced to take sides, forced to break up promising careers in their thirties to start up new lives overseas. Their idea of the intellectual was, as if by necessity, engaged and involved and would stay that way even in America.

For the others, the relations to the 1930s differed, primarily depending on age, but in all cases, there was at least some contact with the idea of partisanship that was so central to the movements of the times. For the older generation, the 1930s represented a turning point, a period of transformation. Mead, Day, Alinsky, Mumford, and Osborn all took part in the 1930s reform efforts—Mead and Mumford through their writings, and Osborn, Alinsky, and Day through changing their lives, the one leaving banking to become a full-time conservationist, the other leaving the university, the third converting to Catholicism. While Mead and Mumford helped to shape the intellectual ethos of the 1930s by defining the issues and providing some of the conceptual frameworks, Osborn, Alinsky, and Day were inspired to give their lives new kinds of meaning and take on new intellectual identities.

Mills, Carson, and McCarthy were students in the 1930s, brought into contact with pragmatic populism through friends or teachers. Each of them would try to re-create, in their writings and in their lives, something of what they thought they had missed out on, while Ginsberg was marked for life by his parents' involvement in the socialist battles of the 1930s. For Baldwin and King, the formative environment was the black church, a source of cultural strength and identity in the

1930s as it would be for both men—in very different ways—in the civil rights movement.

In the 1930s it was important for intellectuals to be engaged in their times, to take sides. With the coming of the Second World War, however, circumstances changed, and it became natural for just about everyone to put differences aside and unite to defeat the external enemy. Only Dorothy Day, as a pacifist, separated the struggle against fascism from the patriotic pathos of the American war effort. Even Leo Szilard managed to obey military instructions to help build the atomic bomb. But perhaps because they were more stubborn, more independent, or simply more committed to the idea of autonomy, the people in this book could never renounce the partisan ideals of the 1930s.

Contextual Tensions

Whether they had actually lived them or only heard about them secondhand, the experiences of the 1930s remained important for all of our subjects. In a very real sense, their lives can be seen as various attempts to resolve the tensions between the partisan ideals that had been fostered in the 1930s and the vastly different contexts for intellectual activity that came to characterize the postwar era.

Every generation of intellectuals faces the task of reinventing itself and redefining its place in society. The intellectual is an emergent category, growing out of past traditions and deep structures in confrontation with changing contextual circumstances. The contemporary context is the starting point for each intellectual generation to go about reinventing itself; but while a generation shares a common historical experience, within each generation, different ideals and traditions are at work. And they are compounded by the different individual experiences as well as by the variegated locations of each intellectual-to-be in the surrounding society. What we refer to as contextual tensions are the types of dissonance between inherited ways of being and new political and institutional environments. The intellectual is formed through the resolution of these tensions, in the process of existentially choosing various strategies for reinterpreting and reinventing traditions. Traditions, we might say, are the raw material out of which intellectual lives are carved.

For the people in this book, the tradition of the partisan intellectual needed to be refitted into the very different circumstances that emerged out of World War II. As we have discussed, American intellectuals were confronted with a new regime after the war: the scientific-technological state with its newfangled experts and its cult of science imposing itself on the homogenized mass society. The new technologies of communication and production were central components of this new regime, making possible but also exacerbating the atomization of people and the destruction of the natural environment. The sources of social conflict, which had provided the basis for the construction of new intellectual roles in the 1930s, had been ameliorated, and in the process the labor unions, the leftist parties and sects, and the small critical journals had all but disappeared. At the same time, the new regime opened up new opportunities for reconstructing intellectual roles and identities. Partisanship had to take a new kind of professional form.

One important vehicle for the reinvention of partisanship was the resurrection of intellectual craftsmanship. Many of our partisan intellectuals derided their colleagues for their subservience to technological rationality and to the standardized, anonymous methodologies of knowledge accumulation that went with it. The intellectual seemed to have become an all too willing cog in the commercial corporate machine, lending his or her skills and talents to the omnipresent military-industrial complex that proved too formidable an opponent even for Dwight Eisenhower, a former general, to keep under control.

Mills, Mead, Mumford, Arendt, Carson, and even Baldwin and McCarthy all stood for an artisanal way of working, projecting into mass society and mass culture a form of professional craftsmanship that many of their fellow writers had come to reject as being old-fashioned and out of date. But they themselves had to change; to reach out to mass audiences, they had to modify their styles, adjust their expectations, and alter their assumptions. They had to enter into a dialogic relationship with the new public, and obviously, some did it better than others. But all of them sought to engage new readers without lowering the standards of their craft.

What many of the people in this book offered was a different identity for intellectual endeavor than was available in the dominant institutional settings. For some of them, the reaffirmation of an older role was central: Mumford's omniscient generalist or Day's moral missionary. For others, new identities had to be constructed: Mills's outlaw academic or Szilard's concerned scientist. For still others, interesting new hybrid identities were busily being formed: Margaret Mead's established outsider, Saul Alinksy's professional activist, Hannah Arendt's philosophical journalist. But what they all shared was the need to redefine themselves as intellectuals in a changed world. Their solutions and their strategies differed, but they were all concerned with resolving that particular kind of identity crisis that confronted postwar intellectuals. What for many of their colleagues was a simple process of accommodation to the new powers-that-be became for the people in this book an existential conflict.

Another kind of tension involved the new institutional context. The partisan intellectuals in the 1930s had broken down the barriers separating intellectuals from the "masses" and formed a number of new organizational structures, from regional development programs to resistance movements and political parties with their partisan reviews and worker education societies. After the war, as universities were transformed into teaching factories and research institutions were bureaucratized, many new intellectual work places opened up, but most of the more partisan ones disappeared. It was at the margins of the multiversities that some of our subjects carved out new institutional niches for their interdisciplinary work, the units that Mead, Szilard, and Mumford helped to create at Columbia and Berkeley; or it was at newer, more "liberal" universities that some of them helped to develop interesting alternative institutions, like Arendt at the New School for Social Research and Marcuse at Brandeis.

In other domains, while some of our subjects contributed to mass circulation magazines and thus carved out spaces for what might be called serious journalism in mass society, others helped Irving Howe and Norman Podhoretz establish new forums for social and cultural debate. Day's mission and city farm and Osborn's farm-in-the-zoo were very different, yet contiguous, ways to redesign the postwar urban landscape, the one by offering refuge and retreat from poverty, the other by providing education and an alternative kind of recreation for city youth. King's efforts to politicize the southern black church is perhaps the most famous example of intellectual institutional innovation in the 1950s; like the others, it grew out of his attempts to resolve the tension between an established institutional setting and the partisan intellectual role. All our subjects had to find a place to continue to reinvent their partisanship. Some of them carved out new spaces, while others tried to keep some already existing spaces open and alive. The partisan intellectual role came to be carried out in a range of innovative locations. That it was carried out at all was largely due to the efforts of the people in this book to resolve contextual tensions.

Seeds of the Sixties

By now, it should be clear that the partisan intellectuals of the 1950s did important things, but can it really be claimed that they all contributed to the social upheavals of the 1960s? What does it actually mean to contend, as we have done throughout this book, that our subjects planted some of the most significant seeds for the wave of activism and mobilization that crashed over America in the 1960s? Let us try to present some answers to these questions in a somewhat more systematic way than we have done in the individual chapters.

As we said in the first chapter, the 1960s represent for us a period of social creativity and experimentation when new ideas were carried into American society and placed firmly on the national agenda. Our claim is that these ideas did not emerge sui generis or as fully sprouted plants. They were, rather, like all ideas, the results of a constructive process of combination, synthesis, and innovation. As we see it, fundamental to the 1960s were the ideas of liberation and participatory democracy and the forging of autonomous realms for individual and collective growth. And we contend that those ideas and experiments were, to a substantial degree, the outgrowth of seeds planted by the people in this book.

The seed planting can be seen in several ways. Most directly, some of the partisan intellectuals kept alive intellectual traditions and modes of thought that would be given new substance and combined in new ways in the 1960s. In this category, we can place the writings of Mills and Marcuse, Arendt and Fromm. In recollecting Marxism, Fromm and Marcuse and even Mills and Arendt were not unique in the American 1950s. There were several other coteries at work, such as the editors and writers of the *Monthly Review* and the contributors to *Dissent* and *Science and Society*. But our subjects managed to free themselves somewhat more effectively than the others from what Bookchin later called "the old crap of the 1930s," that is, dogmatism. For one thing, they aimed for a mass audience and tried to link Marxism to contemporary trends and other ideological traditions. For another, they brought a more philosophical and potentially more personal Marx into postwar America, the humanist Marx that Fromm wrote about and Marcuse's more Hegelian and utopian Marx. From their different backgrounds in German idealism and classical humanism, Fromm and Marcuse could present a kind of socialist theory that spoke to the needs of the lonely crowd of mass society: a psychological Marx who was concerned with feelings and emotions, a personal Marx who gave alienation a name and a focus for oppositional action. This was also the Marx who appealed to Mills and Arendt, a Marx who spoke of universal human needs and attributes.

The poetic experimentation of Ginsberg had a significance of a somewhat different sort. Ginsberg's poetry, based as it was on the romantic subjectivism of Whitman and Rimbaud, helped to bring a new visionary language into postwar America, but it also made poetry itself meaningful and relevant for disenchanted young people. Together with the other Beat writers, Ginsberg constructed a new mode of expressing oneself and of combining art with life and both art and life with politics. Borrowing techniques from William Carlos Williams's earlier descriptions of Paterson, New Jersey, Ginsberg painted pictures of reality with his poetic pen, but it was the reality of the "other America" he portrayed. Those pictures—and even more perhaps, the style of portrayal—would come to be electrified in 1960s rock poetry and inspire the linguistic and existential experiments that marked the counterculture.

On another level, many of the partisan intellectuals of the 1950s came to serve as exemplary role models for the generation of activists that took to the streets in the 1960s. In the ways they lived their lives, taking stands, saying no, protesting injustice and oppression, the early student movement sought to emulate and reproduce on a larger scale the critical process that Alinsky, Day, and King all epitomized. The rules for radicals that Alinsky both produced and practiced were taken to heart by a new generation, which listened with awe and admiration to the moral precepts that King had already begun to articulate in the mid-1950s. The seeds that King and Alinsky planted grew into the collective oppositional practice of the student movement, combining the personal and the political, "living the revolution," as it came to be said, in terms of one's own behavior and existential choices. Day, less famous but no less important, provided another shade of moral altruism by living and working among the poor and keeping alive the tradition of settlement houses that gave intellectual content and significance to the other America.

The seeds that Mumford, Szilard, and Osborn planted were combinations of ideas and role models—Mumford opening up spaces and issues for academic and environmentalist work, Szilard and Osborn reconceptualizing and redefining science and conservation both in their writings and in their actions. Carson, McCarthy, and Mead, the popular writers, managed to do what so few other women managed to do in the 1950s, using the opportunities of the mass media to identify new social problems, giving them life, meaning, and importance. Much of the substantive program of the women's liberation movement and the environmental movement was first articulated in their writings, even though their own rather conventional "life-styles" were rejected by the younger women who followed their lead.

What our subjects provided was not, of course, the whole story. The 1960s were not created by individual acts of conscience, nor were the flower children merely acting on ideas articulated ten or more years before. But to ignore the seeds is equally misleading. Social movements may appear to be spontaneous eruptions of political energy, but they draw on the work of people who, in some crucial ways, served to prepare the way. In the transformation of the individual seeds into the collective harvest, however, the ideas do not remain the same. And, in this respect, the 1960s were most definitely no exception.

What had been individual acts of defiance and moral passion were turned into principles of collective behavior. And it is perhaps there that problems began to develop—not just in the relations between the movements and some of the people in this book but also in terms of the movements themselves. For an individual, partisanship can be, and often is, a survival strategy, a way of keeping honest to oneself, of preserving a sense of personal integrity in an age of conformity. But for a group, partisanship can easily lead to dogmatism; as a source of group identity and solidarity, it often takes a programmatic form, and the flexibility that it must contain when it is at the individual level turns rigid.

In a time colored by "political correctness" and the ascendancy of market liberalism, it is well to remember the partisan intellectuals of the 1950s. They took sides and dissented without becoming dogmatic. May we be able to say the same about ourselves.

REFERENCES

Adorno, Theodor et al. 1950. *The Authoritarian Personality.* New York: W. W. Norton.

Alinsky, Saul. [1946] 1969. *Reveille for Radicals* New York: Vintage.

———. [1971] 1989. *Rules for Radicals.* New York: Vintage.

Arendt, Hannah. 1951. *The Origins of Totalitarianism.* New York: Harcourt Brace Jovanovich.

———. 1958. *The Human Condition.* Chicago: University of Chicago Press.

———. [1963] 1990. *On Revolution.* Harmondsworth: Penguin.

Baldwin, James. 1953. *Go Tell It on the Mountain.* New York: Knopf.

———. 1956. *Giovanni's Room.* New York: Dial Press.

———. 1963. *The Fire Next Time.* New York: Dial Press.

———. 1985. *The Price of the Ticket: Collected Non-Fiction 1948–1985.* New York: St. Martin's.

Bateson, Mary Catherine. 1984. *With a Daughter's Eye: A Memoir of Margaret Mead and Gregory Bateson.* New York: Simon and Schuster.

Bell, Daniel, et al., eds. 1955. *The New American Right.* New York: Criterion Books.

Bernstein, Barton. 1987. Introduction. In Helen Hawkins et al., eds. *Toward a Livable World: Leo Szilard and the Crusade for Nuclear Arms Control.* Cambridge: MIT Press.

Birnbaum, Norman. 1988. *The Radical Renewal: The Politics of Ideas in Modern America.* New York: Pantheon Books.

Blake, Casey. 1991. "Memorial: Lewis Mumford (1895–1990)." *Technology and Culture* (January).

Branch, Taylor. 1988. *Parting the Waters.* New York: Simon and Schuster.

Brooks, Paul. 1972 *The House of Life: Rachel Carson at Work.* Boston: Houghton Mifflin.

Brown, Harrison. 1956. *The Challenge of Man's Future.* New York: Viking Press.

225

Bulletin of the New York Zoological Society.

Bush, Vannevar. 1945. *Science—The Endless Frontier: A Report to the President.* Washington, D.C.: Government Printing Office.

Campbell, James. 1991. *Talking at the Gates: A Life of James Baldwin.* London: Faber and Faber.

Carson, Rachel. 1941. *Under the Sea Wind.* New York: Simon and Schuster.

————. 1951. *The Sea Around Us.* New York: Oxford University Press.

————. 1962. *Silent Spring.* Boston: Houghton Mifflin.

Cone, James. 1991. *Martin & Malcolm & America.* Maryknoll: Orbis.

Davidson, Michael. 1989. *The San Francisco Renaissance.* Cambridge: Cambridge University Press.

Davis, Kenneth. 1984. *Two-Bit Culture: The Paperbacking of America.* Boston: Houghton Mifflin.

Day, Dorothy. [1952] 1981. *The Long Loneliness.* New York: Harper and Row.

————. 1992. *Selected Writings.* Maryknoll: Orbis.

Ehrlich, Paul. 1968. *The Population Bomb.* New York: Ballantine Books.

Eyerman, Ron, and Andrew Jamison. 1991. *Social Movements: A Cognitive Approach.* University Park: Pennsylvania State University Press.

Fraser, Steve. 1989. "The 'Labor Question,'" In Steve Fraser and Gary Gerstle, eds., *The Rise and Fall of the New Deal Order 1930–1980.* Princeton: Princeton University Press.

Fromm, Erich. [1930] 1984. *The Working Class in Weimar Germany: A Psychological and Sociological Study.* Cambridge: Harvard University Press.

————. 1941. *Escape from Freedom.* London: Kegan Paul, Trench, Trubner.

————. 1955. *The Sane Society.* New York: Rinehart & Company.

————. [1956] 1970. *The Art of Loving.* New York: Bantam Books.

Gelderman, Carol. 1988. *Mary McCarthy.* New York: St. Martin's.

Ginsberg, Allen. 1988. *Collected Poems 1947–1980.* New York: Harper and Row.

Green, Martin. *New York 1913.* New York: Scribner's.

Guha, Ramachandra. 1991. "Lewis Mumford, The Forgotten American Environmentalist: An Essay in Rehabilitation." *Capitalism Nature Socialism* (October).

Hayes, Carlton. 1946. "The American Frontier—Frontier of What?" *American Historical Review* (January).

Hays, Samuel. 1959. *Conservation and the Gospel of Efficiency.* Cambridge, Mass.: Harvard University Press.

————. 1987. *Beauty, Health, and Permanence: Environmental Politics in the United States, 1955–1985.* Cambridge: Cambridge University Press.

Herber, Lewis (Murray Bookchin). 1962. *Our Synthetic Environment.* New York: Alfred A. Knopf.

Horowitz, Irving Louis. 1983. *C. Wright Mills: An American Utiopian.* New York: Free Press.

Horwitt, Sanford. 1992. *Let Them Call Me Rebel.* New York: Vintage.

Howard, Jane. 1984. *Margaret Mead: A Life.* New York: Fawcett Columbine.

Hughes, Thomas, and Agatha Hughes, eds. 1990. *Lewis Mumford: Public Intellectual.* Oxford: Oxford University Press.

Hynes, H. Patricia. 1989. *The Recurring Silent Spring.* New York: Pergamon Press.

Kellner, Douglas. 1984. *Herbert Marcuse and the Crisis of Marxism.* Houndmills: Macmillan.

Kerouac, Jack. 1957. *On the Road.* New York: Viking Press.

King, Jr., Martin Luther. 1986. *A Testament of Hope: The Essential Writings of Martin Luther King, Jr.* New York: Harper.

Leopold, Aldo. 1949. *A Sand County Almanac.* New York: Oxford University Press.

Levine, Lawrence. 1988. *Highbrow Lowbrow: The Emergence of Cultural Hierarchy in America.* Cambridge: Harvard University Press.

Lipset, Seymour, and Neal Smelser. 1961. "Recent American Sociology." *British Journal of Sociology* 12:41–51.

Macdonald, Dwight. 1957. *Against the American Grain.* New York: DaCapo.

MacKenzie, Barbara. 1966. *Mary McCarthy.* Boston: Twayne.

May, Elaine Tyler. 1989. "Explosive Issues: Sex, Women and the Bomb." In Lary May, ed., *Recasting America: Culture and Politics in the Age of Cold War.* Chicago: University of Chicago Press.

Marcuse, Herbert. 1941. *Reason and Revolution.* New York: Oxford University Press.

———. 1955. *Eros and Civilization.* Boston: Beacon.

———. 1958. *Soviet Marxism.* Boston: Beacon.

———. 1964. *One-Dimensional Man.* Boston: Beacon.

McCarthy, Mary. 1942. *The Company She Keeps.* New York: Harcourt, Brace and Company.

———. 1949. *The Oasis.* New York: Random House.

———. 1952. *The Groves of Academe.* New York: Harcourt, Brace and Company.

———. [1955] 1980. *A Charmed Life.* New York: Avon Books.

———. 1957. *Memories of a Catholic Girlhood.* New York: Harcourt, Brace, Jovanovich.

———. 1963. *The Group.* New York: Harcourt Brace and World.

Mead, Margaret. 1928. *Coming of Age in Samoa.* New York: William Morrow.

———. 1949. *Male and Female: A Study of the Sexes in a Changing World.* New York: William Morrow.

Miles, Barry. 1990. *Ginsberg.* New York: Harper and Row.

Miller, Donald. 1989. *Lewis Mumford: A Life*. New York: Weidenfeld and Nicolson.

Miller, William. 1982. *Dorothy Day*. New York: Harper and Row.

Mills, C. Wright. 1948. *The New Men of Power*. New York: Harcourt, Brace and Company.

————. 1951. *White Collar*. Oxford: Oxford University Press.

————. 1956. *The Power Elite*. Oxford: Oxford University Press.

————. 1959. *The Sociological Imagination*. Oxford: Oxford University Press.

Mumford, Lewis. 1922. *The Story of Utopias*. New York: Boni and Liveright.

————. 1924. *Sticks and Stones*. New York: Boni and Liveright.

————. 1926. *The Golden Day: A Study in American Literature and Culture*. New York: Boni and Liveright.

————. 1934. *Technics and Civilization*. New York: Harcourt, Brace and Company.

————. 1938. *The Culture of Cities*. New York: Harcourt, Brace and Company.

————. 1944. *The Condition of Man*. New York: Harcourt, Brace and Company.

————. 1947. *Green Memories*. New York: Harcourt, Brace and Company.

————. 1951. *The Conduct of Life*. New York: Harcourt, Brace and Company.

————. 1956. *The Transformations of Man*. New York: Harper and Brothers.

————. 1961. *The City in History: Its Origins, Its Transformations and Its Prospects*. New York: Harcourt, Brace and World.

————. 1979. *Interpretations and Forecasts 1922–1972: Studies in Literature, History, Biography, Technics, and Contemporary Society*. New York: Harcourt Brace Jovanovich.

Niebuhr, Reinhold. 1932. *Moral Man and Immoral Society*. New York: Scribner's.

Osborn, Fairfield. 1948. *Our Plundered Planet*. Boston: Little Brown and Company.

————. 1953. *The Limits of the Earth*. Boston: Little Brown and Company.

Packard, Vance. 1960. *The Waste Makers*. New York: Pocket Books.

Parsons, Talcott. [1948] 1986. "Social Science: A Basic National Resource." In Samuel Klausner and Victor Lidz, eds., *The Nationalization of the Social Sciences*. Philadelphia: University of Pennsylvania Press.

Perry, Lewis. 1984. *Intellectual Life in America: A History*. New York: Franklin Watts.

Riesman, David, with Nathan Glazer and Reuel Denney. 1950. *The Lonely Crowd: A Study of the Changing American Character*. New Haven: Yale University Press.

References

Susman, Warren. 1984. *Culture as History: The Transformation of American Society in the Twentieth Century.* New York: Pantheon Books.

Szilard, Leo. 1961. *The Voice of the Dolphins and Other Stories.* New York: Simon and Schuster.

Trilling, Lionel. [1950] 1976. *The Liberal Imagination.* New York: Scribner's.

Vogt, William. 1948. *Road to Survival.* New York: William Sloane.

Wells, Allan, ed. 1972. *Mass Media and Society.* Palo Alto: Mayfield.

Wills, Garry. 1990. *Under God: Religion and American Politics.* New York: Simon and Schuster.

Young-Bruehl, E. 1982. *Hannah Arendt: For Love of the World.* New Haven: Yale University Press.

INDEX

. . . .

The index refers exclusively to people, academic institutions, and periodicals. For each of the main subjects, subreferences are given to the pages on which the individual's life and works are discussed ("portrait"), as well as to the more specific discussions of the individual's "relation to 1960s."

Abernathy, Ralph, 191
Adams, Ansel, 94
Addams, Jane, 3, 107, 181
Adorno, Theodor, 38, 47, 119–123
Ali, Muhammad, 164
Alinsky, Saul, 16, 23, 181, 194–198, 208, 215–216, 219; portrait, 178–179, 185–192; relation to 1960s, 25, 28, 212, 222
American Museum of Natural History, 79, 130, 136
Arendt, Hannah, 34–35, 61–63, 120, 172, 175, 177, 216, 218–219; portrait, 30–32, 46–54; relation to 1960s, 1, 19, 23–25, 212, 221
Asimov, Isaac, 93–94

Bacon, Francis, 69
Baker, John, 74
Baldwin, James, 19, 20, 23, 176, 180, 200–201, 212–213, 216, 218; portrait, 141–144, 160–168; relation to 1960s, 25, 28
Bateson, Gregory, 104, 131, 134–135, 160
Bateson, Mary Catherine, 135, 210
Baudelaire, Charles, 152

Beard, Charles, 8
Bell, Daniel, 30, 35, 40, 185, 192
Belloc, Hilaire, 195
Bellow, Saul, 48
Benedict, Ruth, 11, 27, 104, 131, 133–135
Bennington College, 61
Bernstein, Barton, 115
Berrigan brothers, 216, 218
Birnbaum, Norman, 11–12
Blake, Casey, 92
Blake, William, 92
Bloch, Ernst, 120
Boas, Franz, 131
Bookchin, Murray, 68–69, 79, 221
Booth, Paul, 191–192
Boston University, 180, 202
Bourne, Randolph, 3
Brandeis University, 103, 219
Brewer, George, 81
Brower, David, 74, 94
Brown, Harrison, 98
Buber, Martin, 56
Bulletin of the Atomic Scientists, 106, 114
Burgess, E. W., 186

Burroughs, William, 19, 28, 143, 150–151, 155, 158
Bush, George, 188
Bush, Vannevar, 14

California, University of, 52–53, 103–105, 207, 219
Camus, Albert, 48
Capone, Al, 178, 186
Carmichael, Stokely, 160
Carnegie Foundation, 9, 18
Carson, Rachel, 64, 68, 79, 135, 212–213, 215–216, 218; portrait, 66–67, 92–101; relation to 1960s, 21, 25–26, 67, 69, 74, 222
Castro, Fidel, 45, 199, 211
Chaplin, Charlie, 149
Chavez, Cesar, 190
Chicago, University of, 52, 112, 115, 178, 185–186, 189
City College (New York), 83
Clarke, Arthur, 93–94
Cleaver, Eldridge, 166–167
Coles, Robert, 119
Columbia University, 30, 37–40, 52, 84, 106, 141, 151–152, 219
Commentary, 52–53, 143, 161–162, 214
Commoner, Barry, 69, 79
Cone, James, 202, 207
Coser, Lewis, 38
Cowley, Malcolm, 168, 194
Crozer Theological Seminary, 201–202

Dahl, Robert, 18
Davis, Miles, 151
Day, Albert, 96
Day, Dorothy, 3, 178, 202, 208, 211, 213, 215–217, 219; portrait, 181–182, 192–200; relation to 1960s, 23, 28, 222
Debs, Eugene, 151
Dell, Floyd, 193
Dellinger, David, 199
Dewey, John, 3, 8, 25, 52, 123, 133, 181, 215
Dial, 4, 83
Dissent, 53, 143, 214, 221
Dos Passos, John, 11, 146, 161

Dreiser, Theodore, 146
Durkheim, Emile, 41
Dylan, Bob, 199

Eastman, Max, 146, 193
Edwards, Jonathan, 107, 181
Ehrlich, Paul, 66, 77, 79
Eichmann, Adolph, 53
Einstein, Albert, 105, 115
Eisenhower, Dwight David, 21, 43, 96, 173, 218
Eliot, T. S., 34
Ellison, Ralph, 53
Ellul, Jacques, 77
Emerson, Ralph Waldo, 3, 66, 83, 87, 107, 157, 181
Engels, Friedrich, 124
Esquire, 20, 158, 162

Fallada, Hans, 41
Farrell, James T., 11, 141, 169
Ferlinghetti, Lawrence, 158
Fermi, Enrico, 105
Ford, Henry, 8, 9, 122
Ford Foundation, 9, 18
Fourier, Charles, 125
Frank, Waldo, 87
Franklin, Benjamin, 107
Freeman, Derek, 129–130
Freud, Sigmund, 31, 35, 55, 57, 59, 110, 118, 124–125, 127–128
Friedan, Betty, 131
Friedman, Milton, 18
Fromm, Erich, 19, 23, 30, 35, 103, 120, 122, 125, 211–214, 216; portrait, 31–32, 54–63; relation to 1960s, 25, 35, 221

Galbraith, John Kenneth, 18, 98
Gandhi, Mahatma, 29, 180, 204–205
Geddes, Patrick, 83, 85
George, Henry, 92
Ginsberg, Allan, 23, 25, 167, 176, 213, 216; portrait, 141, 150–160; relation to 1960s, 19, 28, 143–144, 212, 221
Gitlin, Todd, 191–192
Goethe, Johann Wolfgang von, 72
Gold, Mike, 193–194, 197

Index

Goodman, Paul, 160
Griffith, D. W., 149
Groves, Leslie, 112
Guha, Ramachandra, 89
Guthrie, Woody, 72

Habermas, Jürgen, 123
Haeckel, Ernst, 72
Harding, Warren G., 148
Hardwick, Elizabeth, 172
Harper's, 147, 162–163
Harrington, Michael, 199
Harvard University, 18, 106, 108, 151
Hayden, Corey, 208
Hayden, Tom, 191–192, 208
Hays, Samuel, 95
Hegel, G. W. F., 124, 127–128
Heidegger, Martin, 30, 46, 51, 120, 122
Heilbroner, Robert, 18
Hemingway, Ernest, 154
Hitler, Adolf, 46, 183
Hook, Sidney, 119, 215
Horkheimer, Max, 47, 56, 119–123
Howe, Irving, 18, 20, 26, 143, 214, 219
Husserl, Edmund, 30, 46, 51

Ickes, Harold, 71

James, Henry, 161, 164
James, William, 3, 8
Jaspers, Karl, 46, 51
Jefferson, Thomas, 107
Johns Hopkins University, 92

Kant, Immanuel, 50
Kerouac, Jack, 19, 28, 143, 150–158, 160
Khrushchev, Nikita, 113
King, Martin Luther, Jr., 3, 16, 164, 166–
    167, 178, 182, 190, 195, 197–198, 216,
    220; portrait, 180–181, 200–208; rela-
    tion to 1960s, 25, 28–29, 210, 212–
    213, 222
King, Mary, 208
Kracauer, Siegfried, 56

Lazersfeld, Paul, 37–40
Lenin, V. I., 121

Leopold, Aldo, 71–73, 78, 95
Levine, Lawrence, 145
Levitas, Saul, 161
Lewis, John L., 188
Liebknecht, Karl, 121
Life, 158
Linneaus, Carolus (Carl von Linné), 72
Lipset, Seymour Martin, 40
Lowenthal, Leo, 56, 122
Luce, Henry, 209
Luxembourg, Rosa, 121
Lynd, Robert, 11, 38–39
Lynd, Staughton, 192

McCarthy, Joseph, 61; McCarthyism, 16
McCarthy, Mary, 19, 23, 143–144, 167–
    177, 216, 218; portrait, 141–142, 167–
    177; relation to 1960s, 25, 28, 212,
    222
McKay, Benton, 96
Macdonald, Dwight, 18–20, 36–37, 45, 48,
    143, 149, 189
Mailer, Norman, 167
Malcolm X, 164, 167, 207
Malthus, Thomas, 77
Mandel, Ernest, 160
Marcuse, Herbert, 13, 23, 61, 110, 118–
    128, 131, 211–212, 216, 219; por-
    trait, 103–104, 118–128; relation to
    1960s, 1, 19, 24, 27, 106–107, 138–
    140, 221
Maritain, Jacques, 195
Marsh, George P., 89
Marx, Karl, 31, 35, 45, 55, 57, 120–121,
    124–125, 127–128, 182, 195, 221;
    Marxism, 7, 27, 56–57, 59, 103, 118,
    126, 179, 215, 221
Marx, Leo, 86
Maryland, University of, 36
Massachusetts Institute of Technology
    (M.I.T.), 84
Masses, The, 145–146, 193–194
Maurin, Peter, 195
May, Elaine Tyler, 14
Mead, George H., 8
Mead, Margaret, 9, 106–107, 210, 213,
    216, 218–219; portrait, 104, 128–138;

Mead, Margaret (*continued*)
   relation to 1960s, 25, 27, 138–140,
   212, 222
Melville, Herman, 83
Merton, Robert, 16, 18, 38–39, 119
Mexico, University of, 61
Michigan, University of, 103
Miles, Barry, 155
Miller, Henry, 154
Mills, C. Wright, 15–18, 23, 31–32, 34,
   50–52, 55, 152, 161, 188–189, 199,
   216; portrait, 30, 36–46; relation to
   1960s, 1, 19, 25, 35, 61–63, 211, 218–
   219, 221
Monthly Review, 221
Morehouse College, 200–201
Morris, William, 89–90, 92, 146
Moses, Robert, 88
Muir, John, 71
Muhammad, Elijah, 164–165
Mumford, Lewis, 3, 11, 15–16, 18, 64, 95,
   182, 215–216, 218–219; portrait, 65–
   66, 82–92; relation to 1960s, 1, 19–20,
   23, 25–26, 67–69, 73–74, 100–102,
   212–213, 222
Muste, A. J., 198

Nader, Ralph, 101
Nation, The, 147, 161, 168, 171
New Deal, the, 4, 7, 10, 11, 71, 78–79,
   85, 214–215
New Leader, 30, 36, 161
New Republic, 52, 87, 168, 171
New School for Social Research (New
   York), 4, 31, 52–53, 61, 83, 219
New York Review of Books, 174–175
New York Times, 157
New York Zoological Society (Bronx Zoo),
   64–65, 74–75, 77–81, 101
New Yorker, 20, 52–53, 66, 93, 158, 164,
   172, 175, 214
Niebuhr, Reinhold, 11, 180, 182,
   204–205, 215
Neumann, Franz, 122

O'Neill, Eugene, 179, 194
Oppenheimer, Robert, 105

Ordway, Samuel, 81
Osborn, Fairfield, 23, 26, 89, 98,
   100–101, 216; portrait, 64–65, 74–82;
   relation to 1960s, 67, 69, 212, 222

Packard, Vance, 98
Paine, Thomas, 107
Parsons, Talcott, 17, 18, 42, 55
Partisan Review, 36, 52, 143, 161–162,
   170–172
Peale, Norman V., 14
Peirce, Charles S., 8
Pennsylvania, University of, 84
Podhoretz, Norman, 219
Polanyi, Michael, 112
politics, 37, 149
Princeton University, 52
Progressive, The, 164

Rahv, Philip, 36, 143, 161, 170–171
Reader's Digest, 96
Reed, John, 3, 146
Rexroth, Kenneth, 156
Reynolds, Malvina, 34
Riesman, David, 34, 60, 150
Rimbaud, 152, 221
Rockefeller, Laurence, 81
Rockefeller Foundation, 9, 18
Roosevelt, Franklin D., 7, 14, 32, 105,
   174, 181
Roosevelt, Theodore, 70
Rousseau, Jean Jacques, 50
Russell, Bertrand, 115
Rustin, Bayard, 198

Samuelson, Paul, 18
Sarnoff, David, 147–148
Sartre, Jean Paul, 48
Savio, Mario, 207
Schweitzer, Albert, 89–90, 92
Science and Society, 221
Shaw, Clifford, 186–187
Skinker, Mary, 92
Smelser, Neil, 40
Snyder, Gary, 19, 156–157
Spock, Benjamin, 14
Stalin (Joseph), 47, 113, 141, 151, 183

Index

Stanford University, 84
Steinbeck, John, 11, 146
Steiner, Rudolf, 72

Train, Russell, 81
Trilling, Lionel, 38, 152
Truman, Harry, 105, 183
Trotsky, Leon, 141–142, 169

van Doren, Mark, 152
Vassar College, 168–169, 172–173
Veblen, Thorstein, 3, 52, 83
Vlaag, Piet, 146
Vogt, William, 77

Voltaire, 50
von Hoffman, Nicholas, 190–191

Wallace, Henry, 28, 184
Weber, Alfred, 56
Weber, Max, 17, 41, 43, 45, 51, 56
Wells, H. G., 111
Whalen, Philip, 157
White, Gilbert, 72
Whitman, Walt, 159, 221
Whitehead, Alfred North, 85
Williams, William Carlos, 155, 221
Wills, Garry, 179

Designer: Sandy Drooker
Compositor: Braun-Brumfield, Inc.
Text: 10 / 13 Caledonia
Display: Caledonia, Helvetica
Printer: Maple-Vail Book Mfg. Group
Binder: Maple-Vail Book Mfg. Group